Google™ Sites & Chrome For Dummies®

Cheat Sheet

Google Sites Login Address

User	Address
iGoogle	http://sites.google.com/
Google Apps	http://sites.google.com/a/*your-domain.com*

Google Sites Page Layouts

Page layout	What it's useful for
Web Page	Creating a generic page with text, graphics, gadgets and more.
Dashboard	Sharing gadgets and information from other pages on your site.
Announcements	Sharing news information or blog entries.
File Cabinet	Uploading files and keeping track of multiple versions.
List	Keeping track of projects, assignments, and so on.

Default Addresses For Google Apps Team Edition

App	Address
Sites	http://sites.google.com/a/*your-domain.com*
Start Page	http://partnerpage.google.com/*your-domain.com*
Calendar	http://calendar.google.com/a/*your-domain.com*
Docs	http://docs.google.com/a/*your-domain.com*
Talk	Use the gadget on your Start Page or download the client from http://talk.google.com
Dashboard	http://www.google.com/a/*your-domain.com*

For Dummies: Bestselling Book Series for Beginners

Google™ Sites & Chrome For Dummies®

Cheat Sheet

Google Chrome Keyboard Shortcuts

Keyboard Shortcut	What it does
Ctrl+T	Opens an new tab
Ctrl+W	Closes the current tab
Ctrl+Tab	Cycles through current tabs
Ctrl+N	Opens a new window
Ctrl+Shift+N	Opens a new incognito window
Ctrl+Shift+T	Opens the last tab you closed
Alt+Home	Opens your home page
Ctrl+L	Jumps to the Omnibox
Ctrl+K	Searches for a word in the Omnibox
Ctrl+F	Finds text in an open page
Ctrl++	Increases the font size
Ctrl+-	Decreases the font size
Ctrl+0	Restores the normal font size
Ctrl+B	Shows/hides the bookmarks bar
Ctrl+H	Opens your browsing history
Ctrl+J	Loads your downloads page
Ctrl+X	Cuts
Ctrl+C	Copies
Ctrl+V	Pastes
Ctrl+P	Prints the current tab
Shift+Esc	Opens the Tab Task Manager

For Dummies: Bestselling Book Series for Beginners

Google™ Sites & Chrome

FOR DUMMIES®

Google™ Sites & Chrome

FOR DUMMIES®

by Ryan Teeter and Karl Barksdale

WILEY

Wiley Publishing, Inc.

Google Sites™ & Chrome For Dummies®

Published by
Wiley Publishing, Inc.
111 River Street
Hoboken, NJ 07030-5774
www.wiley.com

WILEY

About the Authors

Ryan Teeter is an accomplished writer and technology trainer. He has worked closely with business teachers throughout the country and consulted with the National Business Education Association, businesses, and school districts on Google Apps implementation. Ryan spent time working at Google in Mountain View, California as an External Training Specialist, developing curriculum used for training Fortune 500 companies.

When he's not conducting training workshops or writing, Ryan's pursuing his passion for teaching and research as a doctoral student at Rutgers University, where he's completing a Ph.D. in accounting information systems. (www.ryanteeter.com)

Karl Barksdale was a former Development Manager for the Training and Certification team at WordPerfect Corporation and a Marketing Manager in the Consumer Products division. He was also the External Training Manager for Google's Online Sales and Operations division. He's best known for authoring and co-authoring 59 business and computer education textbooks. Albeit, the job he enjoys most is teaching at the Utah County Academy of Sciences, an early college high school on the Utah Valley University campus. (www.karlbarksdale.com)

Dedication

Ryan Teeter: This book is dedicated to Erin, the love of my life.

Karl Barksdale: For Hilary, Cory, and Mari, who make it all worthwhile.

Authors' Acknowledgments

This book wouldn't have happened without the inspiration and guidance of Esther Wojcicki of Palo Alto High School and Jeremy Milo, the Google Apps Product Marketing Manager at Google. Nor could we have accomplished so much without the External Training Team at Google, of which we were so fortunate to be a part. Here's to Lance Cotton, Erik Gottlieb, Lauren Frandsen, Kristina Cutura, Charbel Semaan, Tyrona Heath, Mary Hekl, Brian Schreier, and Jared Smith. You guys rock!

We also want to give special recognition to our outstanding team at Wiley Publishing, including Greg Croy, senior acquisitions editor; Chris Morris, senior project editor; Brian Walls, copy editor; Jim Kelly, technical editor and the other incredibly talented and amazing people who made working on this project a real treat.

Along those lines, we want to acknowledge our friends and colleagues at the Rutgers Business School and the Utah County Academy of Sciences for their support.

Finally, we acknowledge you, the reader, for trusting us to help you make the most out of this amazing and incredibly useful technology.

Publisher's Acknowledgments

We're proud of this book; please send us your comments through our online registration form located at `http://dummies.custhelp.com`. For other comments, please contact our Customer Care Department within the U.S. at 877-762-2974, outside the U.S. at 317-572-3993, or fax 317-572-4002.

Some of the .people who helped bring this book to market include the following:

Acquisitions and Editorial

Sr. Project Editor: Christopher Morris

Sr. Acquisitions Editor: Gregory Croy

Copy Editor: Brian Walls

Technical Editor: James Kelly

Editorial Manager: Kevin Kirschner

Editorial Assistant: Amanda Foxworth

Sr. Editorial Assistant: Cherie Case

Cartoons: Rich Tennant
(`www.the5thwave.com`)

Composition Services

Project Coordinator: Kristie Rees

Layout and Graphics: Claudia Bell, Reuben W. Davis, Ana Carrillo, Christine Williams

Proofreader: Bonnie Mikkelson

Indexer: Broccoli Information Management

Publishing and Editorial for Technology Dummies

Richard Swadley, Vice President and Executive Group Publisher

Andy Cummings, Vice President and Publisher

Mary Bednarek, Executive Acquisitions Director

Mary C. Corder, Editorial Director

Publishing for Consumer Dummies

Diane Graves Steele, Vice President and Publisher

Composition Services

Gerry Fahey, Vice President of Production Services

Debbie Stailey, Director of Composition Services

Contents at a Glance

Table of Contents

Part II: Constructing and Sharing Your Google Site 63

Introduction

When most people think of Google, the first thing that comes to mind is Internet search. Millions of people around the globe use Google to find information, learn something new, explore issues, or discover answers to tough questions. We assume that you've used Google Search before — or at least heard of it. If you want to find out how to be a Google Search expert, you've come to the wrong place. We're interested in the other cool tools that Google creates *beyond* its powerful search box. Google Sites and Chrome are two such tools.

Just so you know upfront, Google Sites is a free online service that allows you to easily create Web sites with powerful wiki, file sharing, and collaboration tools. Google Chrome is a free Web browser that you download to your computer and use to access Web sites, including your Google Sites. *Google Sites & Chrome For Dummies* aims to fill the void between what Google thinks is obvious and intuitive and what real people like you need to know to make the most of these two cool tools, including some not-so-obvious tweaks and features.

By the time you finish reading this book, we hope that you not only can master these two spiffy Google products, but also that your eyes are opened to a few of the more than 30 free products and services and how they mesh.

About This Book

This book is designed for all audiences. Whether you're a soccer mom, a college professor, a movie exec, or a skater dude, we have something in here for you. This book helps you understand the tools you need to start building your new site and how to use them.

Although we do our best to make sure what you read in this book is accurate and up-to-date, we can't make any promises. You see, Google likes to update things from time to time. Their products are called *perpetual betas,* meaning that the new bells and whistles discovered by the folks at Google often sneak into these products and change a thing or two. We just thought you should know.

How This Book Is Organized

We divide this book into parts and chapters, organizing the chapters into six parts (which we describe in the following sections).

Part I: Getting Started with Google Sites and Chrome

Part I is the obvious place to start if you're brand new to Google Sites and Chrome. Chapter 1 provides a general overview of Google Sites; we keep it short because we realize that if you have the great wisdom to pick up this book in the first place, you're probably anxious to get started. Chapter 2 gets you up and running with Chrome and highlights the browser's basics. Chapter 3 runs through the process of setting up Google Sites for your business, school, or organization using a Google Account or the Google Apps Team Edition. Finally, Chapter 4 lets you get your hands dirty and shows you the tools you need to start building your site.

Part II: Constructing and Sharing Your Google Site

Chapter 5 covers using the five basic templates to help organize information and files on your site. Chapter 6 goes into adding content from other Google Apps and the Web. When you're feeling creative, look to Chapter 7 for tips on how to choose a new theme and adjust individual colors and graphics. Finally, Chapter 8 shows you how to add other users to the flurry.

Part III: Getting the Most Out of Chrome

The two chapters in this part help you become a Chrome master. Chapter 9 goes into depth on using the Omnibox to search the Web and find your way around Chrome's tools. Chapter 10 gets technical, taking you through the settings and Chrome's advanced features.

Part IV: Building Your Own Scheme

We decided that there's more to Sites than showing you the tools, so this part gives you three practical ideas, which we like to call *schemes,* for creating your site. Chapter 11 gives you ideas for a personal site. Chapter 12 throws out a college course scheme, and Chapter 13 helps you build a business wiki or intranet using Google Sites.

Part V: More Google Apps You Can't Do Without

This part helps you expand your site by using the other Google Apps, including Google Docs, Google Calendar, Gmail, and Google Talk. Chapters 14 through 17 introduce you to the Google Docs Home and discuss how to create and organize your online documents, spreadsheets, and presentations.

Rounding out this part is Google Calendar in Chapter 18, Gmail in Chapter 19, and Google Talk and Contacts in Chapter 20. This part will have you proficient in Google's communications tools in no time flat.

Part VI: The Part of Tens

This part begins by giving ten additional team scheme ideas in Chapter 21. Ending the book is Chapter 22, which suggests more Google Apps and services that you may want to explore. (This final chapter is one of our favorites.)

Conventions Used in This Book

To make using this book as easy and convenient as possible, we set up a few conventions:

- ✔ When we throw a new term at you, we place it in *italics* and define it.
- ✔ We place text that you actually type in **bold**.

✔ Web site addresses and file names appear in a monospace font, like this: `www.dummies.com`. When part of a file name or Web site address varies (depending on what your Web site address is), we use italics to indicate a placeholder. For example, when you see `http://sites.your domain.com`, you type the address of your domain name in place of `yourdomain.com`.

✔ When you need to use a menu to select a command, we use the command arrow (➪). For example, File➪Rename simply means that you should click the File menu and then choose the Rename command.

✔ When we show keyboard shortcuts, we place the plus sign (+) between keys. For example, to use the Cut command, press Ctrl+X. This means to press the Ctrl key and the X key at the same time.

Icons Used In This Book

From time to time, everyone gets distracted, starts to daydream, gets a little hungry, and quits paying attention. In a seemingly futile attempt to regain your attention from that long-overdue Snickers bar, we place icons throughout the book. Each has its own deep-sleep preventive powers:

We mark paragraphs that we think you'll find very useful with this icon. Tips show you shortcuts, timesavers, or something that's otherwise worth noting. So, wake up and pay attention!

When you see this icon, beware. From experience, we know when you can easily make a mistake that may cause irreparable harm or damage to the Internet or national security. Well, maybe the Warning icon doesn't point out something that dire, but you should still pay attention or risk losing data, time, and possibly hair (from pulling it out in frustration).

Rather than repeat ourselves (because maybe you didn't pay attention the first time), we pop this icon in place. Commit the information to memory, and it can help you later.

Okay, we don't use this icon unless we have to. When you see this icon, we're flagging some information that's more technical and nerdy than the rest of the text. You might find the information really cool and very interesting, despite being technical, so read it at your discretion.

Where to Go from Here

We're not going to hold you back any longer. Any of the first four chapters is a great way to dive right in. Start finding out about Google Sites in Chapter 1, install Google Chrome in Chapter 2, sign up for a Google Account in Chapter 3, and begin building your new site in Chapter 4.

Part I

Getting Started with Google Sites and Chrome

The 5th Wave · By Rich Tennant

SOMEWHERE IN THE CITY, SASQUATCH, BIGFOOT AND ELVIS SPEND ANOTHER WARY NIGHT.

"Look—all I'm saying is every time they come out with a new browser with an improved search function, it's just a matter of time."

In this part . . .

Google Sites changes how you share information on the Web and Google Chrome helps you do it at lightning speed. We know you're anxious to dig in, so here's where you can find how to get up and running with Google Sites and Chrome. Find out all about Google Sites, download and install Chrome, sign up for Google Apps, and start building.

If you've previously signed up for a Google Apps or Gmail account and have already installed Chrome, skip ahead to Chapter 4 to start getting your feet wet.

Chapter 1

Befriending Google Sites

Google Sites (http://sites.google.com) is a great online information buddy. After all, buddies watch out for their friends — and Sites
will help take care of you. With a little thought and a few clicks, Google Sites
can help you, your friends, and your co-workers stay on top of projects, meetings, classes, events, clubs, teams, causes, fundraisers, schedules, vacations,
or anything else you can think of. Google Sites fills three related functions:

 ✔ Creates dynamic Web pages with a few clicks

 ✔ Constructs wikis for your users on any topic you may need

 ✔ Generates dynamic file sharing tools on the fly

In this chapter (and this book), we show how Google Sites can be very helpful to you, what that word *wiki* means, and how Google's many online apps
and gadgets can make your life much simpler. You see how Sites compares to
all the other team collaboration tools out there so you can understand why
picking Google Sites is as easy as making a mouse click.

Now for the best part: Google Sites is a free component of Google Apps, along
with Gmail, Calendar, and Docs. As with these other services, you don't need
programming skills, and you don't need any complicated Web design software beyond a Web browser, such as Chrome, Internet Explorer, or Firefox.

What You Should Know Before You Start

Before you can use Google Sites, you must first have a Google Account or
Google Apps account. A Google Account gives you access to a whole bunch
of other free Google online services, such as Google Calendar (http://

`calendar.google.com`), where you can track your appointments and events, Blogger (`www.blogger.com`), which lets you create your own blog, Picasa Web Albums (`www.picasa.com`), where you can share your photos online, and Google Docs (`http://docs.google.com`). If you don't have an account, Chapter 3 shows you how to sign up.

Like many other services offered by Google, Sites is a *perpetual beta*. This means that the clever Google engineers are always improving the way Sites works by adding new features and changing ones that aren't as helpful. If the screen looks somewhat different from the figures that you see in this book, it's okay. The same basic idea should still apply.

To help you understand all that Google Sites has to offer, let us introduce you to three key definitions: *Web pages, wikis,* and *file sharing.*

Web pages

A *Web page* is a file that can be viewed by others in a Web browser. A page can include written text, images, links to other pages, videos, and so on. One way you can use Google Sites is to create a Web page with information you want to share with the world. An example of this type of site is shown in Figure 1-1.

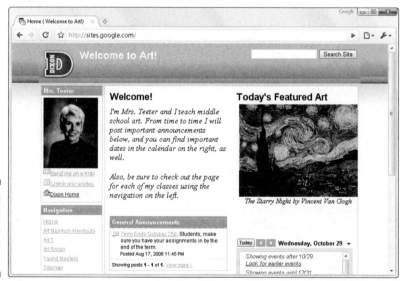

Figure 1-1:
Use Google
Sites to
create a
Web page.

In addition to helping you include your text and images, Google Sites gives you access to hundreds of gadgets that you can add to your page. *Gadgets* are like mini Web pages that show specific information, such as weather, news headlines, calendar events, videos, communication tools, and more. We talk about gadgets in depth in Chapter 6.

Wikis

A *wiki* is a Web page that anyone can add to or edit. Wiki is a Hawaiian word that means quick, and wiki sites are unique because they can be created, edited, and saved very quickly from within your Web browser. They're also very helpful because every member of your group or team needs to go to only one place to find the latest information.

Wikis are becoming more and more popular as companies, organizations, teams, and families work to share information and learn the unique things that people know. In any workplace, employees generally have more collective knowledge about how a company operates than the human resources director or company president. By using a wiki, all employees can share their knowledge with everyone else. The human resources team can then edit and organize it all.

How does a wiki work in Google Sites? Everyone who has the ability to edit a site will see the Create New Page and Edit Page buttons at the top of the page. When anyone in your group clicks the Edit Page button, they can begin making changes to the page by adding a graphic or paragraph. When they are done, all they have to do is click the Save button at the top and the page updates instantly.

If you already have a site and you want to start editing your wiki, head over to Chapter 4. We've also put together a few ideas for creating a wiki for your work, family, class, or group in Part IV.

File sharing

A very important feature that goes hand in hand with wikis is the ability to keep your team's files in a central location. *File sharing* lets members of your team upload any type of file, such as a presentation or video, so everyone else can find it later. When you *upload* a file, you send it from your computer to a Web site. Then other people can *download* the file by saving it from the Web site to their computer.

Define: Wikipedia

The new Internet (also known as *Web 2.0*) is all about sharing information. Instead of simply connecting computers and services, the new Internet connects people and ideas. Look at the most famous wiki: Wikipedia (www. wikipedia.org). When this book was published, there were 2,472,151 articles in English, contributed by more than 7.5 million different users, covering everything from important historical events to pop culture, calculus proofs, and book summaries. Compare that to the meager 120,000 articles found in the Encyclopedia Britannica, which is one of the most comprehensive traditional sources. There's no doubt that connecting people with wikis gives everyone access to more information and helps people feel that they are making a contribution to the world's knowledge.

Google Sites makes it easy to share files using the File Sharing page template, as shown in Figure 1-2. Similar to a editing a wiki page, you add and delete files by clicking the buttons that appear on a File Cabinet page. Additionally, Google Sites keeps track of multiple versions of your files, so if someone makes a change to a file and uploads the new one, you see both the new version and the old one.

To find more about how to use the File Cabinet in Google Sites, check out Chapter 5.

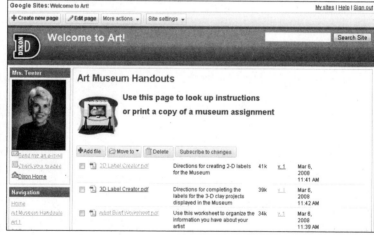

Figure 1-2: File sharing puts all of your important documents in one place.

Comparing Google Sites to Other Team Sites

We're assuming that because you're reading this book, you're leaning toward using Google Sites. In case you're curious, however, here's how the others compare.

Microsoft Office Live Workspace

Microsoft Office Live Workspace (`http://workspace.officelive.com`) — a free service that's probably the most similar to Sites — offers users the ability to share files easily and to comment on projects, as shown in Figure 1-3. Unlike Sites, however, there's no Web page tool, so creating a wiki site isn't part of the package.

The main advantage to using Office Live Workspace is that if you use Microsoft Office, you can download a plug-in that gives you easy access to save your Office documents directly to the site. Office Live's big brothers, Groove and SharePoint, offer additional features for larger companies but also require expensive servers and software.

To use Office Live Workspace, you need a Windows Live ID and password, which you can get free at `http://home.live.com`.

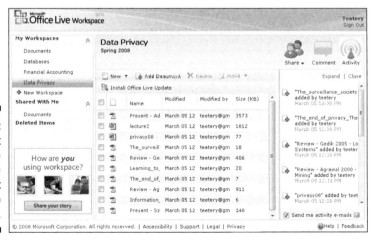

Figure 1-3: Microsoft Office Live Workspace makes it easy to share files.

Blackboard and Moodle

Blackboard (www.blackboard.com) and Moodle (www.moodle.org) are both great tools for teachers to keep track of classes, handouts, quizzes, and grades. (Moodle is shown in Figure 1-4.) They provide tools for pretty much any aspect of your class needs. But they're also very complex and require extensive training every time a new semester rolls around.

Figure 1-4: Moodle has more classroom features, such as quizzes and gradebooks.

Blackboard and Moodle both require servers to run on, and someone to maintain them. You also have to pay a license fee for Blackboard. If your school already uses either one, they have gone ahead and taken care of the cost.

In cases where you don't need all the bells and whistles or if you use other publisher-provided tools, Google Sites gives you the basics to share all of your classroom information with the students in your class. For an example of using Google Sites for a classroom, see Chapter 12.

Acrobat

Adobe takes a slightly different approach to sharing files. They offer five services through their Web site, www.acrobat.com, which allow you to create and share individual files with others:

- ✔ **Buzzword** is an online word processor similar to Google Docs (see Chapter 15).

- ✔ **ConnectNow** lets you host online conferences and share your screen over the Internet.

- ✔ **Create PDF** is a tool to transform your documents into portable document format.

- ✔ **Share** lets you upload and invite others to see your documents.

- ✔ **My Files** gives you a place to keep your files and access them from anywhere.

Instead of using a wiki-like interface, Acrobat gives you the option to enter the e-mail addresses of your team members so they can keep track of your files. Although this is useful for individual documents, it makes running a whole team project a little difficult because every time you want to share a file, you have to remember the addresses of everyone on your team. Still, the black interface is very easy to use and is just plain cool.

Why Google Sites Is the Right Way to Do Things

We mention in the previous section that Google Sites incorporates the best aspects of Web page, wiki, and file sharing technology into an easy-to-use online tool. But choosing Google Sites is about more than playing with a shiny new service — it's also about saving you time and money. In this section, we share with you our two cents, just in case you're not already convinced that Sites is the way to go.

Simplifying your life

The first thing you notice with Google Sites is Google's trademark simplicity. Although other services may have more bells and whistles, Google Sites keeps it simple and gives you the features you need to get your work done without making you master a whole new complicated set of tools and features.

With Google Sites, you can focus more on coordinating group activities to accomplish your tasks and less on figuring out all the extra stuff. Plus, you get all the training you need from this book. Now that's simple!

Saving money

Google Sites is free. Talk about saving money. You don't have to invest in expensive servers and software. All you need is an Internet connection and a Web browser, either of which you could get free at your public library, if you wanted.

All of your pages, wikis, and files are hosted for free, along with your other Google services. The exception, of course, is if you use Google Apps Premier Edition (www.google.com/apps), but in that case, your organization is really paying for the support. (Google Apps Premier Edition, along with all other editions of Google Apps, is discussed in the next section.)

Google can provide these services free because of the money they make on Internet search advertising. Next time you use Google Search, look for the sponsored links to the right of your results. That's what pays the engineers to create these high-quality tools.

How Google Sites Fits with the Other Google Apps

Google Apps (www.google.com/apps) is made up of five fully-functioning online applications: Gmail, Calendar, Docs, Talk, and Sites. Communicating with other people on the Internet is a snap with Gmail and Talk, and collaboration is simple with Calendar, Docs, and Sites. Each of these apps are fully functioning programs that allow you to do your work, such as e-mail and word processing, from any Web browser, instead of relying on your computer's other installed software. Additionally, you can quickly access information you store online by using mini versions of the apps called *gadgets*. There are different editions of the whole Google Apps package, depending on your organization and needs. These include:

✔ **Team Edition:** If you already have a school or work e-mail address, this edition adds Calendar, Docs, Talk, and Sites to the mix. Plus, you can instantly start connecting with other users in your organization that have already signed up. (Click the link for Coworkers or Classmates.)

✔ **Standard Edition:** If your group or business is just starting out or is switching from another service, such as Outlook, this free edition of Google Apps lets you use all five services with your existing domain name with minimal e-mail advertisements. (Click the Business IT Managers link, click the See Details and Sign Up button, and then click Compare to Standard Edition)

✔ **Premier Edition:** This edition costs $50 per user per year, but adds more functionality and security than Standard Edition, more storage space, provides 24/7 support, and gets rid of the ads. (Click the Business IT Managers link.)

✔ **Education Edition.** This is just like Premier Edition, but free for universities, schools, and other nonprofit organizations. (Click the School IT Managers link.)

These apps just so happen to play nice with each other, too, by allowing you to easily share information from one app with another. Some of the features we talk about in this book include alerts, which are sent to your e-mail account, and embedded calendars, which help your team members know what's coming up.

In the next few sections, we give you a taste of what each of the other apps does and provide examples of how you can include them in your sites by using gadgets. You can find more about how to use these apps individually in Part V.

Calendar

Google Calendar (http://calendar.google.com) keeps track of your events. You can easily add new calendar items and access them from anywhere, including your BlackBerry or iPhone. In Calendar, you can create separate calendars for your personal and team-related events and share them with other members of your team.

Displaying your team calendar is easy in Google Sites, thanks to the Calendar gadget. From your site, everyone can quickly find upcoming events or follow up on meetings that happened. Figure 1-5 shows an agenda for a class, using the Calendar gadget.

Skip to Chapter 14 to begin coordinating schedules.

Docs

Create, edit, and store documents, spreadsheets, and presentations online with Google Docs (http://docs.google.com). Google Docs features a surprisingly powerful word processor, spreadsheet editor, and presentations app that provide most of the tools you need. One of the cool things about Docs is that you can share your documents with other team members and work on them at the same time. This way, any changes you make are automatically updated and everyone else can see them right away.

Computer Augmented Accounting

| Today | ◀ ▶ | Monday, May 26 ▼ | 🖶 Print | Week | Mor |

Showing events after 3/1. Look for earlier events

Monday, May 26

Memorial Day Holiday

Tuesday, May 27

10:15am Course Introduction; Chapter 1 Intro to AIS

Wednesday, May 28

10:15am Chapter 1: Intro to Accounting Information ‹

Thursday, May 29

Quiz 1 due

10:15am Chapter 6: Elements of Database Systems

Monday, June 2

Formation of project team due

Quiz 6 due

10:15am Chapter 2: Intro to Microsoft Access (PS)

Tuesday, June 3

10:15am Chaper 7: Systems Analysis and Design (N

Wednesday, June 4

Quiz 7 due

10:15am Chapter 2: Intro to Microsoft Access (PS)

Thursday, June 5

10:15am Chapter 8: Logical Design for Database Sy

Monday, June 9

Events shown in time zone: Eastern Time   ◈ Google Calendar

Figure 1-5:
Place your team calendar on your site.

It should be no surprise, then, that you can include your docs on Google Sites, too. Beyond simply creating links to your individual docs, Google Sites uses gadgets to place the content of your docs directly on your pages, as shown in Figure 1-6. For example, use the Spreadsheet gadget to include a list you have stored in a spreadsheet or the Presentation gadget to play an animated slideshow of a quarterly report.

To find out more about Google Docs, flip to Chapter 15 and begin exploring the Google Docs Home. Chapters 16, 17, and 18 cover the basics for word processing, spreadsheets, and presentations, respectively.

Gmail

Gmail (www.gmail.com) is Google's solution to e-mail. It features a simple interface and a lot of cool innovations, such as conversations and labels. You can also use Gmail with your favorite e-mail program, such as Outlook or Thunderbird. Unlike other free e-mail services, which feature annoying graphical ads, Gmail uses text ads that are less bothersome.

Figure 1-6:
View the
contents of
a document
without
having to
open it.

With Google Apps, Gmail works with your group's domain name. This means that your e-mail can still be *you@yourcompany.com*, but you can use Gmail's intuitive interface and have your e-mail hosted by Google.

Google Sites uses e-mail notifications to let your group or team members know when something changes on your site. When a change is made to a page, Google Sites sends subscribers an e-mail showing exactly what changes were made and gives you a link to open that page directly.

See Chapter 19 to find out more about Gmail.

Talk

When e-mail simply isn't fast enough, use Google Talk (http://talk.google.com). Talk is a really cool instant messaging app that you can either download to your computer or run directly from your site. If you're using Google Apps Team Edition, your co-workers or fellow students are automatically added to your contact list, similar to Figure 1-7. When one of your contacts is online (they'll have a green dot next to their name), simply click their name and start telling them why they're the best member of your team. When you chat with more that one person, each conversation shows as a tab along the top of the Talk gadget.

Figure 1-7:
See
whether
your team
members
are online
and chat
with them
directly.

Add the Talk gadget to any page on your site, and you and your team members are signed in automatically each time you visit.

The second half of Chapter 19 gets you talking with your team and friends. Go there when you want to start talking.

Chapter 2

Getting to Know Chrome

*W*e're going out on a limb here, but if you're reading this book, we're guessing you're more than just a little familiar with the Internet. In your Internet experience, you've no doubt noticed a whole host of new Web services, including wikis, online apps, and social networking, which are changing how we interact with people and information. This new thinking and set of new tools and services is called Web 2.0, and it's light years ahead of the first Web pages of simple text and links. Google thinks it's time for your browser to evolve, too.

The browser is your window to all the information that is created and shared by Web 2.0 services, including Google Sites. Although other browsers have become bulky and slow, Google Chrome provides a fresh, clean view of your favorite sites and services and delivers them fast and efficiently, due to its optimized design.

In this chapter, you get to know Chrome a little better. You find out how to download and install the new Chrome browser. We also show you where all the important buttons and tools are. Part III of this book digs deeper into the settings and features of this lightning-fast browser, so when you're comfortable, skip ahead to check it out.

Choosing Google Chrome

You have many browser choices out there. If you're running Windows, you have likely used Internet Explorer to see the world. If you have a Mac, your Web is powered by Safari. Although both of these browsers do a fine job of displaying your pages and running your apps, there's a better way. Chrome, shown in Figure 2-1, was built from the ground up as a browser for Web 2.0. The developers focused specifically on speed, security, and reliability throughout the design process. Plus, Chrome taps into Google Search to make finding information a breeze. You see what we mean in this section.

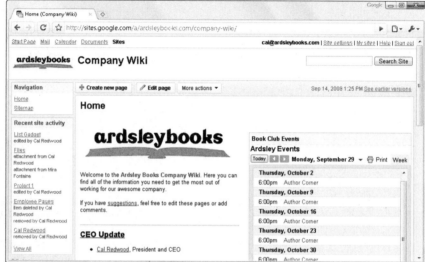

Figure 2-1: Google Chrome's impressive interface.

Using a faster browser

Internet apps use technology that is much more advanced than simple HTML. Older browsers started simple and kept adding new capabilities. Over time, they've become bulky and slow because each app has to load before the browser can load. Who has time to wait for browser windows to open?

Chrome takes advantage of new technology that runs many of these advanced features without using as much computer memory as other older browsers. This means that Chrome starts immediately after you open it and new tabs appear just as quickly. Additionally, many online apps, including Gmail and Google Sites, run much faster in Chrome than in other browsers. Try it and you'll see what we mean.

If you decide Chrome isn't for you, our feelings won't be hurt. You can always go back to Internet Explorer, Safari, or whatever other browser you're used to. However, it's going to take a lot of effort to pry us away from Chrome.

Browser Wars I & II

In the beginning (around AD 1994) there was Mosaic, a small, primitive HTML browser that first popularized the Web. Mosaic was created at the University of Illinois at Urbana-Champaign by a bunch of hotshot programmers, many of whom moved to Silicon Valley and created the next big breakthrough, a much faster browser forever remembered as simply Netscape. Netscape Navigator was the browser of choice until the late '90s when Microsoft released Internet Explorer (IE was first licensed from much of the lingering Mosaic code) and the first browser war ensued.

With a good initial product and its fabled marketing might, Microsoft captured more and more users and pulled ahead as the mainstream Internet browser. Netscape slowly faded into history. While IE began to dominate, however, it added everything and the kitchen sink. The browser bogged down and broke down more than many users could tolerate.

As time went on, the Web was supercharged with 2.0 apps. More and more 'Net apps, such as messaging, voice apps, streaming video, chat, social networking, and online word processing became popular. With Web 2.0, having a fast, reliable Web browser has become more important than ever. In a response to changing needs, a number of alternative browsers have come out to challenge IE. A second browser war is now in full force. This time, Internet Explorer faces stiff competition from Apple Safari, Mozilla Firefox, Opera, and Google Chrome. The focus of these browsers is a return to an efficient, secure, and fast browser that can get the most out of Web 2.0 apps. Regardless of who wins the next browser skirmish, users are the ultimate winners with a better way to view and use the Web.

Making the most of Google Search

The Internet is built around search. Whether you're reviewing products, mastering a new medical procedure, or looking for that special e-mail message, search is indispensable. That's why Chrome builds in Google Search technology everywhere from finding Web sites to locating bookmarks to checking your browsing history.

One of the unique features of Chrome is the Omnibox, as shown in Figure 2-2. The Omnibox combines the browser's address bar, search bar, and search from other Web sites into one location. Whether you know the address or want Google to find it, the Omnibox takes care of you. You find out more about the Omnibox later in this chapter.

 Believe it or not, several other search services are out there that you can use in place of Google, including Yahoo!, Live Search, AOL, and more. When you open Chrome the first time, you have the option to choose Google Search or some other service. You can change it at any time using the Options screen, which we cover in Chapter 10.

Figure 2-2:
The
Omnibox
is your
one-stop
search spot.

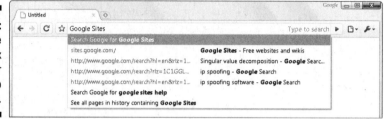

Keeping your computer safe

Chrome even protects you from people who would steal your information or install bad software onto your computer. Every time you use it, Chrome automatically downloads a list of Web sites that Google knows are bad. They either try to get you to give up your personal information or load software to track your behavior. Whenever you come across a bad site, Google blocks the screen and helps you navigate away. If you're certain the site is legitimate, there's an option to continue at your own risk.

Scammers like to make you think you're visiting a popular site, such as your bank or eBay. Although Chrome does its best to protect you from these sites, do not enter personal information, such as PINs or Social Security numbers, on a site that you visit from an e-mail link. When in doubt, visit the site directly (by typing **www.ebay.com**, for example) and log in, or call the organization to see whether the request is valid.

With the Omnibox, you have a handful of ways to tell whether a site is legitimate. In the Omnibox, the domain name of the site you're visiting appears in black letters and the rest of the long address is gray. If you're visiting an eBay page, make sure that the address shows www.ebay.com and not some other address. When you're on a secure site, the Omnibox is yellow and a lock icon appears on the right side. You'll also notice that the "https" letters appear in green.

Downloading and Installing Chrome

Now that you've read a few reasons why we feel Chrome is better than other browsers, it's time to dig in and start using it. This section helps you get up and running in no time flat.

Getting Chrome onto your computer takes just a few clicks. If you're click happy, follow Steps 1 and 2 below and click the buttons that make sense. Chrome installs in a matter of seconds. Otherwise, here are detailed steps to help you set up Chrome just how you want.

1. **Open your browser and navigate to** `www.google.com/chrome`.

2. **Click the blue Download Google Chrome button on the right side of the screen.**

   The Google Chrome Terms of Service screen appears, showing a bunch of legalese text. Optionally, you can grab your lawyer and try to make sense of it.

3. **(Optional) If you want to help Google create better features, click the Optional check box.**

   If you choose this check box, Chrome lets Google know which search suggestions you've chosen and which Web pages cause your browser to crash.

4. **Click the Accept and Install button.**

5. **In the download window that appears, click Run or Open. If another window appears, click Run one more time.**

   The Google Chrome Installer quickly downloads and installs the Chrome browser automatically. When the installation is complete, Chrome opens and the Welcome to Google Chrome window appears.

6. **(Optional) Click the Customize These Settings link and adjust your Google Chrome setup.**

   In the Customize Your Settings window that appears, check the boxes for the settings you want to adjust.

   - *Import settings from:* Check this box and choose your browser from the drop-down list to import your bookmarks, saved passwords, and other settings into Chrome.

   - *Make Google Chrome the default browser:* Check this box to set Chrome as your primary browser. This means that every time you open a Web page, Chrome will open instead of Internet Explorer or Firefox.

   - *Desktop:* Check this option to create a shortcut icon to Chrome on your desktop.

   - *Quick Launch bar:* Check this box to add a shortcut to your Quick Launch bar (to the right of your Start menu).

7. **Click the Start Google Chrome button.**

   The Chrome browser appears, as shown in Figure 2-3. Start browsing right away, or check out the next section of this chapter to find out more about Chrome basics.

8. **(Optional) Choose your default search engine.**

    The first time Chrome launches, you're asked to choose a search engine. Click the Keep Google button if you plan to use Google for your searches, otherwise click the Change Search Engine button. In the Options screen that appears, choose your preferred search engine from the drop-down list to the right of Default Search.

Finding Your Way around Chrome

Remember we said Chrome was fast? You'll notice how fast the window and new tabs appear. The Google engineers were thinking of speed when they built Chrome.

Chrome's interface is designed to be minimal (refer to Figure 2-1). There's no menu bar, no random toolbars, and even the bookmarks only appear on the first page by default. Remember that when you use Chrome, your focus should be the Internet, not the browser.

In this section, we help you make the most of tabs, the New Tab page, and the Omnibox. When you're ready to dig deeper, see Chapters 9 and 10.

Discovering tabs

In Chrome, tabs appear along the top of the window, like folders in a file drawer. Add a new tab by clicking the + (plus sign) button to the right of the set of tabs. Close a tab by clicking the small X on the right edge of that tab. If only one tab is open and you click the X, Chrome will close completely.

Each tab has its own toolbar, complete with navigation buttons and Omnibox, as shown in Figure 2-4. Here's what each button does, from left to right:

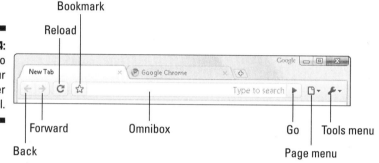

Figure 2-4: Use tabs to keep your pages under control.

- ✔ **Back (left arrow):** Return to the last page you visited.

- ✔ **Forward (right arrow):** Go forward after you've gone to a previous page.

- ✔ **Reload (circular arrow):** Refresh the current page. This is helpful when you're following a breaking news story or the page doesn't display correctly.

- ✔ **Bookmark (star):** Add the current page to your list of bookmarks. Even though a bookmark is added automatically, a popup window appears where you can rename or organize your bookmarks. Chapter 9 has more info on bookmarks.

- ✔ **Omnibox:** Enter your URL or search term here, and then click the Go button.

- ✔ **Go (right-facing triangle):** Load the address or search term found in the Omnibox.

- ✔ **Page menu:** Access common features, such as Copy/Paste or Print.

- ✔ **Tools menu:** Adjust settings or view your browsing history and downloads.

Keeping tabs (no pun intended) on your Internet experience can be a little daunting. While you browse the Internet, chances are you end up with a pile of browser windows that clutter your computer desktop. All the open windows slow down your computer and make it difficult to switch to other programs you may be using. Tabs help alleviate that pain by grouping all of your browser windows into one pane.

If you're used to opening a new browser window each time, start thinking tabs, not windows. For those of you who have the Ctrl+N keyboard shortcut down pat, we'd like to suggest an alternative: Ctrl+T, which creates a new tab. As a bonus, use Ctrl+Tab to cycle through your tabs and Alt+Tab (or Cmd+Tab for you Mac users out there) to flip through your windows.

New Tab page

Where do you go when you open your browser? If you're like most people, you either head to a particular site that you have in mind or want to search the Web for some information. If you're like us, you probably have a handful of Web sites you visit every day. Well, forget using a traditional Home page; the New Tab page can become your new best friend for finding your way easily on the Web.

Every time you start Chrome or open a new tab, the New Tab page loads, revealing all sorts of goodies to enhance your browsing experience. The New Tab page gives you quick access to pages that you're likely to visit. Of course, you can always just start typing in the Omnibox. Here's a highlight of each feature of the New Tab page, which you can also see in Figure 2-5.

Figure 2-5: Use tabs to keep your pages under control.

Bookmarks bar   Searches   Recent bookmarks

Most visited   Recently closed tabs

- ✔ **Bookmarks bar:** Bookmarks to your favorite pages appear in the blue bar, just below the toolbar. When your bookmarks don't all fit, you can find them by clicking the Other Bookmarks button on the right side of the bar.

- ✔ **Most Visited:** Whether it's a blog, your social network, or e-mail, the pages you visit most appear here with little screenshots, so you have a pretty good idea of where you're headed. This section automatically changes as your taste does, based on the number of times you've visited that page. Click the Show Full History link at the bottom of the screen to see where you've been.

- ✔ **Searches:** Quickly find a site in your history or other sites by using the Searches box. Searches will even find text on the page if you don't remember the site name.

- ✔ **Recent Bookmarks:** For bookmark junkies (you know who you are), look here for the latest additions to your treasure trove. Those bookmarks will likely appear on your Bookmarks bar, too.

- ✔ **Recently Closed Tabs:** Accidentally close a tab that you didn't want to? When you open a new tab in the same window, your closed tabs appear. Click the title and it will reappear, complete with that tab's browsing history, so you can go backward and forward right where you left off.

If you really want to see your traditional Home page instead of the New Tab page when you start Chrome, click the Tools menu and choose Options. In the Google Chrome Options screen that appears, look for the Home Page section and select the radio button next to Open This Page. Type your normal Home page address in the box to the right and then click the Close button. *Note:* The New Tab page still loads on all new tabs.

Unleashing the Omnibox

What could be better than a feature called the Omnibox? The Omnibox sits there quietly, waiting to spring into action and take you where you want to go on the Internet. Here are a few reasons why we think the Chrome Omnibox rocks and how you can use it to become a browsing master.

- ✔ **You can use it to load a site.** The Omnibox is an address bar. Type the URL of the site you want to visit, such as **http://sites.google.com**, and you're taken there instantly. When you start typing in the Omnibox, not only does the URL or search term appear, but you also see suggestions for searches, popular pages, recent pages you've visited, bookmarks, and more. Look back at Figure 2-2 to see the Omnibox in action.

✔ **You can use it to activate a search on other sites.** You can also use the Omnibox to search other sites, such as Amazon.com or Wikipedia. First, you have to activate the site, and then you can search the site using Omnibox. Here's how:

1. **To activate search on a site, first visit the main page and perform a simple search.**

   For example, go to www.amazon.com and search for *Google Apps For Dummies*. From now on, you can search the whole Amazon.com site using Omnibox. A search box for your site will also appear in the Searches section of the New Tab page.

2. **Enter the site you want to search into the Omnibox.**

   Type the address of the site you want to search, such as Amazon. com. If your site is activated, you see the Press Tab to Search Amazon.com on the right side of the Omnibox, as shown in Figure 2-6.

3. **Press Tab on your keyboard and then enter your search term in the Omnibox.**

   The site address changes to a blue Search *yoursite.com* bar.

4. **Click the Go button to the right of the Omnibox or press Enter on your keyboard.**

   The results for your search appear directly in the browser window.

Figure 2-6:
Use the
Omnibox
to search
other sites.

When you have the Omnibox down pat, you're ready to enjoy the Internet fully. There's a lot more you can do with Google Chrome. Be sure to check out Chapters 9 and 10 for more info.

Chapter 3

Signing Up for Google Apps and Getting Your Team Online

*G*oogle Sites isn't going to sit there and do everything for you, although we sometimes wish it did. No, you have to get out there and sign up for an account with Google. A Google Account gives you access to Google Sites, as well as to other services such as Google Health (www.google.com/health) where you can track your medical history online, and iGoogle (www.google.com/ig) which keeps your e-mail, news, and so on, all on one page. Don't worry, though; it isn't difficult at all to sign up for an account, unless, like us, you have a hard time reading garbled letters — you see what we mean in a few pages.

You can choose from two types of accounts: a *Google account* and a *Google Apps account*. We know they sound awfully similar, but there really is a difference in what each one does, and we want to make sure that you choose the best one for you. Here's a quick look at the two:

✔ **Google Account:** This type of account is what the typical home user would choose, especially if that user isn't associated with a company, organization, or school. You can use your regular, tried-and-true e-mail address as your Google Account login, although we personally like Gmail and recommend you sign up for it, too. A Google account also lets you create personalized maps and YouTube channels, upload photos, and access other really cool tools and services.

✔ **Google Apps account:** If you work for a company or are part of a school, and you use e-mail provided by your organization, a Google Apps account is the way to go. Your Google Apps account connects you automatically with other people in your organization, assuming they share the same domain name (that's the part of your e-mail address after the @ sign). This connection makes it really easy to share Sites, Calendars, and Docs. You can also chat right away with your colleagues because you share the same contacts list.

Creating a Google Account

You're just moments away from using Google Sites and all the other great services and tools offered by Google. Before you sign up for a new Google account, check to make sure that you don't have an account already. Open your Web browser and navigate to `http://sites.google.com`. If you don't have an account or haven't signed in, your screen should look similar to Figure 3-1. On the other hand, if you see a list of sites or the option to choose your e-mail address, you likely already have an account. Google will double-check your address when you sign up.

Figure 3-1:
Check to see whether you have a Google Account.

There are two ways to sign up for a regular Google account, depending on what else you want to do with it. To use your existing e-mail address, read the first section below. If you don't have an e-mail account (we know there are some of you out there) or if you want to make the switch to Gmail, follow the instructions under "Signing up for a Google account using Gmail" later in this section. When you sign up for Gmail, a Google Account is automatically created using your new Gmail address.

After you've signed up for a Google account, be sure to check out all the other cool stuff Google offers at `www.google.com/options`. To get a sneak peek at some of our favorites, check out Chapter 21.

After you create a Google account, you have to sign in only once to access all the other Google services. You just have to remember your e-mail address and password the first time you log in after you open your Web browser.

Signing up for a Google account using your existing e-mail address

Creating an account with your existing e-mail address is simple. Just follow these steps:

1. **Open your browser and navigate to `http://sites.google.com` (you can also go to `www.google.com/accounts` to create a new account).**

   Your screen should look similar to Figure 3-1.

2. **Click the Get Started link on the right side of the page below the login box.**

   In the textbox that appears, enter your e-mail address and click the Go button that appears on the right. After Google has made sure that your account doesn't already exist, click the Sign Up for a Google Account link that appears below the textbox. You should see a screen that looks like Figure 3-2.

Figure 3-2: Create a Google account using your e-mail address.

3. **In the textboxes on the Create an Account screen, enter your e-mail address and create a password with at least eight characters. From the Location list, choose your country, and then enter the scrambled letters in the Word Verification box.**

If you can't read the letters, try reloading the page to get a new image, or click the wheelchair icon to the right of the box to hear the letters spoken. Deciphering these letters is probably the hardest part of signing up.

The Password Strength bar on the right tells you whether your password is strong enough. A strong password usually has a mix of letters, numbers, and special characters, such as # or ^. For tips on how to choose a secure password, click the Password Strength link.

4. **Read the Terms of Service. If they look good to you and you're ready to create your account, click the I Accept. Create My Account button at the bottom of the page.**

   An e-mail is sent to your e-mail account to verify that you actually own it.

5. **Log into your e-mail and look for a new message from Google titled "Google Email Verification.". Click the long cryptic-looking link in that e-mail to verify your account.**

   The screen that appears thanks you for verifying your account. *Note:* Depending on your e-mail service, you may need to click a button at the top of the message to enable the link. You can also copy and paste the address in a new browser window if that doesn't work.

Congratulations! You now have an official Google account! When you're ready to begin creating a new site, return to `http://sites.google.com` in your browser and skip ahead to Chapter 4 for some helpful pointers.

Signing up for a Google account using Gmail

So you need an e-mail address, huh? Or are you tired of your old one and want to switch to a shiny new one? Either way, we think that Gmail is the way to go and in this section we help you get your very own address . As an added bonus, your Gmail address will act as your login for your new Google account. Here are five easy steps to create your Gmail/Google account:

1. **Open your Web browser and navigate to `www.gmail.com`.**

   Your screen should look like Figure 3-3.

2. **Click the Sign Up For Gmail link on the right side of the screen, below the Sign In box.**

To find out more about Gmail's features, click the About Gmail and New Features! link in the bottom-right corner of the screen (shown in Figure 3-3) before you sign up. You can also find out how to become a Gmail master by reading Chapter 19 of this book.

Figure 3-3:
Sign up
for a Gmail
account.

3. In the textboxes that appear on the Create Account screen, enter your personal information.

Aside from the basic boxes, such as your name, here are some helpful tips for successfully creating a Gmail account.

- *In the box to the right of Desired Login Name, enter the username you would like and click the Check Availability button.* If your name isn't available, red words appear that suggest some available names similar to the username you chose. Choose one of the suggestions by clicking the radio button to the left of it, or enter a new username and click the Check Availability button again. Repeat these steps until you find an available name (the warning text changes from red to blue when your username is available).

- *When you choose a password, the Password Strength bar on the right tells you whether your password is strong.* A strong password usually has a mix of letters, numbers, and special characters, such as # or ^. For tips on how to choose a secure password, click the Password Strength link.

- *Be sure to choose a security question that you'll remember.* If you ever forget your password, you'll need to answer the question correctly to access your account. You can also enter a secondary e-mail address, if you have one, and Google will send a link to reset your password there.

- *From the Location list, choose your country, and then enter the scrambled letters in the Word Verification box below.* If you can't read the letters, try reloading the page to get a new image, or click the wheelchair icon to the right of the box to hear the letters spoken.

4. **Read the Terms of Service. If you agree with them and are ready to create your account, click the I Accept. Create My Account button at the bottom of the page.**

   You're taken to a screen that introduces you to Gmail.

5. **Click the I'm Ready – Show Me My Account link in the top-right corner of the Introduction screen to go to your new Gmail inbox.**

Now that you have an account, go to Chapter 4 to start building your Google Sites. If you want to find out more about Gmail, Chapter 19 is waiting for you now!

Creating a Google Apps Account

Start taking advantage of Google Sites for your team, your classroom, or your company by signing up for a Google Apps account with your school or work e-mail address.

In Chapter 1, we mention four different editions of Google Apps: Standard, Premier, Education, and Team. Your organization may already have signed up for Google Apps Standard, Premier, or Education Edition, in which case your administrator should have given you a username and password. If you haven't received a login or your company doesn't use Google Apps, you can jump right into Google Apps Team Edition.

Google has created a custom address for your Google Apps. The address will look similar to www.google.com/a/*yourschool.edu* or www.google. com/a/*yourwork.com*, replacing *yourschool.edu* or *yourwork.com* with your school or work domain name, of course.

Follow these steps to sign up for Google Apps Team Edition:

If you receive an e-mail invitation to Google Apps from a co-worker or fellow student or professor, click the link in the message and skip to Step 3.

1. **Open your browser and navigate to your Google Apps custom address (www.google.com/a/*your-domain.com*).**

   Your screen should look similar to Figure 3-4.

2. **Click the Create an Account Here link on the left side of the screen, below the login box.**

   The Google Apps Team Edition Sign Up screen loads. *Note:* If you don't see the Create an Account Here link, chances are your organization already has a different edition of Google Apps. Check with your administrator to obtain your login information.

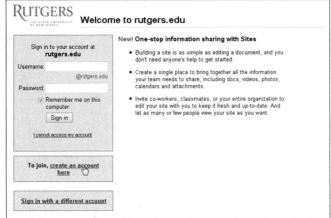

Figure 3-4:
Open your
custom
login screen
to create
a Google
Apps
account.

3. **On the Sign Up screen, enter your current e-mail username and choose a password. Then enter the garbled letters in the Word Verification box and enter your name and location in the boxes that follow.**

When you choose a password, the Password Strength bar below the password box tells you whether your password is strong. A strong password usually has a mix of letters, numbers, and special characters, such as # or ^. For tips on how to choose a secure password, click the Password Strength link. Google recommends that you shouldn't use your work password to protect your security.

4. **Read the Terms of Service and Privacy Policy in the box at the bottom of the screen. When you're ready to create your account, click the I Accept. Continue to Google Apps button below the box.**

An e-mail is sent to your regular work or school address. *Note:* You may have to wait a minute or two for the e-mail to arrive.

5. **Log into your e-mail Inbox and open the message from Google titled "Google Apps: Sign-Up Verification". Click the long, cryptic link to verify your address. On the Thank You screen that appears, click the Click Here to Continue link to return to your Google Apps login screen.**

That's it! You now have a Google Apps account and can start working with your co-workers, study group, or fellow professors. Continue reading to begin exploring the Google Apps dashboard.

Logging In and Finding Your Way around the Dashboard

The Google Apps dashboard gives you access to all your Google Apps, including Sites, Docs, Calendar, Start Page (which is similar to iGoogle), and Talk (Chat), from one convenient Web page. It also connects you with the other users in your school or work domain, and lets you invite your co-workers and classmates to join.

To log into the Google Apps dashboard, open your browser and navigate to your Google Apps custom address (`www.google.com/a/`*your-domain.* `com`). Your screen should look similar to Figure 3-4 in the preceding section. Enter your username (the part of your e-mail address before the @ sign) and password in the boxes on the left side of the screen and click the Sign In button. The dashboard appears, as shown in Figure 3-5.

Bookmark your Google Apps custom address for quick access to your login and dashboard.

In the sections that follow, we help you launch your Google Apps, invite others to join, customize the appearance of your organization's Google Apps services, and last but not least, change your password.

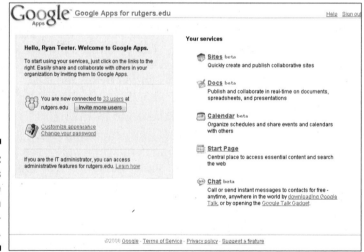

Figure 3-5:
Access your Google Apps from the dashboard.

Launching your Google Apps

From the dashboard, you can launch any of your Google Apps, including Google Sites by clicking the name of the app from the list on the right, as shown in Figure 3-5. You can also download Google Talk to your computer by clicking the Downloading Google Talk link and then clicking the Open or Save File button on the dialog box that appears.

After you open an app, such as Calendar, click any of the links in the top-left corner of your screen to quickly switch between your other apps, such as Docs or Sites. Open your Google Apps custom address (you bookmarked it, right?) to return to your dashboard at any time.

Inviting other users to join Google Apps

Because Google Apps is optimized for teams, getting your co-workers and fellow students to join you online is important if you want to get the most from Sites and the other apps. Here's how you invite other users:

1. **Check to see whether your team members have already signed up for Google Apps by clicking the Users link in the box on the left side of the dashboard.**

   A screen similar to Figure 3-6 appears.

2. **From this screen, click the Invite New Users link to open a screen where you can send a message to other users in your domain.**

   The Invite New Users screen appears. You can also click the Invite More Users link on the main dashboard screen to open this screen.

3. **In the top box, enter the e-mail addresses of your co-workers or fellow students. Then enter a short message in the box below.**

   If you have more than one address, separate the addresses with a comma. Also, your team's e-mail addresses must have the same domain as you for them to receive the invitation. In Chapter 8, we show you how to invite users from outside of your domain to view your Google Sites.

Figure 3-6: View a list of existing Google Apps users in your domain.

Google Apps Google Apps for rutgers.edu   Help Sign out
‹ Back to Home

User accounts

Invite new users
You may invite anyone with a valid email address at rutgers.edu. Learn more

                                                    1 - 30 of 33 Next › Last »

Name	Email address ▼	Date joined
Mark	@ rutgers.edu	May 6, 2008
Adrian	@ rutgers.edu	February 28, 2008
Ajish	@ rutgers.edu	February 8, 2008
Michael	@ rutgers.edu	April 7, 2008
ayez	@ rutgers.edu	Invited on February 8, 2008
cco	@ rutgers.edu	Invited on June 5, 2008
cc	@ rutgers.edu	Invited on June 5, 2008
conrad	@ rutgers.edu	March 25, 2008
Dipesh	@ rutgers.edu	April 23, 2008
Dmitriy	@ rutgers.edu	February 28, 2008

4. **Click the Invite Users button at the bottom of the screen to send your invitation and return to the User Accounts screen or the dashboard.**

   When they open your invitation, they can click on the link and enter their account information in the screen that appears, as described in the previous section. If you decide you don't want to send the invitation, click the Cancel button to discard your message and return to the dashboard.

Customizing your apps appearance

A lesser known, but really cool, feature of Google Apps is the ability to modify how your login screen looks and add your own custom logo to each of your apps. The custom logo replaces the official Google logo that appears in the top-left corner of each of the apps.

With Google Apps Team Edition, anyone in your domain can customize the appearance. Generally, one person adds a logo, and when it's set, everyone else leaves it alone. But, if you or another user gets tired of how things look, here's how to add a little pizzazz to your Google Apps:

1. **Open your browser and log into your Google Apps dashboard.**

   The address for the login screen is similar to `www.google.com/a/yourdomain.com`.

2. **Click the Customize Appearance link in the box on the left side of the screen.**

   A screen that looks similar to Figure 3-7 appears.

Figure 3-7:
Choose a
custom logo
for your
domain.

3. **Choose a set of header logos that you want to use with your Google Apps.**

   To use the default Google logos, click the radio button to the left of Default Logos. To use a custom logo, click the radio button to the left of Custom Logo and do the following:

   a. *On your computer, locate a copy of your logo and save it to your Desktop folder.*

      For best results, resize your logo (using Paint or a similar program) to 143 x 59 pixels and save it as either a PNG or GIF file. You can use a larger, unedited image, but it may appear distorted or fuzzy when it's loaded within Google Apps.

   b. *Return to your Web browser and click the Browse button.*

      A File Browser window appears.

   c. *In the File Browser window, navigate to your desktop and select the logo you downloaded. Click the Open button to return to the Customize screen.*

   d. *Click the Upload button to save your logo to Google Apps.*

      A preview of your logo appears in the Custom Logo box. Be sure to click the radio button next to Custom Logo to make your new logo active.

4. **Select a Sign-in Box Color from the options near the bottom of the Customize screen by clicking the radio button to the left of the color option you want.**

   If you want to create a custom box color, click the radio button to the left of the Custom option and enter a hex number for the colors you want for the border and background.

   Even we don't know what the hex number is except that it's a 6-digit number that identifies one color out of millions. To find the perfect color (and its hex number), open another browser window and navigate to www.colorschemer.com/online.html. Click the colors on the palette at the bottom of the screen to find similar colors. When you find your color, copy the hex number below it (it's the number with the # sign), return to the Customize screen, and paste the number in the Border or Background box.

5. **When you're happy with your new logo and sign-in box colors, click the Save Changes button at the bottom of the screen.**

   When you return to the dashboard or load any of your apps, your new logo appears. It also appears for each of the other users in your domain.

Changing your password

It's a good idea to change your password from time to time. Aside from making you remember yet another new password, it's a good way to keep your information safe. That is unless you keep forgetting your password, and then it doesn't help very much at all. Here's how to make sure that you have the best new password:

1. **To change your Google Apps password, click the Change Your Password link in the box on the left side of the dashboard screen.**

2. **Enter your current password in the appropriate box, and then enter your new password in the two boxes that follow.**

   Keep an eye on the Password Strength meter to make sure that your new password is strong.

3. **Click the Change Password button to save your new password and return to the dashboard.**

If you ever forget your Google Apps password, you can easily create a new one from the login screen. Here's how:

1. **Click the I Cannot Access My Account link at the bottom of the sign-in box.**

2. **Enter your username on the next screen and click the Submit button.**

3. **On the next screen, type the garbled letters that appear in the box and click Submit.**

   Google sends you an e-mail with a link to a page where you can reset your password.

4. **Open your e-mail, look for the message titled "Google Password Assistance," and then click the link that appears in the message.**

5. **Enter your new password twice and click the Save New Password button.**

   A new screen appears indicating that your password has been reset.

6. **Click the Click Here to Continue link to return to the sign-in screen, where you can log in once again to your account with your new password.**

That wasn't too hard, now was it? That pretty much covers the Google Apps dashboard. Make sure that you get your co-workers or study group to sign up, too. That way you can work on your projects, documents, and calendars together.

We won't keep you any longer. Flip the page and get ready to dig into Google Sites and start creating your own Web site, wiki, or file sharing page. You have everything you need to start, so get going, already!

Chapter 4

Exploring Google Sites

. . . .

In This Chapter

▶ Opening your sites

▶ Browsing other sites in your domain

▶ Creating and editing a new site

▶ Familiarizing yourself with the page elements

▶ Adding text, images, tables, gadgets, and more

. . . .

*N*ow that you have a Google Account and have discovered what you can do with Google Sites, it's time to dig in and start exploring. Google Sites is easy to use. If you've ever used a word processor, you already know the basics to making the most of Sites.

This chapter explains how to log into Google Sites and begin creating and editing your very own site. You'll find out how the basic tools work and be on your way to building a useful, powerful site. We also cover how to open other sites that your team has invited you to collaborate on.

Opening Your Sites

Getting into Google Sites is just like logging into any other Web site. After you log in, you can begin creating new sites or edit sites that already exist. When you're ready to create a new site or open your existing sites, open your Web browser and log into Google Sites by doing one of the following:

✔ **Google Account users:** Go to http://sites.google.com and enter your login name and password in the Sign In box on the right side of the screen. Then click the Sign In button.

✔ **Google Apps users:** Go to http://sites.google.com/a/your domain.com and enter your username and password in the Sign In box on the left side of the screen. Then click Sign In.

Google Apps users can also access Sites from the Google Apps dashboard. Log into `www.google.com/a/`*yourdomain.com* and click the Sites link.

The first time you log in, you see a big blue Create a Site button, like the one shown in Figure 4-1. If you've been invited to join a site by a friend or co-worker, you're taken directly to the Google Sites Home, which lists all your sites along with those you've been invited to participate on.

Figure 4-1:
Click
Create a
Site to start
building a
new site.

Note: If you've recently signed into another Google service, such as Gmail, you may be taken directly to your Google Sites Home.

Navigating your Google Sites Home

The Google Sites Home screen, shown in Figure 4-2, lists all the sites that you have access to. These include sites you own, sites you collaborate on, and sites you can view. From the Google Sites Home, you can search your sites, create a new site, or open an existing site. Here are the basic options available on the Google Sites Home:

✔ **Search Sites:** Type a word or phrase in the Search Sites textbox and click the Search Sites button. Your results appear in a list.

✔ **Create New Site:** Click this button to create a new site. We show you how to set one up in the next section.

✔ **My Sites:** Click the site name link in this list to view or edit your site. *Note:* Unless you've already created a site, you may not see any links in this list the first time you log in.

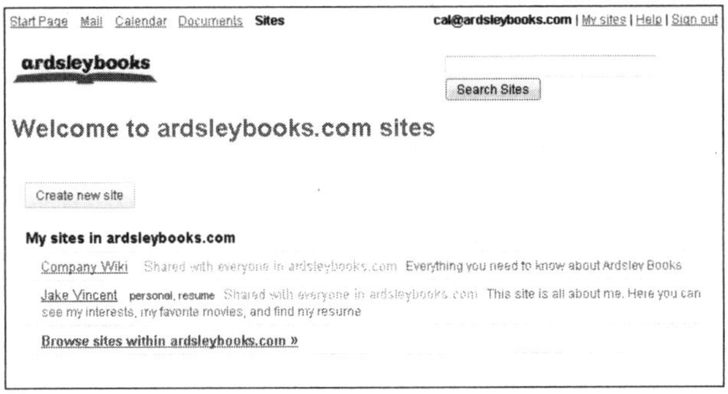

Figure 4-2:
The Google
Sites Home
shows all
your active
sites.

Browsing other sites in your domain

By default, sites created by Google Apps users are automatically shared with everyone in your domain. This means that you can begin browsing through sites that your colleagues have created without having to create one of your own. From the Google Sites Home, here's how to browse those sites:

1. **Click the Browse Sites within *<Yourdomain.com>* link from your Google Sites Home, as shown in Figure 4-2.**

   A screen similar to Figure 4-3 appears.

Figure 4-3:
Click a
category
or use the
Search tool
to find a
site in your
domain.

2. **Click a category link on the left side of the screen.**

   Sites fitting your category appear on the right. You can also use the Search Sites box at the top of the screen. See the section, "Creating a New Site," later in this chapter, to find out more about categories.

3. **Click the title of the site you want to view.**

   That site opens and you can begin browsing through its contents.

Accepting a site invitation

In many cases, it's likely that someone has invited you to collaborate on a site. As a collaborator, you can exercise your wiki power and make changes to the site by adding your insight and ideas.

When you're invited to participate on a site, you generally receive an e-mail invitation, like the one shown in Figure 4-4. The invitation always includes a direct link to the site and may include a brief message from the person who sent the invitation, such as instructions or a description of the site.

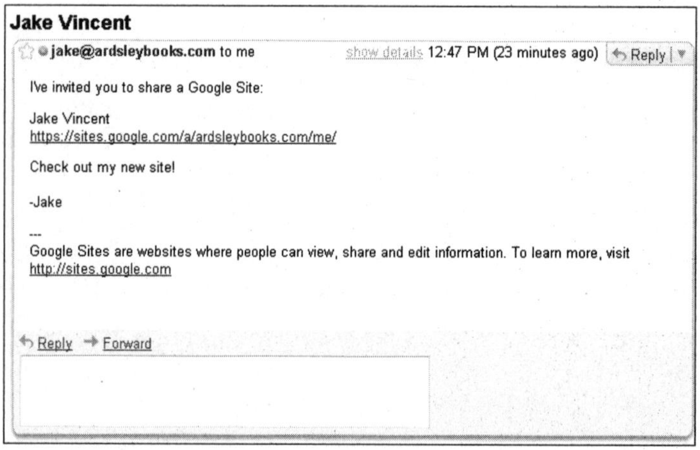

Jake Vincent

jake@ardsleybooks.com to me   show details 12:47 PM (23 minutes ago) ← Reply ▼

I've invited you to share a Google Site:

Jake Vincent
https://sites.google.com/a/ardsleybooks.com/me/

Check out my new site!

-Jake

Google Sites are websites where people can view, share and edit information. To learn more, visit
http://sites.google.com

← Reply → Forward

Figure 4-4:
Open a
site from
an e-mail
invitation.

To open a site you've been invited to, do the following:

1. **From your e-mail client, locate and open your e-mail invitation.**

2. **Click the site link found just below the title of the site.**

   If you haven't already logged into Sites, you're taken to your login screen.

   When you open a site created by a Google Apps user, you're taken to the login screen for that user's domain. If you have a normal Google Account or are not part of that user's domain, make sure that you do the following:

   a. *Click the Sign In with a Different Account link at the bottom of the screen.*

   b. *In the box that appears, enter your e-mail address and click the Go button.*

You're taken to your Google Apps login screen or the Google Account login screen.

3. **Enter your username and password and click the Sign In button to log into Google Sites.**

   On the next screen, you're taken directly to the site you've been invited to. *Note:* Sites that you've been invited to will also appear automatically on your Google Sites Home screen.

Getting back to your Google Sites Home

Any time you want to switch to a different site from the one you're on, click the My Sites link that appears to the right of your e-mail address at the top of your screen. You're taken directly to your Google Sites Home, where you can open the sites you're participating on or browse other sites in your domain.

Knowing your role

Whether you've created your own site or are working on one that someone else has made, you're assigned a role that allows you to make changes to the site . . . or not. As an owner, a collaborator, or a viewer, understanding which role you have is important to knowing what changes, if any, you can make to the site. Here's how you can tell your role:

- ✔ **Owners:** When you create a site, you are the owner. When you log into a site as an owner, you see the Edit buttons, which allow you to create new pages and edit existing pages . Owners also have ultimate power over the site settings and can permanently delete a site when it's no longer needed.

- ✔ **Collaborators:** If you see the Edit buttons on a site that you didn't create, chances are you're a collaborator. You can make changes and add comments but can't change certain site settings, and you can't delete the site.

- ✔ **Viewers:** When you open a site and you don't see the Edit buttons at the top of your page, you're just a viewer. Viewers, as you may have guessed, can't make any changes to the pages on the site. They can only sit back and watch. When you create a public site, other users are viewers by default.

Creating a New Site

After you master logging into Google Sites and finding your way around the Google Sites Home, it's time to begin creating your very own site. Fortunately for you, creating a new site is very straightforward and takes only a few moments. Here's how:

1. **Log into your Google Sites Home.**

2. **Click the Create New Site button.**

   The Create New Site screen appears, similar to Figure 4-5.

3. **Enter your Site information.**

   Here's how that information is used:

   - *Site name:* This name appears at the top of all your pages. It's also the name of the link that appears on your Google Sites Home screen (minus any spaces in the Site name).

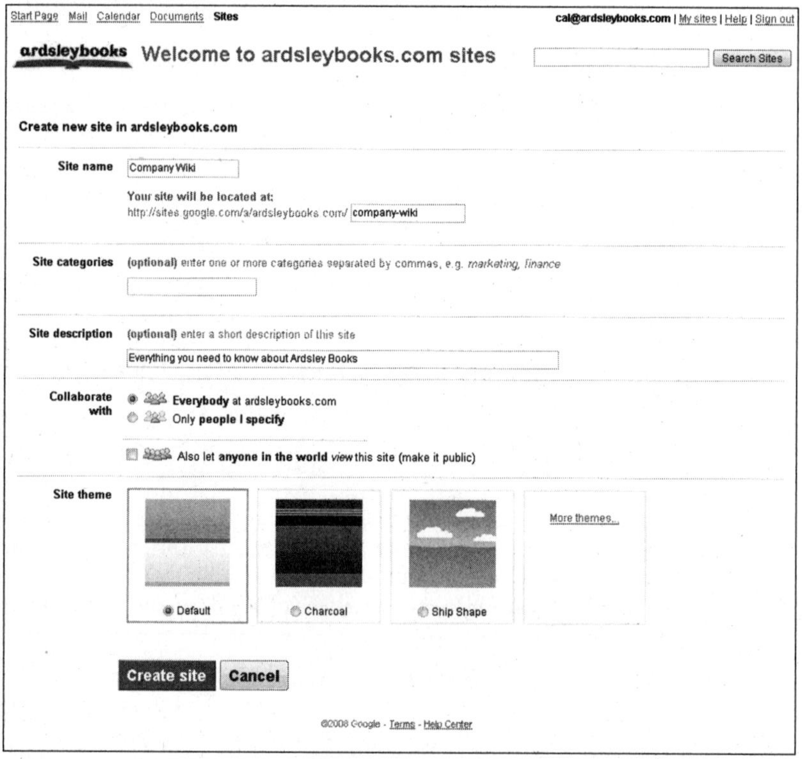

Figure 4-5:
Enter your new site information and choose a theme

- *Site location:* The address to your site includes all the part in gray (refer to Figure 4-5), as well as your custom address. ***Note:*** The site location you choose may already be taken. If you get an error when you try to create your site, try entering a different name or add some numbers or letters to the end.

- *Site categories (optional):* Only Google Apps users see this field. Enter categories here (such as Corporate, or Student Project) to help other users in your domain quickly browse to your site. Make sure that you separate multiple categories with commas.

- *Site description (optional):* Type in a brief description of your site. Descriptions make your site easy to find and appear next to your Site Name link on the Google Sites Home screen.

- *Mature content (optional):* Check this box if you're hosting content that isn't suitable for young audiences. In case you were wondering, Google won't host any ads on sites with mature content.

- *Collaborate with/Share with:* Indicate whom you want to share your site with. To share your site with the world, click the radio button next to Everyone in the World. To keep your site private, click the Only People I Specify radio button. Google Apps users can also choose to share their site with other users in their organization by clicking the radio button next to Everyone at *<Yourdomain.com>*.

- *Site theme:* Select a theme for your site by clicking the site theme box. You can always change your theme or customize your colors and graphics later. To view all the available themes, click the More Themes link and then choose the theme you want.

4. **When you're satisfied with your site information, click the blue Create Site button. *Note:* you may have to type in a garbled code before you can continue.**

   After a few moments, your site is created, and you can begin editing it. Your site now appears on your Google Sites Home screen as well.

If you change your mind about any of your site settings, you can always change them by clicking the Site Settings link in the top-right corner of your screen.

Editing Pages on Your Site

Now that you have a site, you're on your way to creating one of the most useful sites on the Internet — at least for you and your team! This will be where you share your information publicly or keep your team project safe and secure. In this section, we help you know when you can edit pages, what the basic parts of a page are, and introduce the basic formatting tools that are at your disposal.

Using the Edit buttons

When you're the owner or collaborator on a site, the Create New Page and Edit Page buttons appear at the top of each page in the site. These appear in what we call View mode. Click these buttons to begin adding pages and making changes.

- ✔ **Create a New Page:** This button adds new pages to your site. As your project grows, you can add pages that work like regular Web sites, wikis, and file sharing sites. We cover how to use these new pages in Chapter 5.

- ✔ **Edit Page:** Click this button to enter Edit mode, as shown in Figure 4-6. When you're in Edit mode, the Edit Page button is replaced by the Edit Page toolbar. Editable areas on your page are highlighted yellow and appear with a dotted outline.

Header   Body

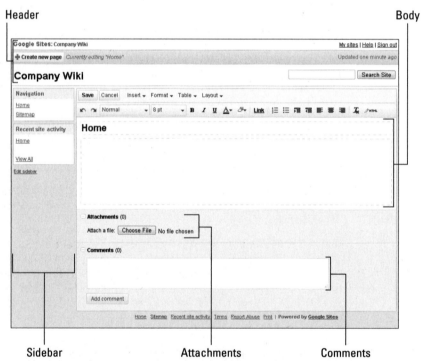

Figure 4-6:
In Edit mode, the Edit Page toolbar appears.

Sidebar   Attachments   Comments

- ✔ **More Actions:** The More Actions button is really a menu. Click it and you see several tools that let you organize your page and subscribe to changes. These tools are used in later chapters.

- ✔ **Site Settings:** This is also a menu that allows you to access your site sharing and appearance options. Chapter 7 digs deeper into customizing your site settings.

When you're in Edit mode, the Edit Page and More Actions buttons are replaced by the Edit Page toolbar. After you've made edits to your page, click the Save or Cancel button to return to View mode.

Web browsers crash from time to time. We recommend you save your page often. Google has your back, though, and in the case of an unexpected glitch, Google Sites will recover your latest work the next time you enter Edit mode.

Checking out your page elements

A basic page in a site has five main parts, as shown in Figure 4-6 in the preceding section.

- ✔ **Header:** This is where the name of your site goes, as well as a custom logo, if you choose. We show you how to customize a header in Chapter 7.

- ✔ **Sidebar:** The Sidebar appears on either the right or left side of the body. Usually, you'll see the Navigation box (which lists the important pages) and the Recent Site Activity box (which show pages that have been updated recently). We show you how to customize your Sidebar in Chapter 7.

- ✔ **Body:** The body contains all the information on a given page. The body of a page can contain paragraphs of text, lists of links, files, Web clips, and gadgets. When you're in Edit mode, the body is the only part of the page that you can change. The body also has a spot for a page title.

- ✔ **Attachments:** You and your collaborators can upload files from your computer to any pages that you to allow attachments. Attachments appear on the page below the body.

- ✔ **Comments:** Get feedback on your page or share your ideas with comments. The Comments section appears below attachments.

When you enter Edit mode, the body is the only area that can be edited directly. However, you can customize many of the other elements as well. See Chapter 7 when you're ready to make adjustments for your whole site.

Using the right toolbar for the job

Users familiar with Google Docs will notice that the tools that appear in Edit mode are very similar to those found in Google Docs. Table 4-1 identifies what each of the tools on the Edit Page toolbar does. In addition to these tools, four menus provide additional options for formatting your page. These include Insert, Format, Table, and Layout. In the next sections, we cover how to use these tools to format your text and objects.

TIP

The Edit Page toolbar always appears at the top of the window, even if you scroll down on a page. This way, you have easy access to your tools even when you're not at the top.

Table 4-1	Edit Page Toolbar Commands and Shortcuts		
Button	**Command**	**Keyboard Shortcut**	**What It Does**
Save	Save		Saves your page and exits Edit mode
Cancel	Cancel		Exits Edit mode without saving any changes you have made
↰	Undo (Last Edit)	Ctrl+Z	Undoes the last change you made
↱	Redo (Last Edit)	Ctrl+Y	Undoes the last undo
Sans Serif ▼	Font		Changes the style of the font
Size ▼	Font Size		Increases or decreases the size of the font
B	Bold	Ctrl+B	Applies bold formatting
I	Italic	Ctrl+I	Applies italic formatting
<u>U</u>	Underline	Ctrl+U	Underlines words
A▼	Text Color		Changes the color of your text
✎▼	Text Background (Highlight) Color		Adds a color behind words just like a highlighter pen

Button	Command	Keyboard Shortcut	What It Does
Link	Add or remove link	Ctrl+K	Creates a hyperlink in your page so that readers can click to view a related Web page or other resource
	Numbered List		Creates a numbered list
	Bullet List		Creates a bulleted list
	Decrease Indent		Moves paragraphs or lists half an inch to the left
	Increase Indent		Moves paragraphs or lists half an inch to the right
	Left (Align Left)		Aligns text to the left margin of a page
	Center (Align Center)		Aligns text to the center of a page
	Right (Align Right)		Aligns text to the right margin of the page
	Remove Formatting	Ctrl+ Space	Strips any formatting, such as bold, underlIne, or font changes, from selected text
HTML	HTML		Edits the HTML code for the selected editable area

Applying Text Formatting to Your Page

Most of the buttons on the Edit Page toolbar are used for formatting. Formatting makes pages more interesting visually and makes them easier to read. You can apply formatting to your text by doing either of the following:

✔ Select any text you want to format and click the desired button.

✔ While you're typing, click a formatting button first to turn on the feature, enter your text, and then click the formatting button again to turn off the option.

Changing your body text style

The body text that appears on each new page uses a font called Normal, size 10. Normal is a basic Web font without any frills. The point size refers to how big or small a font appears on-screen and in print. The higher the number, the larger the font. The default 10 point (10pt) font is large enough for most readers.

To change the way your text appears, first highlight the text you want to change. Click the Font drop-down list (by clicking the little triangle shown in Figure 4-7) and choose a different font from the list, such as Georgia, Trebuchet, or Verdana. In similar fashion, to change the text size, click the Size drop-down list and choose a different point size, such as 12 or 14.

Figure 4-7:
Choose your font and size options from their drop-down menus on the Edit Page toolbar.

The same procedure applies for changing the color of your text or placing a highlight color around your words. To change the color of text, click the Text Color button and select a color from the color palette that appears. To add a highlight color around your words, click the Highlight Color button and select the color you want from the palette. Be sure the highlight color contrasts with the color of your text so that it can be read easily.

Adding emphasis

There's nothing more basic than applying bold, italic, and underline formats to your words to help you make a point.

✔ **Bold:** Makes your words appear more important, with darker, thicker letters.

✔ *Italic:* Slants your text onto its side to offset it from other text.

✔ **Underline:** Used for titles and headings, underline adds a line below the text. Underline should be used sparingly because other users may mistake it for a link, which is usually underlined on Web pages.

Removing unwanted formats

 Font style, color, bold, and other formats can be removed easily by selecting your text and clicking the Remove Formatting button. You can remove formatting by either clicking the Remove Formatting button from the Edit Page toolbar or you can choose Format⇨Clear Formatting.

Creating lists

 To begin a list, click either the Numbered or Bulleted list buttons, enter the first list item, and then press Enter. Each time you press the Enter key, a new bullet or the next number appears. You can also create the entire list first, select the list, and then tap the appropriate button. Bulleted lists perform these functions (and look like this one):

✔ Display information in no particular order or sequence.

✔ Provide an easy way to organize similar types of information.

✔ Make complicated lists of information easier to read and take in.

Numbered lists imply a sequence of events. You can start this kind of list by

1. **Pressing the Numbered List button.**
2. **Entering your text.**
3. **Pressing Enter at the end of each paragraph.**

 To turn bulleting or numbering off, click the buttons again. You may need to press Enter after your list ends and also tap the Decrease Indent button a few times to realign your text to the left margin, which we discuss next.

Aligning your paragraphs

 The Increase Indent button moves a selected paragraph ½ inch to the right of the current margin. This is often used for long quotes. The Decrease Indent button does just the opposite by moving an entire paragraph ½ inch to the left. This button is often needed to correct paragraphs that may slip out of alignment. For example, if the bullets or numbers are removed from a list, oftentimes the paragraphs remain indented improperly. Simply select the misaligned paragraphs and then click the Decrease Indent button.

 The Edit Page toolbar offers three one-click alignment possibilities:

- ✔ **Left align:** By default, text on pages is aligned to the left margin. This means that the text appears straight on the left margin yet is ragged on the right side, as a quick glance at the toolbar icons reveals. To move centered, right-aligned, or justified text to the default left margin, select the text and click the Align Text Left button.

- ✔ **Center align:** To center a title or an image, select your text or image and then click the Center button. You can also click the Center button first and then enter your text.

- ✔ **Right align:** Align your text on the right margin by clicking the Align Text Right button. This option is rarely used because it's often hard to read text that is ragged on the left side of a page.

 The Format menu provides alternative ways of selecting the left, right, and center align commands. For example, to justify left, click Format⇨Align⇨Left.

Power formatting with styles, superscripts, subscripts, and more

The Format menu provides text styles that can help you quickly locate important information on your page. Styles are used primarily to organize your content. They are particularly handy if you want to add a table of contents for quick page navigation.

The following styles can be applied by selecting your text and choosing one of these options from the Format menu:

- ✔ **Heading (H2):** The largest heading style; generally used for titles.

- ✔ **Sub-heading (H3):** A smaller heading style; sub-headings are often used for section titles.

- ✔ **Minor heading (H4):** The smallest heading style. Slightly larger than normal text, apply this style to less important section headings.

- ✔ **Normal paragraph text:** The default style for normal text. Apply the normal paragraph style to remove other styles, such as H2, H3, and H4.

In the lower section of the Format menu are some other important, yet specialized, formatting commands:

- ✔ **Strikeout:** Apply this style to put a line through (or strike out) words.

- ✔ **Superscript:** Apply this style to raise text above the line. This style is used often for footnote references and exponents in mathematics, such as $2^3=8$.

- ✔ **Subscript:** Use this style to lower the text below the line. This style is used for such things as chemical notations, as in H_2O.

Inserting Images, Links, Table of Contents, Lines, and Other Gadgets

Sites are about more than just words. They're meant to be dynamic, colorful, and very useful. The Insert menu helps you do just that. To see what we mean, click the Insert menu and look at all the options. This menu allows you to insert a host of elements: images, links, table of contents, horizontal lines, content from other Google Apps, and other gadgets.

Before we jump into this detailed list, it may be good to preview what some of these features actually do. Take a look at Figure 4-8. We will refer back to this figure several times in the next few pages.

Figure 4-8: Elements that can be applied from the Insert menu.

Adding images

Inserting images is a breeze. You can insert images that already appear on other Web pages, or upload your own pictures from your computer. Follow the steps below.

If you're adding an image from another Web page, make sure that you have permission to use it on your page. *Note:* Clip art and images from Wikipedia are generally okay to use.

1. **Click your mouse where you want the image to appear on the Page.**

2. **Click the Insert menu and then click the Image option.**

   The Add an Image screen appears.

3. **Select either the Uploaded Images radio button or the Web Address (URL) radio button.**

   Depending on which radio button you select, the steps change a bit:

   a. If you select the Uploaded Images radio button, click the Browse button. In the File Upload dialog box that appears, browse to your file, select it, and then click the Open button, which places the path to the file in the Browse box.

   b. If you select the Web Address (URL) radio button, type or paste the URL into the Image URL textbox. A preview of the image appears in the dialog box.

4. **Click the Add Image button to place the image on your page, or choose Cancel to abandon the process.**

5. **(Optional) To make changes in how your image appears, click the image.**

   A blue bar appears below the image with several options, as shown in Figure 4-9.

Figure 4-9: Click an image to show its formatting bar.

Align: L C R - Size: S M L **Original** - Wrap: on **off** - Remove

- *Align:* Aligns your image to the left, right, or center of the text adjacent to the image.

- *Size:* Changes how large your image will appear by clicking the S, M, or L options. You can also click the little white boxes around your image to resize the image manually.

- *Wrap:* Allows the text to appear around or alongside the text. If you don't check this option, the text is pushed below the image.

- *Remove:* Deletes the image from your page.

Google Sites can also access images directly from the Internet, so you don't have to upload the file and you save space. When you find an image on another Web page that you want to add to your site, right-click the image and choose Copy from the menu that appears. Return to your site and open your page in Edit mode. Click where you want your image to appear and choose Edit⇨Paste from your browser menu, or press Ctrl+V. Like magic, your image appears and you can make any adjustments you like.

Linking to other pages

Links are very useful when you want to locate frequently used Web pages, e-mail addresses, or other online resources. To create a hyperlink on your page, select the text you want to turn into a link and click the Link button on the Edit Page toolbar or choose Insert➪Link. The Create Link window appears.

From the list that appears, choose from the options below. The textbox changes depending on the option you select.

✔ **Existing Page:** Links to another page in your site. From the list, click the name of the page you want to link to and then click the OK button to insert the link. You can also click the Create New Page button at the bottom of the window to add a new page on the fly.

✔ **Web address:** Enter the URL in the textbox that appears, such as `www.wikipedia.org`. (Google Sites automatically adds the `http://` for you.)

If you need to change any of the settings above, click the linked text and click the Change link in the blue box that appears. Remove the link entirely by selecting the link and clicking the Remove link.

Adding a table of contents

A table of contents lists all the headings that appear on a page. When you add a table of contents to a page in Google Sites, all the titles to which you added an H2, H3, or H4 heading by using the Format menu will be listed as links; refer to Figure 4-8. Visitors can click a heading from the table of contents to skip directly to that section on the page. This is especially helpful for pages with lots of text, such as handbooks or manuals.

To insert a table of contents, choose Insert➪Table of Contents. The Insert Table of Contents screen appears. Enter a width for your table of contents and then click Save. A placeholder for your table of contents is added to your page. As with images, to adjust the wrapping and alignment, click the placeholder and choose your options from the blue bar that appears.

The table of contents does not show your links in Edit mode. When you click the Save button and preview your site, you can make sure that your table of contents appears correctly. The links are automatically updated every time you add or remove headers and click Save.

Inserting horizontal lines

Horizontal lines can be placed on a page to separate sections or paragraphs. It's like drawing a line with a pencil horizontally across a piece of paper. (To see a sample, refer to Figure 4-8.) Add a horizontal line to your page by choosing Insert⇨Horizontal Line.

Fitting Your Stuff in Tables

Tables create little boxes in a grid pattern inside a page. By using columns and rows, tables organize certain types of information in a valuable and visual way.

Follow these steps to create a table:

1. **Click the Table menu and choose Insert Table.**

   A grid appears where you can select how large you want your table to be.

2. **Highlight the number of rows (down) and columns (across) that you want for your table and then click the square in the bottom-right corner.**

   Your new table appears on your page and you can begin entering lists, numbers, and more.

After you create your table, you can format the text by using the Edit Page toolbar and then insert images, links, or anything else with the Insert menu.

The Table menu gives you further control over your table. From the menu you can modify, move, insert, or delete an entire table, one or more columns, one or more rows, and one or more cells.

- ✔ **Inserting rows and columns:** Place your insertion point in the column or row where you want the new row or column to appear. Click the Table drop-down list followed by Insert Row Up, Insert Row Down, Insert Column on the Left, or Insert Column on the Right.

- ✔ **Deleting rows and columns:** Select the column or row you want to delete. Click the Table drop-down list followed by Delete Table, Delete Row, or Delete Column.

Moving existing columns is more problematic than moving rows. Start by inserting a new column as explained above. Select and copy the column you want to move and then paste the information into the new column. Only then should you delete the original column of information.

Fitting More Stuff on Your Page

Although you can create an unlimited number of pages and stretch your page as long as you like, you may find it useful to keep more gadgets and other useful information at the top of your page. This is especially true for your main Home page. For this reason, you can choose between one column, which keeps things simple, or two columns, which gives you twice the space.

To change the number of columns on your page, click the Layout drop-down list and choose either One-column or Two-column. The two-column layout adds an extra editable area to the body of your page. Click inside either column to add text, graphics, or other gadgets as you normally would.

Part II

Constructing and Sharing Your Google Site

The 5th Wave — By Rich Tennant

In this part . . .

Here we cover the bread and butter of Google Sites. Three chapters are dedicated to helping you tweak your style and fill your site with content, gadgets, and more. You also see how to add stuff from Google Docs and Google Calendar.

The last two chapters help you share your site with the world. Get your team on board with your project, let your family in on the excitement, or create a site that only you can change. We show you how here.

Chapter 5

Mastering Page Layouts and Tools

• •

• •

*W*e mention at the beginning of this book that Google Sites combinesall the tools you need to create dynamic Web pages, construct powerful wikis, and easily share files with your team, class, or family. To help make these functions possible, you can choose from five different layouts and create a site that does everything you need to get your project done or share your stuff. Each layout combines elements of the basic wiki page with a specific set of easy-to-use tools to help you share your work and keep on top of your projects.

Here's a look at your layout choices. To see these pages in action, look for the sections in this chapter dedicated to each of these layouts.

✔ **Web Page:** Use a Web page to share information. Web pages are great for manuals or handbooks, notes, and other information. Images and gadgets add pizzazz to any Web page.

✔ **Dashboard:** The dashboard page brings together all the great Google Gadgets, which are like mini Web pages with dynamic content. You choose which gadgets you want, and Google takes care of updating and showing off your stuff.

✔ **Announcements:** When you want to make important information known, the Announcements page works wonders. This layout allows you to post news and comments in much the same way you do with a blog.

✔ **File Cabinet:** To make file sharing easy, the File Cabinet layout keeps your documents neat and tidy. The File Cabinet even keeps track of different versions of your files so you can find an older copy if you need to.

✔ **List:** The List layout is very flexible and lets you create virtually any type of list. From To Do lists and rosters to checklists and deadlines, you can keep track of it all with a List.

After you create a new site, adding new pages and expanding your site is a breeze. This chapter starts with steps to easily add new pages to your site. Then in the following sections, you see how to use each of the tools that are specific to each layout.

If you don't have a site already, Chapter 4 goes through the steps to create one.

Adding New Pages to Your Site

Depending on what kind of site you want, adding a variety of pages can help you keep all of your important information handy and help you get your project done in a flash. We won't tell you how you should organize your pages, but Part II of this book has some great suggestions for personal, work, school, and project sites.

After you fill your home page and are ready to expand your site, adding pages and choosing a new page layout is simple. Here's how:

1. **Open your browser and log into your site.**

2. **Click the Create New Page button at the top of the page.**

   You see a screen similar to Figure 5-1. *Note:* If you don't see the Create New Page button on a site you didn't create, you may not be allowed to make changes to the site. First, make sure that you're logged in (there's a login link at the bottom of the screen); then if you still can't make changes, ask the site owner to add you as a collaborator.

3. **Type the name of your new page in the Page Name textbox.**

   You can adjust your page name later by editing the page title.

4. **Click the radio button inside the box of the page layout you desire.**

5. **Choose where you want to put the page:**

   • *Put page at the top level.* Pages that are general to your site, such as announcements or main project pages usually go here.

   • *Put page under current page.* If the page you're creating is related to the page you were just viewing, choose this option to create a sub-page. Grouping similar pages together helps you keep your site organized.

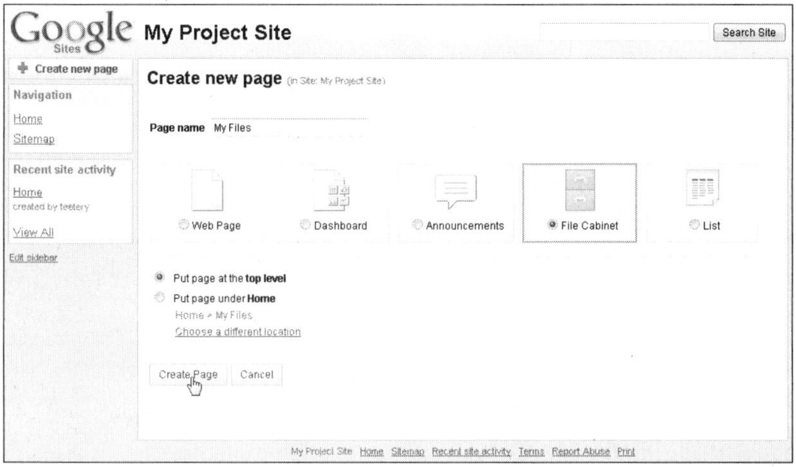

Figure 5-1:
Choose a
page layout
for your new
page.

- *Choose a different location.* This is helpful if you want to create a
  sub-page, like the preceding option. Click this link to group your
  page with another existing page on your site, as shown in Figure
  5-2. From the list that appears, click the name of the page you want
  to group with and then click the Select button.

Figure 5-2:
Group
pages by
clicking
an existing
page from
your site.

6. **Click the Create Page button to add the new page to your site.
   Otherwise, click Cancel if you don't want a new page after all.**

Crash course in site organization

A word on Web site structure: You may want to draw a diagram of your site before you begin creating it. If you don't know how many pages to create, look for some ideas in Part IV. When you start creating your site, you make a new page for each function you want your site to have.

The structure shown in Figure 5-2 may work as a good start for a project site, but you ultimately decide whether you want more pages or fewer pages, depending on your organization and how much information you want to share. Don't be limited to the options we show you in this figure.

Adjusting page settings

Each page has several options that allow you to tweak and personalize the elements that appear on your page. These settings let you show or hide elements, such as the header or attachments, and allow you to add your page to the Navigation box on your site's Sidebar.

1. **Open the page whose settings you want to adjust.**

2. **Click the More Actions button at the top of the page and choose Page Settings from the list that appears.**

   Note: If you are currently in Edit mode, you won't see the More Actions button until you click Save or Cancel on the Edit Page toolbar.

3. **Check the boxes next to the settings you want to enable. Uncheck the boxes to disable specific settings.**

   Each option does something a little different. Read on to find out what each of them does. *Note:* Depending on the page layout, you may not see all these options.

   - *Show This in "Navigation" in the Sidebar:* By default, the Navigation box appears on the Sidebar and contains shortcuts to important pages. However, new pages aren't automatically added to the Navigation box. Check this box to create a new link for your current page. The new link appears at the bottom of the list.

   - *Show Page Title:* Check this box to show the page title. Uncheck the box to hide any information found in the title box. **Note:** The title won't be deleted; you can still edit it, you just won't see it when you view the page.

   - *Show Links to Sub-Pages:* When you check this box, a bar appears along the bottom of the page with links to sub-pages. These links are convenient when you want to show additional information but don't want it to take up space in the Navigation box. **Note:** This option may not appear for all pages.

- *Allow Attachments:* Check this box to enable yourself and other users to upload files to your page. When attachments are allowed, you see the Attachments bar along the bottom of the page. See the "Working with Attachments" section later in this chapter to find out how attachments work.

- *Allow Comments:* When this box is checked, users can make comments to the page, including questions and suggestions. When comments are allowed, the Comments bar appears along the bottom of the page. See the "Making comments" section later in this chapter for more information.

- *Page URL:* Each page has a specific address, usually based on the page title. Edit the shortcut name for your current page in the box below this option. The page URL appears at the end of your site address. For example, the page URL for "project-1" shows up as `http://sites.google.com/site/yoursite/project-1` for Google Account users and `http://sites.google.com/a/yourdomain.com/yoursite/project-1` for Google Apps users.

The page URL for your page can be found at any time on the Address bar of your Web browser.

4. **When you're finished making adjustments, click the Save button. If you don't want to save, click the Cancel button.**

Working with attachments

Attachments are files that you upload to a page. With Sites, they're similar to attachments that you send to a friend or co-worker as part of an e-mail message. Just as an e-mail attachment usually has something to do with the e-mail message being sent, attachments on Google Sites are generally related to the page you upload them to. For example, if you create a page for a school field trip or a company retreat, users can attach files that include maps, itineraries, permission forms, and so on, without having to create separate pages for them.

When enabled, the Attachments bar appears at the bottom of the page, as shown in Figure 5-3. Anyone you've shared your site with can see and open attachments, but only collaborators can upload files of their own.

If you don't see the Attachments bar at the bottom of a page, you can add it by following the steps in the preceding section.

To attach your file to a page, follow these steps:

1. **Click the + to the left of the title in the Attachments bar.**

   The upload tool appears (refer to Figure 5-3).

Fun Stuff

- Staff Book Club
- Special Events

Attachments (1)

Directions.pptx 27k - on 7/23/2008 12:23PM MDT by Cal Redwood (version 1) Remove

Attach a file: [   ] [Browse...]

Comments (2)

mira - 7/23/2008 12:25PM MDT - Remove
Where can we find information on Project 1?

cal - 7/23/2008 12:25PM - Remove
Check out the sitemap link

[   ]

[Add comment]

Figure 5-3:
Add files
and com-
ments to a
page with
the Attach-
ments and
Comments
bars.

2. **Click the Browse button.**

   A dialog box appears, allowing you to open a file on your computer.

   Google won't allow you to attach certain types of files, such as files ending in `.exe`, which may cause harm to other users' computers. If you have trouble uploading a file, look for an orange bar at the very top of the page that describes why your file couldn't be added.

3. **On your computer, locate the file you want to attach.**

4. **Click the Open button.**

   The file is automatically uploaded and attached to your page.

Google keeps track of multiple versions of your attachments. When you attach a file with the exact same name as an attachment that already exists, a new Earlier Versions link appears to the right of the file. Click that link to view all revisions of the attachment. To delete an attachment, click the Remove link to the right of the attachment information.

Making comments

When you work on a project, post photos, and create amazing Web pages, comments allow other users to add their two cents or ask questions. As with attachments, only collaborators can post comments, but everyone that has access to your site can see them.

1. **Click the + to the left of the title on the Comments bar found at the bottom of the page.**

   A textbox appears, allowing you to add comments, similar to the one in Figure 5-3 in the preceding section.

2. **Enter your comment in the textbox.**

3. **Click the Add Comment button to add your suggestion or question.**

If you don't like your comment or want to get rid of it, click the Remove link to the left of your name on the Comments bar.

Designing a Web Page

The Web page template is the most straightforward layout available. It basically consists of an editable header and body. When you create a new site, your Home page uses the Web page template by default, similar to Figure 5-4.

Adding text and images to your page is a snap. To find out how or to review the tools available for editing your Web page, see Chapter 4. Web pages are also great places to include gadgets, which are like mini Web pages that show specific information, such as weather or docs. Check out Chapter 6 for more information on how to use gadgets.

Each of the other templates begin with the basic Web page elements at the top and then have specialized tools that allow you to upload files, post announcements, and so on.

There may be times where you want to do more with your Web page than the basic tools allow, such as adding a red background color to a table. If you know a thing or two about HTML (the coding used to design Web pages), then you can add your own special touch to a page.

If you want to master HTML, perform a Google search for *"Learning HTML"* and you will find several great resources that take you through basic HTML and style sheets.

To make changes to the HTML, you must first click the Edit Page button to enter Edit mode. Click inside the header or body box and on the Edit Page toolbar, click the HTML button on the far right. A window appears that looks similar to Figure 5-5.

Look for the tag you want to change and make your edits. To see what your changes look like, select the radio button in the Preview tab at the top of the window. When you're satisfied with your changes, click the Update button at the bottom. If you decide you like your page the way it was, you can always click Cancel instead.

By the way, to change your table's background color to red, look for the <table> tag in the HTML window and add <table *bgcolor=red*>.

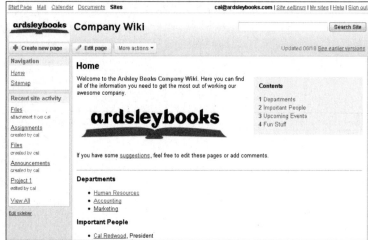

Figure 5-4:
Use the
Web page
template to
share basic
information.

Figure 5-5:
Dig into the
HTML to
tweak your
page.

Steering toward a Dashboard

Projects, personal sites, and class sites have the tendency to have a lot of information spread around on several different pages. After all, you probably want a combination of Announcements pages, File Cabinets, Web pages, and Lists. If you're like us, it's nice to see all your important information in one place without having to click through a bunch of pages. This is where the dashboard layout comes in handy.

A *dashboard* is a Web page that is filled with gadgets. Besides displaying weather and mini-games, gadgets let you see information from other pages at a glance. For your class page, a dashboard might show you recent announcements, course documents, and the semester calendar, similar to Figure 5-6.

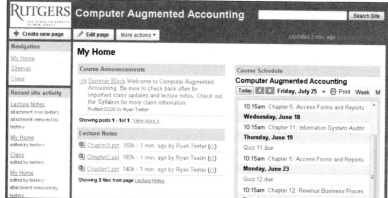

Figure 5-6:
A dashboard shows all your information in one place.

When you choose the dashboard layout, a new page is created with two columns and four placeholders for gadgets, as shown in Figure 5-7. Replace the placeholders with the gadgets of your choice to create a dashboard that works for you.

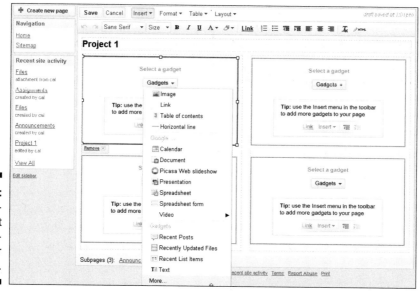

Figure 5-7:
The dashboard layout adds placeholders for gadgets.

If you want your gadgets to take up more space, you can change the layout so that it shows only one column. Click the Layout drop-down list and choose One-column.

Note: Dashboard layouts do not show attachments or comments by default, but you can add them by clicking the More Actions button at the top of the page and choosing Page Settings from the list.

Adding gadgets

An advantage of the Dashboard template is that adding gadgets is a snap, using the gadget placeholders. To turn a placeholder into a gadget, click the Gadgets button in the center of the placeholder and then select a gadget from the list that appears. The Insert Gadget window appears, allowing you to enter your gadget settings. After you enter your settings, click Save to add the gadget or click Cancel instead.

In most cases, your gadget won't show any information until you exit Edit mode by clicking the Save button at the top of the screen.

If you want to add additional gadgets, return to Edit mode and click your mouse inside one of the columns where you want to insert the gadget. Click the Insert drop-down list on the Edit Page toolbar and choose additional gadgets.

Adjusting gadgets

You may have noticed that when you add a new gadget, you enter specific information for the gadget, such as a Web address, or size dimensions. If you change your mind and want to change a setting, enter Edit mode on your page and click the gadget. A blue bar appears either above or below the gadget; in Figure 5-8, the bar appears below the gadget. Each link in the blue bar performs a specific function.

Figure 5-8:
Make
changes
to gadgets
using the
links in the
blue bar.

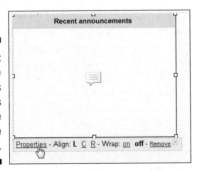

- ✔ **Properties:** Click this link to change the settings for your gadget, such as the size or page it is accessing. When you click Properties, the Edit Gadget window appears.

- ✔ **Align:** Choose which side of the page you want your gadget to hang out on. *L* means left, *C* means center, and *R* means right. Click each letter to find the alignment you like best.

- ✔ **Wrap:** When you have other text and graphics on your page, you can choose to have that content wrap around your gadget. *On* means text appears above, to the side, and below your gadget. *Off* means your gadget has its own space and text only appears above and below it.

- ✔ **Remove:** Click this link to make your gadget disappear. There is no undo option here, so if you accidentally remove a gadget, you must add it again using the instructions in the preceding section.

Deleting gadgets

It's perfectly understandable if you want to change your page or get rid of an old gadget. To remove a gadget from your page, first enter Edit mode. Click the gadget you want to delete and wait for the blue bar to appear (refer to Figure 5-8). Click the Remove link and, in a flash, your gadget disappears into thin air. Now you can replace it with something more elegant or flashy . . . or not!

Using Announcements

Keep your colleagues, team members, or friends up-to-date with the Announcements layout. Announcements pages are similar to blogs. The main Announcements page lists all your posts or individual announcements, and each post is its own page. Use announcements to share your past adventures or to notify others of upcoming events.

Your newest posts appear at the top of your Announcements page. Each announcement shows who wrote it and when they posted it, similar to Figure 5-9.

You can edit the title and body of your Announcements page just as you would a normal Web page. Click the Edit Page button to get started.

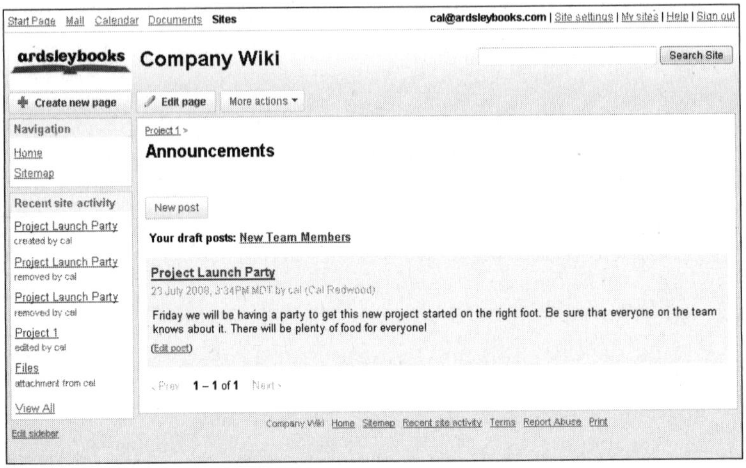

Start Page Mail Calendar Documents **Sites**   cal@ardsleybooks.com | Site settings | My sites | Help | Sign out

ardsleybooks **Company Wiki**   Search Site

✚ Create new page   ✎ Edit page   More actions ▼

Navigation   Project 1 ›
Home   **Announcements**
Sitemap

Recent site activity   New post
Project Launch Party
created by cal   **Your draft posts:** New Team Members
Project Launch Party
removed by cal   **Project Launch Party**
Project Launch Party   23 July 2009, 3:34PM MDT by cal (Cal Redwood)
removed by cal
Project 1   Friday we will be having a party to get this new project started on the right foot. Be sure that everyone on the team
edited by cal   knows about it. There will be plenty of food for everyone!
Files
attachment from cel   (Edit post)

View All   ‹ Prev **1 – 1 of 1** Next ›
Edit sidebar
                        Company Wiki Home Sitemap Recent site activity Terms Report Abuse Print

Figure 5-9:
Keep
friends up-
to-date
with
Announce-
ments.

Writing a new post

When you're ready to start writing your announcements, browse to your Announcements page and follow these steps:

1. **Click the New Post button.**

   A new post is created, as shown in Figure 5-10.

2. **Enter a title for your post and add any information in the body below.**

3. **(Optional) Click the Save Draft button on the Edit Page toolbar.**

   Drafts don't appear in the announcements list nor can users see them. You can always edit your drafts later. Skip to the next section for more information on drafts.

4. **(Optional) Add any file attachments or comments to the bottom of the page. These features are only available if you've enabled attachments and comments for the page.**

5. **When you're ready to publish your post, click the Save button on the Edit Page toolbar.**

Each post is its own page on your site. Click the Sitemap link in the Navigation box on your Sidebar to locate a specific post. You can also search for posts using the search box at the top of the screen.

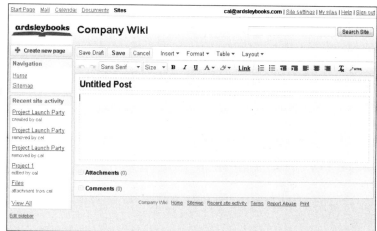

Figure 5-10:
Edit a new announce-
ment just
like you
would a
normal
Web page.

Dealing with drafts

When you edit new announcement posts, you'll notice an extra button in the Edit Page toolbar that reads Save Draft. Drafts are helpful when you write a new post and don't want to publish yet. This gives you a chance to add, edit, or change information before everyone sees it.

After you create a new post, click the Save Draft button on the Edit Page tool-bar. When you return to your Announcements page, you'll see a link to your draft posts below the "New Post" button to the right of "Your Draft Posts" (refer to Figure 5-9). Click the title of a draft post to begin editing it.

After you click the Save button in a draft post, your announcement is posted. You'll no longer see the Save Draft button when you go to make changes.

Deleting old announcements

When you finish with your old posts, or decide you really didn't want to announce that surprise birthday party, you can easily go back and clean up your announcements in a jiffy.

1. **Navigate to the Announcements page where the post you want to delete is located.**

   In the Navigation box on the Sidebar, click the Sitemap link to quickly locate your Announcements page.

2. **Click the title of the post you want to delete.**

   You are taken to that post's page.

3. **Click the More Actions drop-down list at the top of the page and choose Delete from the list that appears.**

A box appears asking you if you really want to delete your post. Make sure that you really don't want to see that post again because after you click the Delete button, you won't be given a chance to undo your action.

4. **Click the Delete button to remove your post or click Cancel if you decide you want to keep it after all.**

When your post is deleted, you return to the Announcements page.

Filling Your File Cabinet

A project can be simple or complex, but regardless of its size, your team is likely going to need to keep track of all sorts of documents to get it done. That's where the File Cabinet template comes in handy. Any of your team members can add documents, spreadsheets, archives, PDFs, music files, and so on, to your File Cabinet. The File Cabinet is also a great place to back up your important files in case something happens to your computer. All in all, the File Cabinet is one of the most useful templates on your site. (See Figure 5-11.)

Figure 5-11:
Keep track of multiple files with the File Cabinet.

Each Google Site holds up to 100 megabytes of pictures, documents, and other attachments. For most projects that's plenty of storage space. However, you may have to go back and delete files if your site stops accepting your files.

Just as you can with a normal Web page, you can edit the title and body of your File Cabinet page. Click the Edit Page button to get started.

Adding files

Uploading your documents is a cinch. Just follow these steps and you'll have everything you need for your project in one place in no time.

To add any of your Google Docs to your page, look at Chapter 6.

1. **Click the Add File button.**

   The Add File window appears.

2. **(Optional) Choose the file you want to add from your computer. Here's how:**

   a. Click the radio button next to the option for Your Computer.

   b. Click the Browse button.

   c. In the dialog box that appears, locate the file on your computer.

   d. Click Open. You return to your File Cabinet page.

3. **(Optional) Choose the file you want to add from the Web. Here's how:**

   a. Click the radio button next to the option for The Web (Paste in URL).

   b. In another browser window or tab, navigate to the file you want to attach.

   c. In your browser's address bar, highlight the URL where the file is located and then choose Edit➪Copy or press Ctrl+C on your keyboard.

   d. Return to your File Cabinet page.

   e. Click inside the first box and choose Edit➪Paste or press Ctrl+V on your keyboard to paste the URL.

   f. (Optional) In the textbox next to Text to Display, type a short name for your file.

4. **(Optional) In the File Description field, enter a brief description of your file's contents.**

5. **Click the Upload button.**

   After a few moments, the window closes and you return to your File Cabinet page. Your file should appear. ***Note:*** If you upload a file with the same name as a file that already exists in your File Cabinet, the old file is backed up and the newest version appears in the list. See "Tracking Files" later in this section for more information.

Organizing files

Life can get a little crazy at times, and your File Cabinet can quickly become overrun by unruly files. Fortunately, there's an easy way to group files into folders so that you can keep on top of your projects or files collection.

To move files to a folder, check the box next to the file or files you want to move. Click the Move To button at the top of the list. If you already have a folder, you can choose it from the list. Otherwise, click the New Folder option from the list. In the New Folder window that appears, enter a name for your folder and click the Save button. Your folder is created and your selected files are automatically added to it.

To get rid of a folder, click the Remove link to the right of the folder name. A warning dialog box appears, letting you know that all the files in that folder will be deleted. Click the Delete button to remove your folder and related files.

If you want to delete a folder but not the files in it, check the box to the left of the files you want to keep and then move them to another folder. You can then remove your old folder without worrying about losing your files.

Deleting files

To remove files from your File Cabinet, check the box to the left of the file names and then click the Delete button at the top of the list.

After you delete a file, no one can access previous versions of the file until another copy is uploaded. All previous versions of the file are hidden, and there's no quick undo option when you delete the file.

Tracking files

When a file has been uploaded more than once, the File Cabinet page automatically archives the old version and replaces it with the new one. This is helpful when you want to keep track of progress on a project or look up information that is found only in an older version.

To track files, click the little version number (v. #) link to the right of the file name. (The file shown in Figure 5-11 shows a v.5 link.) You'll see a list of all the previous versions of the file, similar to Figure 5-12.

Click any Version link to open that version of the file. Newer versions appear at the top of the list. When you finish, click the Back to Page link at the top of the page to return to your File Cabinet.

Figure 5-12:
Keep track
of multiple
versions
of your
documents.

Following changes to your File Cabinet

You shouldn't have to check your File Cabinet every day to see what has
been added and changed. Let Google Sites notify you automatically when
changes happen. Click the Subscribe to Changes button. You receive an
e-mail from the site identifying the file name and who added or changed the
file. The e-mail also contains links that take you directly to the file or File
Cabinet page.

If you don't want to cramp your Inbox, return to your File Cabinet page and
click Unsubscribe from Page Changes. You can also click the Unsubscribe Me
link in any of the notification e-mails.

Tracking Projects Using Lists

The last layout available for your new page is a List. Everyone loves lists.
Whether you're going grocery shopping, assigning people things to do, or
making sure that your project is moving along at a good rate, the List layout
can help.

When you create a new List page, you have several predefined list templates
to choose from, as follows:

 ✔ **Action Items:** After your high-powered meeting with your team, use
   an action items list to follow up. The default columns are Owner,
   Description, Resolution, and Complete. With Action Items, you always
   know what still needs to be done before your next meeting.

✔ **Issue List:** For projects that have issues in need of support, the Issue List is very helpful. Columns include Raised by, Owner, Priority, Issue, and Resolution. In a classroom setting, an Issue list could be used to keep track of student topics or questions.

✔ **Unit Status:** Use Unit Status to keep track of different items, such as widget components. (See Figure 5-13.) The Unit Status list has the following columns: Status, Owner, Feature, and Design (URL). The URL is useful for linking documents, Web sites, or order pages needed for your project.

✔ **Custom List:** Let your imagination go wild with custom lists. Choose as many columns as you like, name them what you like, and select from different field types.

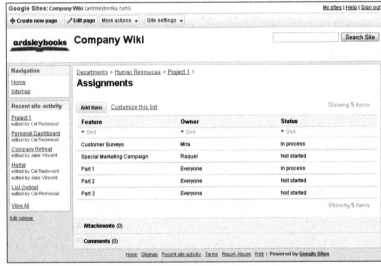

Figure 5-13:
A Unit Status list helps you keep track of projects.

To start adding items to your new list, click the Use This Template button or the Create a Custom List button under the template. You find out more about Custom Lists in the next section.

You can edit the title and body of your List page just as you would a normal Web page. Click the Edit Page button to get started.

Customizing your list

To make sure that your list keeps track of exactly what you want it to, you have the option of creating a custom list or changing an existing list. Here's how:

1. **Click the Customize This List link to the right of the Add Item button.**

   The Customize Your List window appears.

2. **Enter the column name in the Column Name field.**

3. **Choose a column type from the Type drop-down list.**

4. **(Optional) Add a new column by clicking the Add a Column link below your column list.**

5. **(Optional) Change the order of the columns by clicking a column title and then clicking the white up or down arrow that appears to the right of your column name.**

   Note: The column title at the top of the list will be the farthest to the left on your page.

6. **(Optional) To delete a column or field, click the name of the column you want to delete and then click the white X that appears to the right.**

7. **When you're done customizing your list, click the Save button.**

   You can also click the Cancel button if you want to discard your changes.

Adding list items

To add list items, click the Add Item button. A screen appears containing fields for each of the columns on your list.

Here are some things to keep in mind when you fill in information:

- In textboxes, enter text as you want it to appear on your list. You can enter small items, such as names, or large paragraphs and descriptions.

- For check boxes, click the box and a check appears on your list.

- URLs use two fields. Enter the address of the Web page you want to link to in the first box and enter a short description of the page in the second box. The description appears as a link to the long Web address.

Updating list items

Lists change. While your project progresses or when tasks get accomplished, you'll likely want to update your list items. Hover your cursor on the list item you want to change. Click the list item to make the Edit Item screen appear, as shown in Figure 5-14.

Add item Customize this list		Showing 5 items
Feature	Owner	Status
Sort ▼	Sort ▼	Sort ▼
Customer Surveys	Mira	In process
Special Marketing Campaign	Raquel	Not started
Part 1	Everyone	In process
Part 2	Everyone	Not started
Part 3	Everyone	Not started
		Showing 5 items

Figure 5-14: Click a list item to begin editing it.

When you finish updating your list item, click the Save button to return to your list. If you decide you don't like your changes, click the Cancel button instead.

Deleting list items

When you finish with a list item or want to delete an item, click the item, and then click the Delete This Item link at the bottom of the Edit Item screen. The item disappears immediately.

If you delete an item by accident, don't fret — Google Sites allows you to undo your last action. Look for the orange bar that appears at the very top of your screen and then click the Undo link.

Sorting your lists

Ordering your lists is a piece of cake. Sorting comes in handy when you want to group lists by people, dates, or other criteria. The Sort bar appears below the column titles (refer to Figure 5-13). Click the Sort drop-down list below the column you want to organize and then click the order you want from the list that appears:

✔ **A–Z:** Sort the column in ascending order. Numbers appear at the top of the list.

✔ **Z–A:** Sort the column in descending order. Numbers appear at the bottom.

Chapter 6

Adding Gadgets

Gadgets are the bread and butter of Google Sites. They make it easy to add engaging content, share important files, and keep on top of projects. Add that you don't need to know any computer code to add gadgets, and you've got a recipe for success.

Adding gadgets is a snap. When you're editing a page, simply choose a gadget from the Insert menu, enter a few details in the window that pops up (such as how much space you want the gadget to take on your page), and voilà! Your gadget magically appears, making your site more useful than ever.

This chapter helps you harness the power of gadgets. You add content from other Google Apps (which you find out about in Part V), mix up information from other pages on your site, and insert gadgets that share information from the Internet, including weather, news, games, and more. By the time you're finished, we're confident that you'll be a gadget master.

Inserting Gadgets

In case you missed it, gadgets on Google Sites are like mini Web pages that share specific pieces of information. Whether you use a dashboard layout, as we mention in Chapter 5, or simply share some information on a page, gadgets are sure to make your site more engaging. Figure 6-1 shows an example of a page with multiple gadgets.

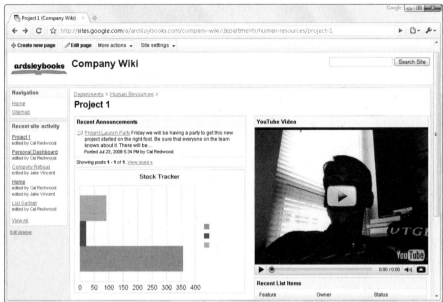

Figure 6-1:
Gadgets add
punch to
your site.

The process of adding gadgets is pretty straightforward. Basically, you open a page on your site, click the Edit Page button and then begin inserting gadgets. Although each gadget may deviate a little from the examples we include here, they tend to have some common elements we explain upfront so we don't have to repeat ourselves.

Here are the basics of adding a gadget to your page:

1. **Open your browser and navigate to the page on your site where you want to add a gadget.**

2. **Click the Edit Page button to enter Edit mode.**

3. **Click the Insert menu at the top of the screen and choose a gadget from the list that appears.**

   An Insert Gadget screen appears.

4. **Enter the settings you want to customize.**

   Each gadget may have different settings, but a few common ones exist:

   • *Height:* Indicate how many points or pixels (px) high you want your gadget. If you want your gadget to fit on the screen, keep in mind that standard Web browsers are about 670px high.

   • *Width:* Enter the number of pixels wide you want your gadget. If you leave this number blank, the gadget will adjust to fit its content or stretch across and fill the column or screen.

- *Include Border Around Your Gadget:* Check this box to show a thin border around your gadget. The color of the border will match your site's scheme. To change the color, see Chapter 7.

- *Include Title:* Check this box and enter a title for your gadget to have that name appear in the top border of the gadget.

5. **Click the Save or Insert button, whichever appears.**

You're taken to your site and a placeholder for your gadget appears on your page. To see your gadget in action, click the Save button at the top of the screen.

That's it. Some gadgets require a few more steps or details than this, such as a page or calendar; we walk you through the more complicated ones in the next sections.

To adjust your gadget settings later, click the Edit Page button on the page with your gadget to begin editing. Click the placeholder for your gadget and then click the Properties link in the blue bar that appears. When you're done, click Save. From this blue bar, you can align your gadget by clicking the L (left), C (center), or R (right) links, and also turn text wrapping on or off.

Meshing Content from Other Pages on Your Site

Let's face it — you can create a lot of different types of pages — Lists, Announcements, File Cabinets, and more. After a while, it can become overwhelming to keep track of them. Although the Sitemap link on the Sidebar helps you find everything fast, and the Search Site tool points you to the right spot even faster, we know how nice it is to have all of your important information together on a page. Chapter 5 Introduces you to the dashboard page. Here we help you make the most of your dashboard and the gadgets you really need to keep your family, friends, or team on the right track.

In the next section, we cover the options you need to know to show off information from your Announcements, File Cabinets, and Lists, and we show you how to create textboxes with extra tidbits for your visitors or collaborators.

Incorporating announcements

When you have an Announcements page, you can add an Announcements gadget to a Web page or dashboard to quickly show your most recent posts. This is particularly helpful for relaying your most recent posts to your family and friends or updating your team about a project, as shown in Figure 6-2.

Figure 6-2:
Keep track
of your
project with
gadgets.

Insert the Announcements gadget as you would any other gadget. First, open the page you want to add the gadget to and click the Edit Page button. From the Edit Page toolbar, choose Insert⇨Recent Posts. The Insert Recent Announcements screen appears. Adjust your settings, in particular these two:

- ✓ **Show Posts from:** From this list, choose the Announcements page you want to see headlines from. All the Announcements pages on your site appear in this list.

- ✓ **Number of Posts to Show:** Enter the number of entries you want to show.

When you're done, click Save to add your gadget. Click Save on the Edit Page toolbar to see the gadget in action on your page, displaying the most recent posts from your Announcements page.

Previewing the File Cabinet

The File Cabinet helps you keep track of files, but like Announcements, sometimes you want quick access to the most recent additions or changes. The File Cabinet gadget, shown toward the bottom in Figure 6-2, lets you do just that.

1. **Open the page on which you want to display your most recent files and click the Edit Page button.**

2. **From the Edit Page toolbar, choose Insert⇨Recently Updated Files.**

   The Insert Recent Files screen appears.

3. **Choose your settings and then click Save.**

   Be sure to choose which File Cabinet page you want to show, and how many files you want to see. A placeholder appears on your page for your new gadget.

4. **When you're finished, click Save at the top of the page to reveal your recent files.**

Abbreviating your lists

Use the Lists gadget to display the most recent additions or changes to a list on your page. This is very helpful when you want to keep track of how a project is progressing or to quickly see what's on your To Do list.

On your page, click the Edit Page button and then choose Insert⇨Recent List Items on the Edit Page toolbar. The Insert Recent List Items screen appears. Choose the settings you want for your lists. Here, you have a few more options to keep track of:

- ✔ **Show List Items from:** Choose the list page you want to show items from by clicking this menu and clicking the page title.

- ✔ **Select the Columns You Wish to Display:** When you've chosen your list, all the columns from that page appear. Check the box next to each column title to show it on your page. If you only want to see a few or have limited space on your page, check only the most important columns.

- ✔ **Number of List Items to Show:** Enter the number of items you want to show. Only the most recent additions to your list will appear on your page.

- ✔ **Sorted by:** From this drop-down list, choose the column by which you want to sort your list items.

When you finish adjusting the Lists gadget, click Save; a placeholder appears on your page. Click Save on the Edit Page toolbar to see your gadget in action, with your list items all in a row!

Creating your own textbox

When you have content to place on your page but don't know exactly what to do with it, there's one more gadget we like that you can use — Text Box. Think of this gadget as you would a textbox in your word processor. It provides a place where you can highlight a point, add a quote, or set aside random stuff that you just can't find a place for on your page.

To add a textbox to your page,

1. **Click the Edit Page button on the page.**
2. **Choose Insert⇨Text Box from the Edit Page toolbar.**

    The Insert Text Box screen appears.

3. **Use the Edit Page toolbar in the Insert Text Box screen to add any images, links, and other tidbits you want to appear. When you're done, click the Save button.**

    A placeholder appears on your page.

4. **Click the Save button on the Edit Page toolbar to see your textbox with the rest of your gadgets and page content.**

Sharing Information from Other Google Apps

If you're using Google Sites to help your team stay on top of its game, chances are you've toyed with the other Google Apps. Specifically, Google Calendar is extremely useful in helping organize your time, and Google Docs is a perfect app to share up-to-date documents, spreadsheets, and presentations.

In this section, you discover how to add a Calendar gadget to your site and insert documents, spreadsheets, and presentations.

Showing a calendar on your site

One of the most useful gadgets we've found shows events from your Google Calendar right on your page. Whether you want to keep track of meetings or let family know about important events, the Calendar gadget is perfect for keeping everyone up-to-date.

You have three views to choose from when including your calendar. Week and Month views are useful when you want to dedicate a whole page to your calendar. However, when you want to keep things concise and not take up a lot of space, we recommend you look at Agenda view, as shown in Figure 6-3. Agenda view shows all of your events for the next 30 days with the upcoming appointments at the top.

Figure 6-3:
Agenda
view
shows your
upcoming
events in
a scrolling
list.

To find more about creating and using a Google Calendar, be sure to check out Chapter 18. Here's how to add a Calendar gadget to your site:

1. **Open your Calendar in a new browser window or tab.**

2. **In the My Calendars list, click the down arrow to the right of the calendar you want to share.**

3. **Choose the Calendar Settings link from the menu that appears.**

4. **Scroll down the Calendar Settings page and click the blue HTML button in the Calendar Address section.**

    A new screen appears, revealing your calendar's Web address.

5. **Right-click the address link and choose Copy or Copy Link Address (depending on your browser) from the menu that appears.**

6. **Open your Google Sites and locate the page where you want to place your calendar.**

7. **Click the Edit Page button at the top of your screen to switch to Edit mode.**

8. **On your page, click your cursor where you want your calendar, and then choose Insert⇨Calendar.**

    The Calendar Properties screen appears.

9. **Right-click the first box in the Insert Calendar screen and choose Paste from the menu that appears.**

   Your calendar address should now appear in the box.

10. **Adjust these settings to your liking:**

    • *View:* Choose an option in this drop-down list to change your calendar view. Week shows a week's worth of events. Month shows a full month, similar to a wall calendar. Agenda adds a scrolling list of all the events coming up in the next month with the closest events at the top(refer to Figure 6-3).

    • *Show Week, Month, and Agenda Tabs:* Check this box to show tabs on the top of your calendar. Anyone who views the calendar on your Site will be able to change the view to show the week, month, or agenda view.

    • *Show Calendar Name:* This option reveals the name of your calendar at the top of the gadget.

    • *Show Navigation Buttons:* Navigation buttons allow anyone who sees your calendar to move forward and backward through months and weeks. When this option is checked, a back button and a forward button appear in the top-left corner of your Calendar gadget.

    • *Show Current Date Range:* This option shows the dates, for a given period, on the top of the Calendar gadget.

11. **Click the Save button to insert your calendar and return to your site.**

    A placeholder for your gadget appears until you save your page. Click Save on the Edit Page toolbar to see your calendar as it will appear normally.

Presenting a document, spreadsheet, or presentation

Google Docs is an online office suite with which you can create and edit documents, spreadsheets, and presentations from any computer with an Internet connection. One of the reasons to use Google Docs along with Google Sites is that you can share the most up-to-date version of your documents, spreadsheets, and presentations on your site without having to re-upload files or constantly publish new changes. This is because when you save your changes to your documents online, your site automatically updates and shows the latest information.

The gadgets for documents, spreadsheets, and presentations actually display your entire document within a small frame on your page, similar to Figure 6-4. In the case of presentations, a small slideshow frame appears, allowing visitors and team members to view your most current presentation.

Figure 6-4:
Show off a
spreadsheet
directly from
your page.

Because Google Docs is key to sharing information on your site, we dedicate four chapters of this book to getting you up to speed. See Chapters 14–17 for more about Google Docs.

When you're ready to share a document, spreadsheet, or presentation, here's how to place it on your page:

1. **In your browser, navigate to the page on your site where you want to share your document.**

2. **Click the Edit Page button at the top of the screen to begin editing your page.**

3. **From the Edit Page toolbar, choose Insert⇨Document (or Spreadsheet or Presentation).**

   The Insert screen appears.

4. **Choose a document from the list on the right of the screen and click the Select button.**

   After you click the Select button, the Insert Document screen appears.

   Note: Use the list on the left side of the screen to navigate through your Google Docs. You can also search for a document by entering a term in the Search box at the top of the Insert screen and clicking Search.

5. **Adjust any of your gadget settings (shown in Figure 6-5) and then click the Save button.**

   A placeholder for your document, spreadsheet, or presentation appears on your page.

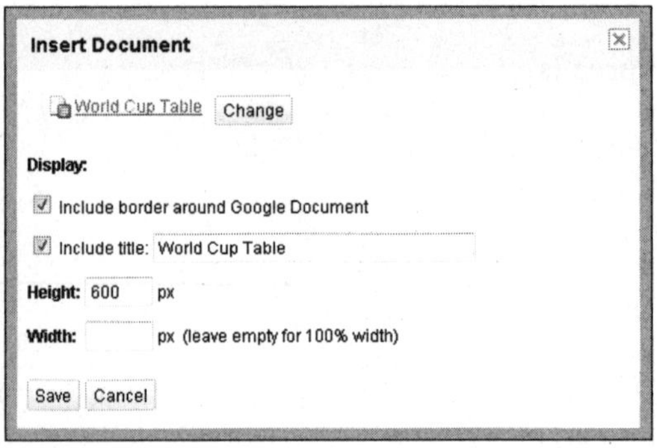

Insert Document   ☒

　🗎 World Cup Table   Change

Display:

☑ Include border around Google Document

☑ Include title: World Cup Table

Height: 600   px

Width: px (leave empty for 100% width)

Save   Cancel

Figure 6-5:
Adjust your
document
gadget
settings.

6. **Click the Save button on the Edit Page toolbar to see your document,
   spreadsheet, or presentation as it will appear on your site.**

   You can always change your settings later by clicking the gadget placeholder and clicking the Properties link that appears.

Linking to your documents

If you don't want to show your whole document within a gadget, you can insert
a link to your document instead. This is particularly helpful when you want to
share a Web presentation and have other users join in and follow along.

Here's how to link to your document:

1. **Open your document in Google Docs.**

2. **Click the Share button at the top and choose Publish as Web Page
   from the popup menu that appears.**

3. **On the next screen, click Publish Document.**

   A link to your document appears.

4. **Right-click the link and choose either Copy Link Address or Copy
   Shortcut (depending on your browser) from the menu that appears.**

5. **Return to your site and click the Edit button.**

6. **From the Edit Page toolbar, choose Insert⇨Link.**

7. **Click the Web Address option in the window that appears and then
   paste the link to your document in the Link to This URL box.**

8. **Click OK and then click Save to save your page.**

   Visitors to your site can now open the document directly from your page.

Inserting charts

In addition to adding spreadsheets, it's possible to show charts and gadgets from Google Docs as well. Like your other Google Docs, spreadsheet charts and gadgets are automatically updated on your site whenever you change the document itself. Here's how to add a chart or gadget:

1. **Open your Google spreadsheet containing a chart or graph in a separate browser window.**

2. **Click the chart, and from the Chart drop-down menu that appears above it, choose Publish Chart.**

3. **Click OK on the dialog box that appears (you'll be re-publishing your spreadsheet) and the Publish Chart screen appears, revealing the URL for the chart image.**

4. **Select only the URL text found inside the quotes and copy it.**

5. **In another browser window, navigate to the page on your site where you want to add the chart and click the Edit Page button.**

6. **From the Insert menu, choose Image.**

   The Add an Image screen appears.

7. **Click the Web Address (URL) link on the left side of the screen.**

8. **Inside the Image URL box, select the http:// text and paste the address of your chart.**

   A preview of your chart image appears in the box underneath. If you don't see your chart, check your chart's address.

9. **Click the Add Image button to insert your chart and return to your site.**

10. **Click the Save button to save your changes and view your chart.**

Gather information with a spreadsheet form

Another great use of Google Docs is collecting information from your site into a spreadsheet. This is useful for conducting informal polls, creating a mailing list, or having guests you've invited RSVP to a party.

This is a two-part process. To start collecting information, you need to create (and save your responses into) a spreadsheet. Check out Chapter 16 to find more about spreadsheets.

Here's Part 1:

1. **In your browser, open Google Docs.**

2. **Click the New button and choose Form from the list that appears.**

    The New Form screen appears in a new window, similar to Figure 6-6.

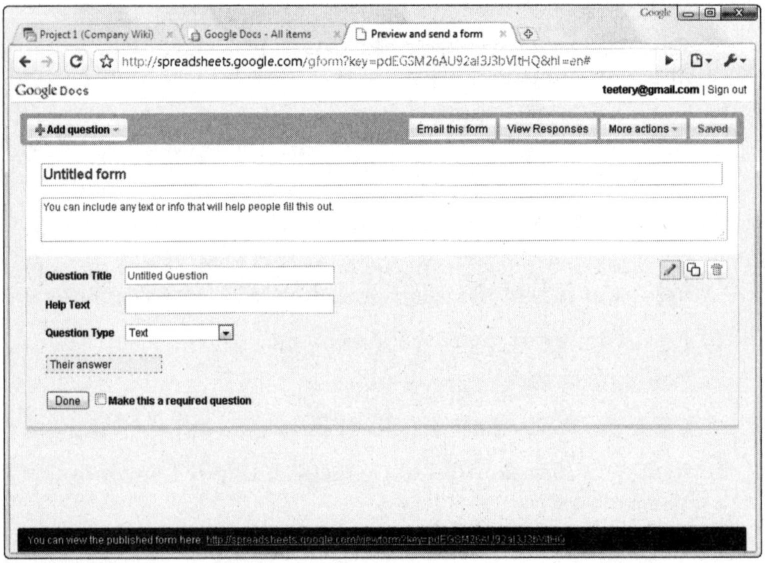

Figure 6-6:
Create a
new form
in Google
Docs.

3. **Enter a form title and description in the first two textboxes, provide the Question Title and Help Text information, and then choose a question type from the Question Type drop-down list.**

4. **(Optional) For list questions, enter the items you want your respondents to choose from.**

5. **Click Done when your question looks good.**

6. **(Optional) Click the Add Question button to create additional questions by repeating Steps 3 through 5.**

7. **Click Save to save your new form.**

8. **At the bottom of the screen, right-click the link inside the black box and choose either Copy Link Location or Copy Shortcut (depending on your browser) from the menu that appears.**

Now that you have a form, it's time to add it to your page. Here's Part 2:

1. **Open the page where you want to insert your form and click the Edit Page button.**

2. **From the Edit Page toolbar, choose Insert⇨Spreadsheet Form.**

   The Insert Spreadsheet form appears.

3. **In the first textbox, paste the address for your spreadsheet form by pressing Ctrl+V on your keyboard or right-clicking your mouse and choosing Paste from the menu that appears.**

4. **Adjust any other settings and then click Save.**

   A placeholder for your form appears on your page. Click Save on the Edit Page toolbar to see your form in action.

Any visitors to your site can now answer your questions and give you the information you're looking for. To review the responses, return to Google Docs, open your form, and then click the View Responses button.

Grabbing Video and Photos from the Web

There was a time when the Internet was just about words — text on pages that linked to text on other pages. Although it's true that most of the information on the Web is text, video and photos have become an important source of information, entertainment, and sharing. If you don't believe us, check out YouTube (www.youtube.com) or do a search on Google Video (http://video.google.com) and see how many millions of videos are out there.

Showing video to your group with YouTube or Google Video

While you've browsed the Internet, you've undoubtedly come across a blog or Web site that includes a little video clip. Welcome to the YouTube generation. You can join in the fun and show off clips of your own on your site using the Google Video gadget.

Before you can place a clip on your site, you have to find the video clip first. Go to either www.youtube.com or http://video.google.com and search for the video clip you want on your page. Highlight the URL in the address bar and copy it.

Open the page where you want the video clip to appear and click the Edit Page button. From the Edit Page toolbar, choose Insert⇨Video⇨Google Video or YouTube, depending on where you found your original clip. The Insert YouTube Video screen appears. Paste the URL in the first textbox, adjust any of the other settings, and click Save to insert your video. Click Save on the Edit Page toolbar to view your video.

Managing your photos online and offline

Picasa Web Albums (http://picasaweb. google.com) is a free service from Google that allows you to upload and share your photos online. In addition to storing your photos online, Google provides free photo-editing and photo-organizing software called Picasa (www. picasa.com).

After you download and install Picasa, it takes only a few clicks to enhance your photos, organize them into folders, and e-mail or print them. Best of all, Picasa syncs your photos with your online Picasa Web Albums so you can share them with the world, or more important, add them to your site with the Picasa Web Slideshow gadget!

Viewing slideshows with Picasa Web

If a photo is worth a thousand words, imagine what a whole album of photos is worth! Google Sites is a great place to show off your photos, especially if your site is personal or shared with your family. The Picasa Web Slideshow gadget is a Google gadget for photo albums that displays images from Picasa Web Albums, Google's free online photo-storage service.

Although we don't cover creating Picasa Web Albums in this book, we recommend you play around with it if, like us, photos play an important role in your life or project.

After you create some Picasa Web Albums and upload your photos, here's how to show them on your page:

1. **In your browser, navigate to the Picasa Web Album you want to share.**

   You can create and access your albums at `http://picasaweb.google.com`. Click the album cover of the album you want to share to view your photos.

2. **Highlight the album URL in the address bar and copy the address by pressing Ctrl+C on your keyboard or right-clicking the address and choosing Copy from the menu that appears.**

3. **Navigate to the page on your site where you want to add the Slideshow gadget.**

4. **Click the Edit Page button to reveal the Edit Page toolbar.**

5. **From the Edit Page toolbar choose Insert⇨Picasa Web Slideshow.**

   The Insert Picasa Web Slideshow window appears.

6. **Paste the URL of your Picasa Web Album in the first textbox.**

   Press Ctrl+V on your keyboard or right-click the box and choose Paste from the menu that appears.

7. **Adjust your other presentation options:**

   • *Select Slideshow Size:* Choose how large you want the Slideshow gadget to appear. You can always try different sizes by adjusting your gadget later.

   • *Show Captions:* If the photos in your Picasa Web Album have descriptions or long file names, you can click this option and they will appear in the presentation at the bottom of each photo.

   • *Autoplay:* Choose this option to have your presentation cycle through your photos automatically. If you don't check this option, a play button appears on your Slideshow gadget and visitors to your site will have to start the presentation manually.

8. **When you finish adjusting your Slideshow gadget options, click the Save button.**

   A placeholder for your gadget appears on your page. Click the Save button on the Edit Page toolbar to see the Slideshow gadget in action.

Browsing the Google Gadgets Directory

Adding other Google gadgets is a snap. Google maintains a directory of hundreds of gadgets that companies and users have created that put useful and entertaining tools at your fingertips. Some gadgets can even let you access information from all of your Google Apps on one page.

Checking out the gadget directory

To access the gadget directory, click Insert on the Edit Page toolbar and choose More from the bottom of the list that appears. The directory appears, similar to Figure 6-7. (The gadgets that appear may vary because Google users create new gadgets all the time.) Browse through the categories, and when you find a gadget you like, click the gadget link or preview image to begin adjusting the gadget's settings.

In addition to browsing these categories, you can enter a search term at the top of the gadget directory and click the Search button to find a specific gadget. If you're interested in making a gadget for your page, search Google for *make your own gadget* or visit www.google.com/ig/gmchoices.

If you're using Google Apps, you can create your own version of a Start Page by adding gadgets that give you access to your personal calendar and docs or allow you to chat with your contacts. The following sections show you how.

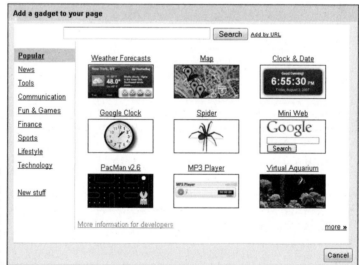

Figure 6-7: Find gadgets in the gadget directory.

Don't confuse the following gadgets with the ones we discuss earlier in this chapter. Although the earlier gadgets let you share your public documents or calendars, the following gadgets are for your eyes only. When you open your site, the following gadgets show you your personal files and only you can see them, similar to Figure 6-8.

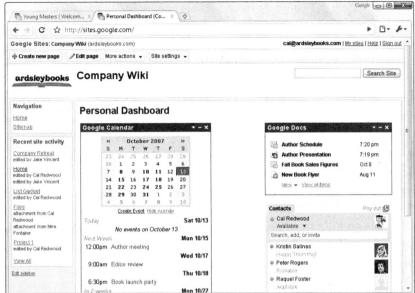

Figure 6-8:
Use gadgets
to create
your own
personal
dashboard.

Seeing what's happening on your personal calendar

Use the Google Calendar gadget to keep on top of what's going on. In the gadget directory, search for *Google Calendar*. If you access your page after you log into your Google Account, you see the following additional features:

- **Create Event:** Opens a new window and lets you add a new appointment directly to your calendar.

- **Show/Hide Agenda:** View your upcoming events in the gadget. You can also click a day on the mini calendar to see events for that day. Click Hide Agenda if you don't want to see your events here.

If you don't see the Google Calendar gadget on your page, click the Add Stuff link, click the Google Apps link, and finally, click the Add It Now button below the Google Calendar gadget. Turn to Chapter 18 to discover more about Google Calendar.

You can customize your calendar settings to edit your date and time format, as well as show and hide the mini calendar.

Viewing your latest docs

The Google Docs gadget displays your most recent documents, spreadsheets, and presentations. To access the Google Docs gadget, first click the Edit button on your page, and then choose Insert⇨More, search for *Google Docs.* Click the Google Docs link for the first gadget that appears, and then click OK.

This gadget may ask you to sign into Google Docs before it shows your current list. Click the Sign In link to go to your docs. When you return to the page (simply reenter your page's Web address in your browser), your list will show your recent docs. Here are the key Google Docs links:

- ✔ **New:** Click this menu to create a new document, presentation, or spreadsheet directly from the gadget.

- ✔ **View All Items:** Go directly to your Docs Home and view all your documents.

The Google Docs gadget shows five documents by default. You can edit the gadget settings to preview more or less, and to hide or show the last edit date.

Chatting with your contacts

Use the Google Talk gadget to see whether your contacts are online and to chat with them. The Google Talk gadget, shown in Figure 6-8, gets a whole section in Chapter 20, so we don't go into details about how to use it here.

To add the Google Talk gadget to your page, click the Edit Page button, and then choose Insert⇨More from the Edit Page toolbar. Search for *Google Talk,* click the Google Talk link for the first gadget that appears, and then click OK. When you're done, click Save.

Note: You may need to click the Sign In link to load Google Talk the first time.

Chapter 7

Customizing Your Site's Look and Feel

*Y*our site should be special, have a splash of personality, and be inviting to everyone who collaborates on or visits it. Or, you can opt for a utilitarian approach, where function and a clean presentation are essential. Whatever your preference, Google Sites has a set of simple tools to make your site look just how you want.

In this chapter, we look at changing your site's theme, choosing how the page elements appear, and tweaking the colors to match your personality or team scheme. Figure 7-1 shows a sample site where the logo, theme, and layout have been personalized to fit the needs of a classroom site. If you're still looking for ideas after exploring this chapter, check out Part IV for more customization goodness.

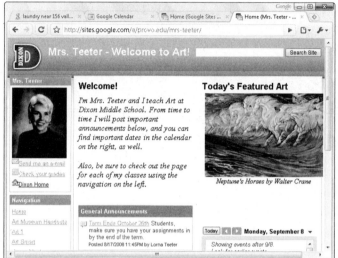

Figure 7-1:
A custom theme adds personality and pizzazz to your site.

Sticking with a Theme

When you first create a site, you have the option to choose a Google-designed theme. Fortunately, if you're tired of your theme or want to mix things up a bit for your team, you're just a few clicks away from applying a fresh coat of color. These steps will have you going with a new theme in no time at all:

1. **Log into your site.**

2. **Click the Site Settings button at the top of the screen and choose Change Appearance from the list that appears.**

   A new screen appears, allowing you to adjust your site settings.

3. **On the blue bar, click the Appearance link.**

4. **Click the Themes link.**

   You see a large grid of designs used in each theme, as shown in Figure 7-2.

5. **Select the radio button next to the theme you want to use and then click the Save Changes button at the top of the screen.**

To see what your site looks like with any of the themes available, click the Preview link below the theme title. A new window appears, showing your site with the new look. Before you save your changes, it's a good idea to make sure that the theme you've selected is the right one by clicking the Preview button at the top of the screen.

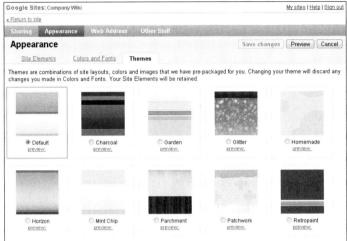

Figure 7-2:
Preview
and select a
new theme
from Site
Settings.

6. **When you finish, return to your site by clicking the Google Sites logo or the Return to Site link in the top-left corner of the screen.**

   Your site now appears with your new theme, including colors and background images. If the new theme doesn't appear right away, click the refresh button on your Web browser.

Working Magic with Site Elements

In Chapter 4, we explain the different site elements, including the header, sidebar, and body of a page on your site. With a little bit of tweaking, the different parts of your site don't need to be the same as everyone else's.

This section is dedicated to helping you customize the physical location of all the content on your site, as well as add a custom logo for your project or team.

To begin tweaking your site elements, follow these steps to dig into your site settings:

1. **Log into your site.**

2. **Click the Site Settings link in the top-right corner of the screen.**

3. **On the blue bar, click the Appearance link.**

   The Appearance screen appears.

4. Click the Site Elements tab.

The Site Elements screen appears, similar to Figure 7-3. Here you notice the Change Site Layout button, and options to adjust the Header, Sidebar, and Page Content. We cover these in this section.

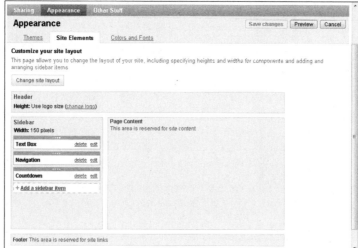

Figure 7-3:
The Site Elements screen lets you adjust your site layout, logo, and sidebar.

5. When you're finished making adjustments on this screen, click the Save Changes button at the top of the screen and then click the Return to Site link to see your new layout.

If your site has the Sidebar enabled, you can go straight to the Site Elements tab by clicking the Edit Sidebar link below the Sidebar on any page in your site.

Changing your site layout

Each of the elements on your site takes up a certain amount of space on your screen. Click the Change Site Layout button on the Site Elements screen to change how much space each of the elements uses. The Change Site Layout screen appears. This is where you'll adjust the page.

The Change Site Layout screen offers the following options:

✔ **Site Width:** You have the option to have your site stretch across the screen or fill a fixed width. A fixed width centers your content on the page, similar to a blog (see Figure 7-4). Enter a number and choose Percent to have the contents of the site stretch, or enter a number of pixels (700–900 is pretty standard) to create a centered page.

✔ **Header:** Check this box to show the header, which includes your logo, site name, and search box.

✔ **Sidebar:** Check this box to use the Sidebar and Sidebar items, such as Navigation, Countdown, and other gadgets. Also, select a radio button to place the Sidebar on the left or right side of the screen. Additionally, indicate how wide you want the Sidebar to be; 150px is the standard.

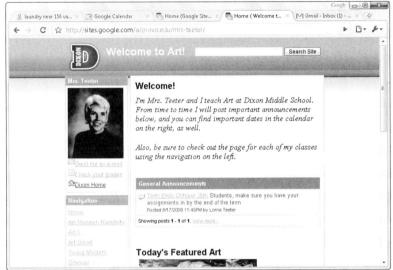

Figure 7-4:
A fixed-width page looks more like a blog.

After you adjust your site layout, click OK to return to your site settings. Click the Preview button to see your new settings in a new window, and then click Save Changes if you like what you see.

Choosing your site logo

A generic site shows the Google Sites logo in the top-left corner of every page you create. Although it's nice to promote Google, we prefer having our own image there, whether a company logo, school mascot, or team photo. The page shown in Figure 7-4 has a school logo, and we think it suits that page.

Before you choose a custom logo, you must save the logo image to your computer and adjust the size to your liking. Acceptable logos should also be in JPEG, GIF, or PNG format. On a Windows computer, you can use Paint to resize your image, and then save it as one of these three formats. If your group has a logo available on the Web, navigate to the page where the image is, right-click the image, and then choose Save As or Save Image (depending on your browser). Name your image and save it in an easy-to-remember location, such as your desktop or Documents folder.

Only use images that you have the right to use. You could get in trouble for using copyrighted and other restricted images on your site.

When you're ready to choose a new logo, follow these steps:

1. **Navigate to the Site Elements page in your Site Settings.**

2. **In the light blue Header box, click the Change Logo link.**

   The Configure Site Logo screen appears, similar to Figure 7-5.

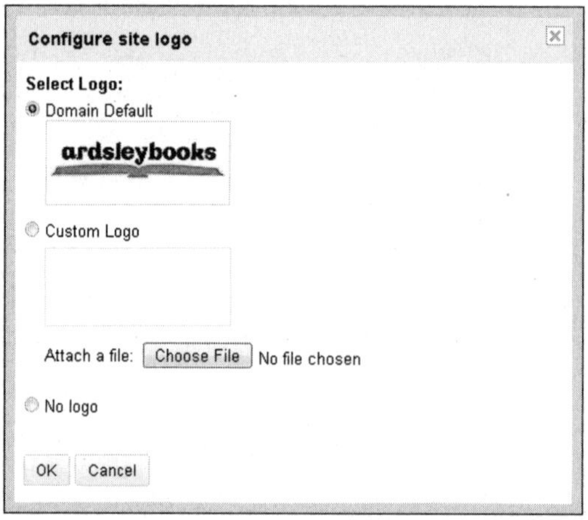

Configure site logo ☒

Select Logo:
◉ Domain Default

ardsleybooks

◯ Custom Logo

Attach a file: [Choose File] No file chosen

◯ No logo

[OK] [Cancel]

Figure 7-5:
Choose the default logo, a custom logo, or no logo.

3. **Select the radio button next to your logo option.**

   Domain Logo shows your organization's logo if you're using Google Apps. Custom Logo displays the logo of your choosing. No Logo removes any logo from your site.

4. **(Optional) For a custom logo, click the Browse button.**

   The Open dialog box appears, allowing you to find your logo on your computer.

5. **(Optional) In the Open dialog box, locate and select your logo image and then click the Open button.**

   After a few moments, your custom logo uploads and appears on the Configure Site Logo screen.

6. **Click the OK button to select your logo and return to your site settings.**

7. **Click the Preview button to view your new logo on your site in a new window. If you're satisfied, close the window and click the Save Changes button. Otherwise, close the window and click Cancel.**

Adding Sidebar elements

The Sidebar is a handy location to place links, countdown calendars, or other gadgets that you want to appear on all of your site's pages. Some elements can help motivate people whereas others let you see how your project is progressing.

To add a new Sidebar element, navigate to the Site Elements screen in your Site Settings, and then click the Add a Sidebar Item link on the left side of the page, as shown in Figure 7-6. Choose a Sidebar element from the screen that appears and click the Add button to attach it to the Sidebar.

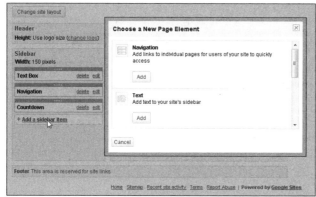

Figure 7-6:
Add a new
element to
the Sidebar.

When your Sidebar element appears in the list, click the Edit link to the right of the element name to start adjusting its settings. Here's what each element does, as well as settings you can edit:

✓ **Navigation:** Shows links to popular pages on your site.

To reorder pages to the Navigation box, click a page from the list that appears and then click the arrows to the right of the list.

To delete a page, highlight the page in the list and then click the X box below the arrows on the right.

To add a page, click the Add Page to Sidebar Navigation link. In the list that appears, highlight the page you want to add and click OK. You can then reorder the page to your liking.

✓ **Text:** Creates your own mini Web page with links, images, and so on.

On the Configure Text Box screen, use the Edit toolbar to format your textbox to your liking, similar to Figure 7-7. Click OK when you're done.

If you have experience with HTML, click the HTML button to add other custom tags, styles, and so on. Sadly, you cannot insert <IFRAME> or <EMBED> tags into a Sidebar textbox.

✔ **Recent Site Activity:** Displays a list of new pages, site changes, and recently uploaded files.

On the Configure Recent Site Activity screen, enter a number of recent activities to show and then click OK.

✔ **My Recent Activity:** This box shows the activity of the currently logged in user, including page edits and comments.

On the Configure My Recent Activity screen, enter a number of recent activities to show and then click OK.

✔ **Countdown:** Show a countdown of days on your Sidebar that is automatically updated. When your date is reached, the countdown will start counting backwards from when the event passed.

From the Configure Countdown screen, enter the name of the event and then click the Choose Date button. Use the arrows on the popup calendar and click your desired date. Click OK to update your countdown.

Figure 7-7:
Create custom Sidebar content using the Text element.

Although it's possible to add as many Sidebar elements as you want, we recommend that you only use elements that are useful to your project. Otherwise, your site can become very cluttered and unfriendly.

Changing Sidebar elements

You can adjust your Sidebar elements to your liking any time you like by clicking the Edit Sidebar link on any of your site's pages. When you've returned to the Site Elements screen, you can reorder, edit, or delete your items.

To reorder your Sidebar, click and hold the blue bar located above the element you want to move. Drag the element to where you want it and let go of your mouse button. The other elements automatically move above and below your final resting spot.

To edit an item, click the Edit link to the right of the element name. Make any adjustments you want. (See the preceding section for more info).

To delete an item, click the Delete link to the right of the element name. The item disappears. If you delete an item accidentally, click the Cancel button and your Sidebar will remain unchanged.

Sprinkling a Dash of Color and Fonts

In some cases, the themes provided by Google for your site may not be what you're looking for. Whether you favor off-the-wall colors, lovely pastels, or something more in line with your school or corporate setting, you're likely going to have to get a little more personal with Google Sites' settings.

Fortunately, changing colors is pretty easy. Although we won't vouch for your own taste, we're confident that you'll find it a breeze to make changes to your color scheme, add background pictures, and choose a font that fits you.

The colors you choose are up to you. Before you begin changing colors, we recommend that you choose a theme that most closely matches your desired set of colors. This way you only have to adjust a few elements instead of all of them.

To change your colors and fonts, follow these steps:

1. **Log into your site and click the Site Settings link in the top-right corner of the screen.**

   The Site Settings screen appears.

2. **Click the Appearance link in the blue bar and then click the Colors and Fonts link.**

   Your screen looks similar to Figure 7-8.

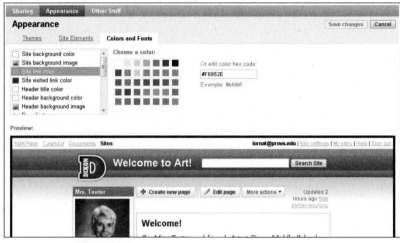

Figure 7-8:
Use the
Colors
and Fonts
screen to
fine-tune
your color
scheme.

3. **(Optional) Adjust a site color element, as described here:**

a. *Select a site color element, such as Site Link Color from the list on the left.*

b. *Choose a color from the palette.* Your new color appears in the Preview section. See Figure 7-9.

c. *(Optional) Enter the color hex value in the box to the right of the color palette.* If you're having trouble finding a color code, check out www.colorschemer.com/online.html.

4. **(Optional) Adjust a background image of the Site, Header, Page, or Sidebar title, following these steps:**

a. *Select a site element from the list on the left, such as Site Background Image.*

b. *Choose a background image by selecting the radio button next to the option you want.*

From Theme uses the background associated with your current theme. None removes your background image and uses the background color instead. Custom lets you choose an image from your computer.

c. *(Optional) Click the Choose File button and locate a file on your computer.* When the Open dialog box appears, choose your image file and then click Open.

Like other image elements, your background image should be in JPEG, GIF, or PNG format.

   d. Click the Repeat drop-down list to choose how the image will repeat.

     Horizontal stacks the image and is useful for the Sidebar. Vertical repeats the image from left to right across the page and is useful for shadows or fades. Horizontal and Vertical repeats the image throughout the entire page.

   e. Select a horizontal and vertical position by clicking the Horizontal Position and Vertical Position drop-down lists.

     Horizontal Position repeats the image along the left side, center, or right side of the screen. Vertical Position repeats the image along the top, center, or bottom of the screen.

5. (Optional) Choose a font for your body or Sidebar, as described here:

   a. Highlight a site element from the list on the left, such as Page Font. Your screen looks similar to Figure 7-9.

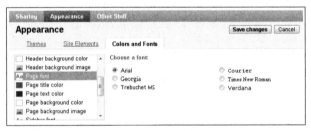

Figure 7-9:
Select a
font for your
page and
Sidebar.

   b. Click the radio button to the left of the font you want to use. Your new color appears in the Preview section.

6. After you choose the new colors, images, and fonts you like, click the Save Changes button at the top of the screen. Otherwise, click Cancel to leave your site how it was previously.

Looking for a good background image? Do a quick Google search for *background images*. When you find an image that suits you, give it a right-click and choose Save Image As or Save As (depending on your browser). Choose a folder to save your image in and then click Save.

Chapter 8

Bringing Collaboration to a New Level

In This Chapter

▶ Defining relationships within a collaboration

▶ Seeing your site through others' eyes

▶ Keeping track of file changes, and page and site updates

*A*t the beginning of this book, we discuss that Google Sites is all about sharing. Remember that the best wikis are the ones where lots of people share what they know about a topic, project, or event. Unless you plan to keep the site to yourself and have a one-way conversation with your visitors, you want to keep everyone in the loop and encourage them to edit pages and share ideas.

The previous few chapters focus on creating your site and perfecting your design; in this chapter, you bring the rest of your team, family, class, or adoring public on board. Here, we cover sending invitations to others, viewing your site from a public perspective, tracking updates, and managing subscriptions.

Defining Relationships

You can invite people to join your site at any time after you create your site. In fact, if you chose to allow anyone in your domain to edit your site when you created it, you already have some collaborators.

How people interact with your site is important. After all, you may not want everyone changing your color scheme, or some people making any changes at all. This section shows you how to invite others to join in and how to adjust your site permissions to allow or restrict access to whomever you like.

Only site owners can send invitations and change a user's access privileges. If you are a collaborator or viewer, you won't be able to make these changes.

Sending invitations to others

Invitations are the primary way for other users to know that they can view or edit pages on your site. When you add new users, you receive the option to send them an e-mail message. Invitees also receive the Web address of your site so they can start working on your site immediately.

Your site URL can become rather lengthy, especially if you're a Google Apps user. When you send an invitation to others, why have them remember `http://sites.google.com/a/`*`yourdomain.com/site/page`* when you can create a shorter URL using a shortcut service, such as TinyURL (`http://tinyurl.com`)? Paste that long address into the TinyURL home page and that long URL turns into something as miniscule as `http://tinyurl.com/4vw22u`.

Here's how to start sending invitations:

1. **Navigate to a page on the site you want to share.**

2. **Log into the site, if you haven't already, by clicking the Login link at the bottom of the page.**

   The Edit buttons appear on your page.

3. **Click the Site Settings button and choose Share This Site from the list that appears.**

   The Site Sharing screen loads, similar to Figure 8-1.

4. **Choose one of the permissions you want your users to have:**

   • *As Owners:* Owners can view and edit your site. They can also change site settings (including the look and feel) and invite other people to join.

   • *As Collaborators:* Collaborators can only view and edit your site, and create new pages. They cannot change site settings or invite others to join.

   • *As Viewers:* Viewers can only, you guessed it, see your site. They cannot make any changes or invite others.

5. **Enter the e-mail addresses of the people you want to invite.**

   It they're in your Contacts, their address automatically appears when you start typing. Alternatively, you can click the Choose from Contacts link below the box to open the Contact Picker (shown in Figure 8-2) and search your contacts.

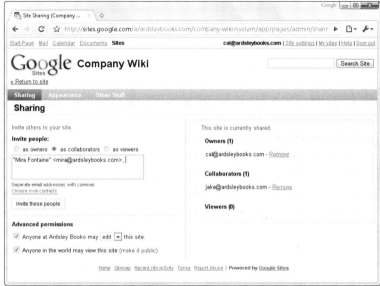

Figure 8-1:
Add other
users from
the Site
Sharing
screen.

Figure 8-2:
Search for
collabora-
tors with
the Contact
Picker.

6. **Click the Invite These People button.**

   An e-mail screen appears where you can enter a brief message.
   Remember that a link to your site is included automatically in your mes-
   sage. If you want to receive a copy of the message, check the box next to
   CC Me.

7. **(Optional) Click Send to send your invitation.**

   The message is sent and you return to the Sites Sharing screen.

8. **(Optional) Click Skip Sending Invitation.**

   A message is not sent, but your site now appears in their Google Sites list. They'll see it the next time they log in (or you'll have to verbally inform them that they have access). You return to the Sites Sharing screen.

9. **(Optional) Rinse and repeat Steps 4 through 8 for each remaining permission: owners, collaborators, or viewers.**

After you invite users, they can view or contribute to your site. Your current owners, collaborators, and viewers appear in the gray box on the right side of the Site Sharing screen (refer to Figure 8-1). Click the Return to Site link to go back to editing your site.

You can change the level of access to users at any time using the Site Sharing screen. Follow Steps 4 through 8 above, using the new permissions level and the same address. When you're done, your list reflects the changes you make.

Advanced permissions

While you're on the Site Sharing screen, feel free to adjust the Advanced Permissions, which specify the permissions for the rest of the world. This may be helpful if you want different settings than those you chose when you first created your site. You can check one or more of the following options. *Note:* The first two options are available only to Google Apps users.

- ✔ **Anyone at *yoursite.com* may view this site.** Allows your site to appear in the list of all the users in your organization. Users are able to view but not make any changes to your site.

- ✔ **Anyone at *yoursite.com* may edit this site.** Same as the last option; however, anyone at your site can make changes to the pages.

- ✔ **Anyone in the world may view this site (make it public).** Allows everyone in the world to see your site. If not selected, only those who you invite can see your site.

Removing users from your site

When a team member leaves or you decide to block someone from your site, you need to manually remove him from the Sites Sharing list. When you remove them, they can no longer access your site unless your site is public to begin with. Here's how to do it:

1. **If you're an owner, log into your site.**

2. **Click the More Actions button and choose Site Sharing from the list.**

3. **On the Site Sharing screen that appears, click the Remove link to the right of the e-mail address of the user whose access you want to revoke.**

Seeing Your Site Through a Viewer's Eyes

You are the owner of the sites you create, which means that every time you go to your site, you see the Edit buttons and can make changes. When you're sharing your site with many viewers, having to log in and out to see the page how they see it can be annoying. This is especially true if you're making several tweaks to the page and have a specific look in mind.

Fortunately, you can quickly preview each of your pages as a viewer. This allows you to quickly see your updates with two clicks. From any page on your site, click the More Actions button, and choose Preview Page as Viewer from the list that appears.

A new tab appears, similar to Figure 8-3. In viewer preview, notice that the Google bar along the top of the page disappears, as well as the Edit buttons. This is how your page appears to all of your noncollaborating visitors.

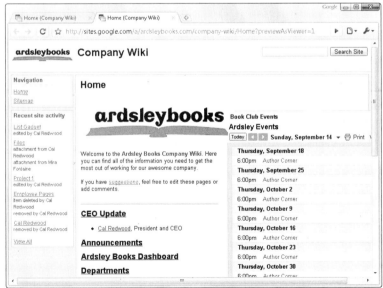

Figure 8-3:
A page in viewer preview.

When you're finished with your page view, return to Edit mode by closing this new tab or by clicking any of the links on the page.

Tracking File Changes

With many people working together and making changes to the same files, sooner or later someone will delete something critical or your original idea becomes so thoroughly altered it's no longer recognizable. Thankfully, Google Sites keeps track of all the changes made to a page since it was created, which makes sorting things out much easier.

Conflict management

It's generally not good to make changes to a page while someone else is making changes. Fortunately, if you try to edit a page that's being changed, Google locks the page and warns you that another user is busy with that page, as shown in the figure here. A message appears, telling you who's hogging your space so you can deal with him properly.

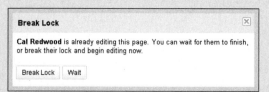

At this point, either you can be polite and click the Wait button, or you can be bullish and click the Break Lock button. When the other person tries to save their changes, they see an Edit Conflict warning, shown in the figure here, where they can either click Yes and override your changes or click No and leave you to your madness.

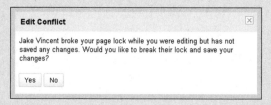

The moral of this story is that it's usually better to wait and check with the other person before you attempt to overwrite their poetic masterpiece or reimbursement procedure.

In the top-right corner of the page, you may notice a date or time attached to each page. This indicates when the last update to that page was made. To the right of the date you find the See Earlier Versions link. This link is key to restoring information or reverting to an older version. In this section, we cover how to view, compare, and revert to older versions of a page on your site.

Viewing a past version of your page

When you click the See Earlier Versions link, a screen similar to Figure 8-4 appears, listing the ten most recent versions of your page. To list even older versions, scroll to the bottom of the page and click the Prev link. The list shows a link to each version, when that version was last edited, and who made those changes. You can use this information to find the specific version you're looking for.

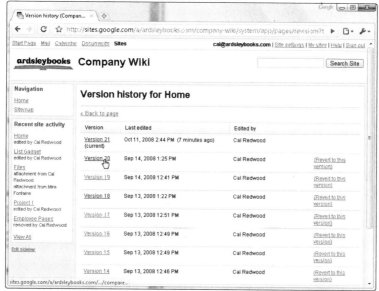

Figure 8-4:
Browse through different versions of your page.

Clicking a Version link reveals what the page looked like at that point in time. From this new screen, you can quickly load other versions of the page by clicking the Version drop-down list and choosing another version.

To return to the latest version of the page, click the Back to Version History link at the top of the page. After you return to the Version History page, click the Back to Page link.

Comparing different page versions

When you're certain that something on the page has changed, but you just can't lay a finger on it, try comparing versions. The new addition or deletion jumps right out and you can rest easy.

From the Version History screen, click a Version link to open a version of the page. Then, click the Compare Two Versions link at the top of the page. A new drop-down list appears. Choose a version from the Select First list and another version from the Select Second list to compare changes.

Text and other items that were deleted have a line through them. Insertions and other added items are highlighted, as shown in Figure 8-5. If no changes occurred, the page appears blank.

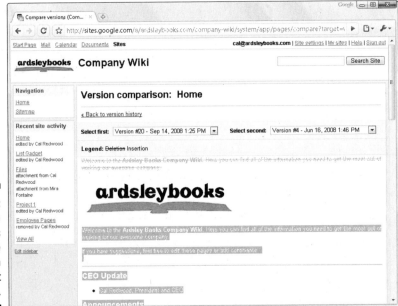

Figure 8-5: Compare changes made between two different versions.

From this screen, you can choose any two versions you like and look for whatever it is you're looking for.

Reverting to an older version

When you find the older version that you want to restore, click the Back to Version History link, and then click the Revert to This Version link to the right of the version you want that page to look like.

When you revert to an earlier version, what's really happening is that a new version of your page is being created based on that version. Therefore, if you decide you like a newer version better, you can still access that version later.

Keeping Tabs on Page and Site Updates

Who doesn't want to feel like Big Brother occasionally? One of the most enjoyable features we discovered is the ability to receive e-mail updates when our pages change. You get that giddy feeling that comes from not only knowing you and others are using your site, but also from the joy of seeing what changes were made and how the site is evolving.

You have two ways to subscribe to changes on your site, which we show you in this section:

✔ **Individual pages:** Receive updates on changes made only to specific pages you subscribe to.

✔ **Entire site:** See changes made on any page within a site.

With the right subscription, you receive updates every time someone (including yourself) does any of the following:

✔ Uploads attachments

✔ Makes comments

✔ Edits a page

✔ Creates a new page

As an added bonus, everyone who collaborates on a site can subscribe to page or site updates as well. (Viewers just have to keep checking manually.) This way, everyone is in the know, and that's cool. Now that we've whet your appetite, here's how you can join in on the fun.

Subscribing to individual page changes

Subscribing to individual page changes is your best option when you're only concerned with a page or two and don't want to receive updates from other pages. (Are you sure you really don't want to see when Grandma updates her meatloaf recipes?) A few quick steps and you'll be the first to know when the page changes:

1. **Open the page from which you want to receive updates.**

   If you're not signed in, click the Sign In link at the bottom of the page.

2. **Click the More Actions button at the top of the page.**

3. **From the list that appears, choose Subscribe to Page Changes.**

That's it! An orange bar appears at the top of the screen letting you know that you'll start receiving notifications when the page changes.

Watching for site changes

In some cases, you may want to be notified when any of the pages on your site change. Rather than subscribing to all the different pages individually, follow these steps to subscribe to site updates in two clicks:

1. **Open the page you want to receive updates from.**

2. **Click the More Actions button at the top of the page.**

3. **From the list that appears, choose Subscribe to Site Changes.**

The orange bar at the top of the screen lets you know that you'll start receiving notifications when any page on your site changes.

Don't take our word for it. To test the notification system, subscribe to a page or site changes, and then edit and save a page. Finally, check your e-mail Inbox within a few minutes and you should see the update. The message looks similar to the one shown in Figure 8-6.

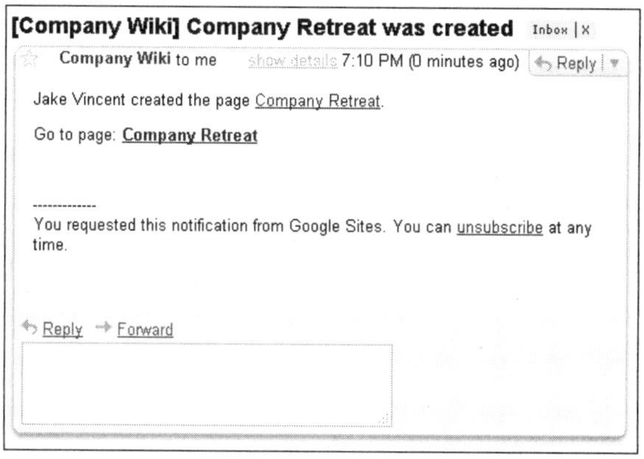

> **[Company Wiki] Company Retreat was created** Inbox | x
>
> Company Wiki to me   show details 7:10 PM (0 minutes ago) ↩ Reply | ▼
>
> Jake Vincent created the page Company Retreat.
>
> Go to page: **Company Retreat**
>
> -----------
> You requested this notification from Google Sites. You can unsubscribe at any time.
>
> ↩ Reply → Forward

Figure 8-6:
An e-mail
notifies you
when a new
page is
created.

Managing subscriptions

We realize that very active sites are updated all the time and soon your
e-mail Inbox can be overrun by update notifications. If this becomes too
much for you, it's time to let go. Unsubscribing is your only option —
unless you have Gmail.

The easiest way to unsubscribe from a page or site is to click the
Unsubscribe link in any of the e-mail messages you receive from that page or
site. Refer to Figure 8-6 if you're uncertain.

Alternatively, you can unsubscribe from any page directly with these three
simple steps:

1. **Navigate to the page from which you want to unsubscribe.**

2. **Click the More Actions button at the top of the page.**

3. **Choose Unsubscribe from Page/Site Changes from the list that appears.**

A familiar orange bar appears at the top of the screen letting you know that
your action has been completed.

If you still want to receive updates from your page or site, but don't want to
clutter your Gmail Inbox, we have a quick suggestion for you. To protect your
Gmail Inbox from e-mail overload of the Google Sites variety, you can create
filters to have the messages skip the Inbox and appear in the Labels box on
the left side of the screen, as shown in Figure 8-7. This way, you know when
changes are made, but you don't have to look through all the updates to find
your real messages.

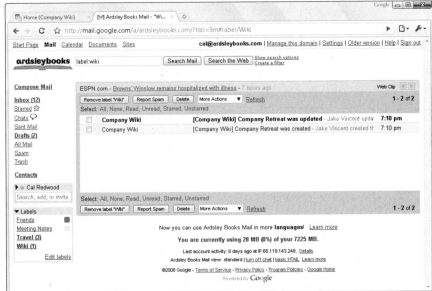

Figure 8-7:
Filter your
messages
in Gmail
to prevent
Inbox
overload.

We recommend that you use filters in your Gmail Inbox. Here's how:

1. **Log into Gmail.**

2. **Open an update message from your site.**

   Messages from your site show the title of your site in the From field, as well as the subject. If you subscribe to updates and haven't seen any yet, open a page on your site, make a change, and then click Save.

3. **Click the More Actions button above your message and choose Filter Messages Like These from the list that appears.**

   The Create a Filter screen appears with a list of related e-mail notifications. Your screen might look similar to Figure 8-8.

4. **(Optional) To limit the messages to a specific site, enter the site name in the Subject box.**

5. **Click the Next Step button.**

6. **On the next screen, check the boxes next to Skip the Inbox and Apply the Label.**

7. **Click the Choose Label drop-down list to the right and choose New Label.**

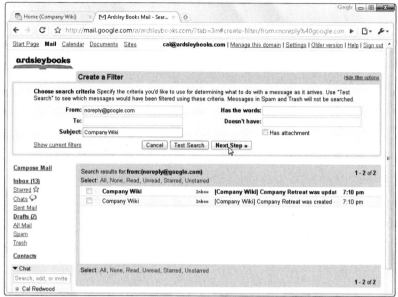

8. **In the blue box that appears, enter the name of your new label and click OK.**

   We like to use something along the lines of "Site Updates" or "Company Wiki."

9. **Check the box next to the Also Apply Filter to Conversations Below option and then click the Create Filter button.**

   Your new label appears in the Labels box on the left side of your Gmail screen, and all new notifications will go directly to your new folder label. When new messages arrive, the label appears in bold and the number of new messages appears to the right of the label. Neat, huh? You can read more about Gmail labels and filters in Chapter 19.

Part III
Getting the Most Out of Chrome

"So, you want to work for the best browser company in the world? Well, let me get you a job application. Let's see...where are they? Shoot! I can never find anything around here!"

In this part . . .

If you've had a chance to take Chrome for a spin, then look no further than this part to find the tweaks you need to make the Internet purr. Two chapters here help you uncover Chrome's power and finesse. With a few adjustments here and there, we help you take on the latest and greatest the Web has to offer.

Chapter 9

Perfecting Chrome Browsing

*W*hen it comes to browsers, it's time for something different. Let's face it; we've all been caught in a slow, confining, crash-prone and bloated browser rut for a decade. To pave the road in a new direction, Google created Chrome.

When you first use Chrome, you'll be surprised that things look and react differently from your old browser; however, in a few seconds, you'll start muttering to yourself, "I like that," "Why didn't they think of that before," and the ever-cheerful, "Nice." In this chapter, we show you some of these ah-ha features.

Teaching Chrome Your Habits

When you first start Chrome, it looks stark — almost empty — as shown in Figure 9-1. Don't panic; this is a good thing. Chrome is waiting for you to fill the void. Within seconds, you'll start teaching Chrome your preferences and habits, let Chrome know the pages you want to see right away, and quickly turn the stark environment into the most efficient browser interface you've ever seen.

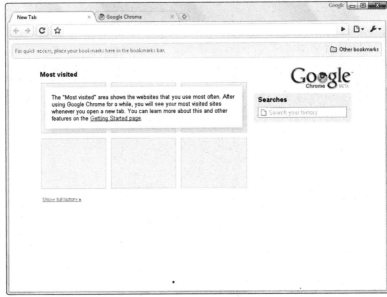

Figure 9-1:
Chrome
starts out
deceptively
stark.

Every page you visit is remembered by Chrome. Your most frequently viewed pages are prioritized in the New Tab start page so you can get back to them in a flash. (See Figure 9-2.) To get your favorite sites into the system, try our 60-second start that we explain next.

Try the 60-second start

Start by entering the Web addresses of five or six key sites that you visit frequently. Enter the first Web address (URL) into the address box on the toolbar. The address box appears next to the little star — you can't miss it. Press Enter or click the triangular-looking Go button at the end of the address box to download your page.

To enter your second page, click the + sign that follows the last open tab and enter a new URL in the toolbar. Enter one URL right after the other, glancing at the screen just long enough to see each of your pages zip in quickly, each on its own tabbed page.

Chrome starts searching for possibilities as soon as you start typing your URL by immediately launching the Omnibox below the toolbar. Watch the Omnibox for clues about the page you are looking for so you don't have to enter the entire Web address. If you see the URL that you want in the Omnibox, stop typing and click it.

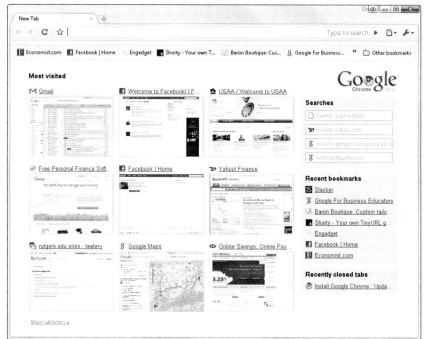

Figure 9-2:
Chrome
remembers
your brows-
ing habits
and records
your pre-
ferred sites.

If you can't remember the URL to a favorite site, just enter search words describing the site in the address box on the toolbar rather than a URL. You'll get a typical Universal Search listing of Google search results. Pick a Search result and — *presto!* — you have a page of related information. (Read the expanded Search Tips section, "Search Effectively with Chrome's Omnibox," at the end of this chapter.)

Chrome immediately starts analyzing your behavior patterns; therefore, your most frequently viewed sites will be on the new tab screen whenever you hit the New Tab button or the + sign. All the pages displayed as thumbnails in Figure 9-2 were visited within 60 seconds after starting Google Chrome.

Each day you use Chrome refines Google's understanding of how you work online and prepares an increasingly valuable list of frequently visited pages. The most frequently visited pages are displayed as thumbnails on the New Tab page. Click any of the thumbnails to return to a page quickly. If you need to see all of your previously viewed pages, click the Show Full History link at the bottom of the New Tab screen. Scroll down the list that appears until you find the page you're looking for. It's broken down by day and every page vis- ited has a timestamp to make searching easier.

Play the Tab shuffle

You can do many fun things after you have several tabs open in a Chrome session. First, you can drag tabs to the left and right, and change the order of tabs at the top. That's very helpful in certain situations. For example, if you're giving a presentation and need to view several Web sites, you can have them queued and ready to go in the order you want them to appear.

Another easy option with tabs is to drag them completely out of Chrome and create separate windows for them. Clicking and dragging on a page's tab and pulling it out of Chrome opens a new session of Chrome, as shown in Figure 9-3. You can close the old session and still preserve the page you just dragged from the original Chrome session. You can then open more tabs in the new session and repeat the process if necessary.

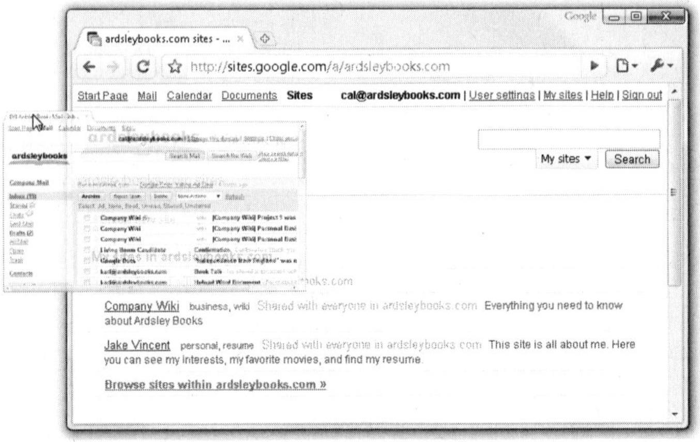

Figure 9-3:
Change the
order of
tabs or drag
tabs out to
create new
Chrome
sessions.

Tips on the toolbar

Chrome offers the usual Forward and Backward buttons on the toolbar. It also has a Reload button right next to the Forward button. So if a page doesn't come in properly, or you need to update its content, just click the Reload button, which looks like an arrow that curves clockwise. (Look for it in Figure 9-4.)

Next to the Refresh button is the Bookmark Star button. We detail the use of the Bookmark Star button in a dedicated section later in this chapter. At the end of the address entry box, you see the Go button, which looks like an arrow or a triangle. Click this button after you enter your Web address or URL. While a page is loading, the icon changes into a Stop icon; clicking that icon stops a page from loading. If things are coming in too slowly for your liking, click the Stop icon.

Figure 9-4:
Chrome
offers a
clean and
efficient
toolbar.

We present both of the menus shown on the far right side of the toolbar in Figure 9-4. The menu that looks like piece of paper bent at the edge is the Page menu. The Page menu is a combination of the File and Edit menus on a traditional browser. The other menu — the Tools menu — looks like a wrench, and is a combined settings and options menu for Chrome's more advanced features.

Using the Page menu

The Page menu is found on the right side of the toolbar. This important menu, displayed in Figure 9-5, combines many of the features found on the File and Edit menus of a typical browser. To keep our explanations clear, we refer to it throughout as the Page menu.

Figure 9-5:
The Page
menu.

Here are the key elements of the Page menu:

✔ **New Tab:** This option opens a new tab. (However, it's easier just to click the + that follows the previously opened tab.)

- **New Window:** This option opens a new browser window; in other words, this option launches a new Chrome session.

- **New Incognito Window:** Choose this option to go incognito, just like James Bond. More on this later.

- **Create Application Shortcuts:** This option turns Web page apps into easy-to-access applications. More on this later.

- **Cut, Copy, and Paste:** These options perform these three common Web text-, picture-, and page-editing tasks.

- **Find in Page:** This option locates a portion of text within an existing Web page. For example, you can search for keywords in a long article to find the exact quote you need.

- **Save Page As:** If you need to save a copy of a Web page to your computer, click this option.

- **Print.** This option prints the current Web page.

- **Text Zoom:** Makes text on a Chrome Web page appear larger or smaller. More on this later.

- **Encoding:** Changes the character set used on a page. This option is mostly for sites that use non-Western characters, such as Chinese or Arabic.

- **Developer:** Views the page source and debugs JavaScript. You can also access the Task Manager here, which we discuss in Chapter 10.

- **Report Bug or Broken Website:** This option helps Google police the Internet by reporting bugs or broken Web sites.

Going incognito: James Bond's browser

Unless you're James Bond, we can't imagine why you might want to view pages incognito. Albeit, when you go incognito, the pages you visit aren't recorded in your History file. In fact, Google Chrome makes no record of your travels. However, the sites you visit do keep a record, and you should always be mindful of that. To go incognito, from the Page menu choose New Incognito Window.

Create application shortcuts

Zillions of new Web applications (called *apps*) are available online. Most can be launched and treated like the traditional programs on your PC by using the Application Shortcuts feature. Selecting this option does two things. The Application Shortcuts feature first creates a shortcut to help you launch a

Web app from your desktop or Start menu just as you can with any other program. Second, the feature opens the app in a separate window for quick and easy access. Here are a few quick examples of apps to which you can apply this feature:

✔ Google Docs

✔ Google Finance

✔ Google Sites

✔ Gmail

✔ Lots more

Application shortcuts are made possible by a tool built into Google Chrome called Google Gears. In addition to creating application shortcuts, Google Gears also allows you to access some of your apps even when you're not connected to the Internet. See Chapter 10 for an example of this.

To make an application shortcut, follow these steps:

1. **Open the page that contains your application.**

2. **Click the Page menu and choose Create Application Shortcuts.**

   The Google Gears dialog box opens, as shown in Figure 9-6.

Figure 9-6:
Create
application
shortcuts in
the Google
Gears dialog
box.

3. **Decide where you want the shortcut to appear. Click any combination of the Desktop, Start Menu, or Quick Launch Bar boxes.**

4. **Click OK. (Click Cancel if you change your mind.)**

   Your current app reopens in its own window and the shortcut link to your app appears in the locations you designate. Any other time, double-click the shortcut to open the app. For example, the Google Finance App, when opened, looks like Figure 9-7.

Saving time with keyboard shortcuts

Use these keyboard shortcuts to take some stress off your mouse. Look for these on the Cheat Sheet at the beginning of this book for a quick reference.

Ctrl+T	Open a new tab.	Ctrl++	Increase the font size.
Ctrl+W	Close the current tab.	Ctrl+-	Decrease the font size.
Ctrl+Tab	Cycle through current tabs.	Ctrl+0	Restore the normal font size.
Ctrl+N	Open a new window.	Ctrl+B	Always show the Bookmarks bar.
Ctrl+Shift+N	Open a new incognito window.	Ctrl+H	Open your browsing history.
Ctrl+Shift+T	Open the last tab you closed.	Ctrl+J	Load your Downloads page.
Alt+Home	Open your Home page.	Ctrl+X	Cut.
Ctrl+L	Jump to the Omnibox.	Ctrl+C	Copy.
Ctrl+K	Search for a word in the Omnibox.	Ctrl+V	Paste.
		Ctrl+P	Print the current tab.
Ctrl+F	Find text in an open page.	Shift+Esc	Open the Tab Task Manager.

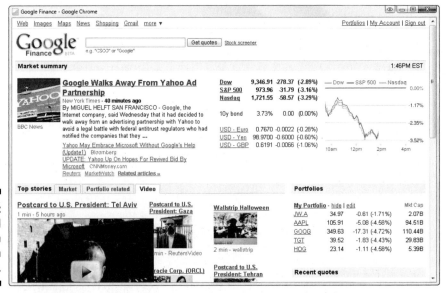

Figure 9-7:
An opened app from an application shortcut.

After you decide to make an app appear as a normal application window, all the links to your other Google services appear across the top. You'll need to use the Sign In link in the top-right corner to gain access to your full range of Google Apps. You can now link to Google's other apps like Gmail, News, Maps, or the Web. Click the More down arrow to link to Sites, Documents, and other Google Apps.

Zoom, zoom, zoom

Some of us are as blind as bats and need to see bigger type on our Web pages. The fix is built into Chrome. To make the font larger on Web pages, click the Page menu and choose Text Zoom. This opens a popup menu that lets you make the text larger or smaller, or return altered text to its normal size.

The right-click menu

Like most other apps, you can right-click a Chrome Web page to gain access to the popup menu commands. The popup menu changes depending on what kind of page element you click. For example, Figure 9-8 shows two right-click menus. The first appears when you click plain text; the second appears when you click a picture that is also a hypertext link. Choose the option you need. For example, if you want to copy a picture, choose Save Image As.

Figure 9-8:
Choose commands from popup contextual menus.

Power over popups

There is another kind of popup that isn't as helpful as the right-click popup menu explained in the preceding section. The Web is full of popup and pop-under ads, spam, and malicious things that need blocking. Google Chrome blocks popup spam, advertising, and other windows that magically appear on top of or under a Web page.

However, some popups with specific interest to you may be a necessary part of a Web site you're visiting. So that you don't miss something important, Chrome lets you know when a popup has been blocked by displaying a Blocked message at the bottom of the screen.

To access a blocked page:

1. **Spot the message bar in the lower-right corner of Chrome announcing that the popup has been blocked.**

2. **Click the message bar once to find out more about the blocked information.**

   This snippet of information can help you decide whether the popup is safe and contains something you're interested in.

3. **Click the Maximize button, double-click the message, or drag the message into your Chrome window and Chrome will display the blocked information.**

Getting the Most from the Fastest Bookmarks in Browser Town

Some of your most important sites can be bookmarked. Internet Explorer (IE) calls a bookmark a "Favorite," which is a distinct departure from tradition. *Bookmark* is the preferred term used by the original Mosaic browser, Netscape Navigator, Firefox, Safari, and now Chrome.

Bookmarking tells Google Chrome which sites you value the most so you can get to them quickly. Bookmarks are added to the Bookmarks bar on the New Tab page. Chrome also creates a Recent Bookmarks list and places it in a column next to the Most Visited sites thumbnails (refer to Figure 9-2). What's more, when you close tabs you no longer need, Chrome starts a new list below the bookmarks list just in case you close a tab in haste and need to return to it quickly.

Single-click bookmarks

Traditional browsers make bookmarking or creating favorites lists too difficult. Chrome simplifies the process without losing any of the functionality avid bookmarkers thrive on.

To add a bookmark, follow these steps:

1. **Open the page you want to bookmark.**
2. **Click the Bookmark Star button to the left of the Omnibox.**

   That's it. The page is bookmarked!
3. **Click Close to close the Bookmark Added balloon.**

Refining and editing your bookmarks

Editing a bookmark is easy in Chrome. Gone are the endless dialog boxes of options that must be tackled in other browsers. In Chrome, just open any already bookmarked page and click the Bookmark Star button. You're greeted with a notice that the bookmark has already been added. (See Figure 9-9.)

Figure 9-9: Rename, remove, or edit a bookmark.

In this balloon, the following editing options are at your service:

- ✔ Click the Name box to rename the bookmark.
- ✔ Click the Remove link to remove the bookmark.
- ✔ Click the Folder drop-down list to place a bookmark into another folder.
- ✔ Click Edit to open the Edit window shown in Figure 9-10. (More on that in a second.)

The Bookmarks Bar and optional folders

By default, bookmarks are placed in the Bookmarks Bar folder. These bookmarks appear just under the toolbar in the New Tab page for one-click access to key bookmarks.

However, not all your bookmarks can fit on the Bookmarks bar. To organize bookmarks further, you need to create folders. To create folders, follow these steps:

1. **Click the Bookmark Star button.**

2. **Click Edit in the bookmark balloon to open the Edit Bookmark window shown in Figure 9-10.**

Figure 9-10:
The Edit
Bookmark
dialog box.

3. **In the Name box, change the name of your bookmark as needed.**

4. **In the URL box, enter or change the Web address of the bookmark you're trying to update.**

5. **Click the New Folder button to create a subfolder of the Other Bookmarks folder.**

6. **Name the folder.**

7. **Click OK.**

Place your bookmarks in folders

After you create your folders, you need to use them. Google's propensity for simplicity is evident in how it handles your management of bookmarks as it takes the pain out of this previously tedious task.

Here's how to place your bookmarks in folders:

1. **Open any page you want to bookmark.**

2. **Click the Bookmark Star button.**

3. **Click the Folder drop-down list.**

4. **Choose your target folder.**

Deleting bookmarks

You have several ways to delete bookmarks. First, if you open a previously bookmarked page, you can click the Bookmark Star button and choose the Remove link. You can also go directly to the Bookmark bar and right-click any bookmark you decide to discard. From the resulting popup menu, choose Delete from the list and — *poof!* — your bookmark is digital dust.

Always show the Bookmarks bar?

One of the problems with modern browsers is that the toolbars at the top of the screen occupy a good part of the viewing area of any Web page, and take away from the online experience. Google's minimalist tendency has tried to avoid stealing screen space with its clever use of the New Tab page. By default, this is the only place where you see the Bookmarks bar. That makes sense because the Bookmarks bar appears when you're making the decision about what new page you want to open. This is probably how most people will want to leave it — keeping the Bookmarks bar out of the way, not obscuring the amount of screen space dedicated to viewing a Web page or a YouTube video.

However, if you want to see the Bookmarks bar on every page, right-click the Bookmarks bar in the New Tab page and choose Always Show Bookmarks Bar or press Ctrl+B.

Even if you've bookmarked hundreds of pages, you can use the search tool to find any one of them either in your history or in your bookmarks list. Chrome even keeps track of recently closed tabs, so if you close something accidentally, you can restore it with a click. You can also search your entire browsing history for lost pages with the Search box.

Use the Tools Menu

The button that looks like a wrench opens a settings menu called the Tools menu. Click the wrench shown in Figure 9-11 to open the menu and see these essential tools:

- **Always Show Bookmarks Bar:** Allows the Bookmarks bar to appear on every open tabbed page.

- **History:** Shows a detailed history of every site you've visited online.

- **Downloads:** Lists all of the files you've downloaded to your computer using Chrome.

✔ **Clear Browsing Data:** A helpful feature that clears out your browsing history, cookies, system cache, or password recall files.

✔ **Import Bookmarks & Settings:** Allows you to import any bookmarks, favorites, or settings from other browsers, such as Firefox or Internet Explorer.

✔ **Options:** Opens the Options dialog box, the details of which are explored in Chapter 10.

✔ **About Google Chrome:** Launches the copyright and version screen. Open this screen and Google Chrome checks to see that you're running the latest version. If there's an update available, an Update button appears. Click the button and restart your browser to use the latest version.

✔ **Help:** Visit Google and read the online Help files. There are some great videos and even a few cartoons you'll find entertaining.

✔ **Exit:** Click to exit the Chrome browser.

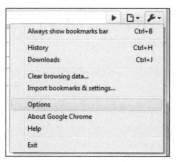

Figure 9-11:
The Tools menu gives you access to Chrome options.

History

Keeping track of everything is in Google's DNA and the History feature is no exception. Open the Tools menu and choose History. A tab screen similar to Figure 9-12 appears. Scroll down the list and go back to any specific day you like. To open any page over again, click on it. To delete the entire list, choose the Delete History link on the right-hand side of the open tab.

Don't scroll down looking for an obscure Web site you visited in the past. Enter a keyword and click the Search History button instead. All the pages related to that word appear, making it much easier to find the page you're looking for.

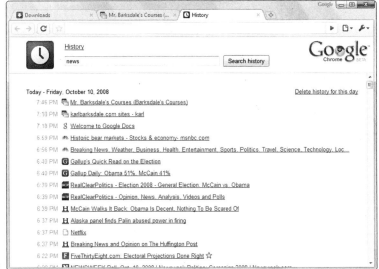

Figure 9-12:
Chrome's
detailed
History list
shows sites
you've
visited.

Downloading files

Chrome opens a special tab, the Downloads tab, the second you download a file. This same page keeps track of every file you download during a session so that you can jump to any downloads you've initiated. Clicking the downloaded file once opens it. If you click the drop-down arrow on the right of the downloaded file button, you find more options in the menu that appears:

- ✔ Click Open to open the file.
- ✔ Click Show in Folder to open the folder where the file is saved.
- ✔ Click Always Open Files of This Type to open certain file types automatically during the current session.

Now, this is going to sound repetitive — Google keeps track of everything, including every file you've downloaded, even files you downloaded weeks or months ago. To search for one of these lost downloads, open the Tools menu and choose Downloads. A Downloads history page listing all of your previous downloads appears, as shown in Figure 9-13. From this page, you can easily search for long-lost downloads.

On this tab, you can open any previously downloaded file by clicking its link. You can also locate the file from its online location link (or URL) or open the folder where the file has been saved on your computer. If you need to download several files, you'll find this to be a very useful screen.

Figure 9-13:
The
Downloads
history page
allows you
to search
and find
long lost
downloads.

Clear browsing data

Most users will never know or care about the Clear Browsing Data screen, but for some, clearing browsing data is a vital feature. To remove items from your browsing history, open the Tools menu and choose Clear Browsing Data, as shown in Figure 9-14.

Figure 9-14:
Clear his-
tory, cache,
cookies, and
passwords
from the
same menu.

Select each category you want to delete or clear:

- **Clear Browsing History:** Clears the History file, erasing your tracks to where you've searched and sites you've visited.

- **Clear Download History:** Clears the Download history file.

✔ **Empty the Cache:** Deletes Chrome's memory of the pages you've visited. This feature also clears the New Tab page of all your most visited pages.

✔ **Delete Cookies:** Deletes the little files supplied by the sites you visit. *Cookies* often provide authentication information to a site, track your activities and browsing habits, and create a personal profile for some sites that you visit.

✔ **Clear Saved Passwords:** Removes any login information you have stored.

The Clear Data from This Period drop-down list lets you specify exactly how far back you want to go for your deletions. You can choose to delete everything or isolate the last day, week, or month for your checked items.

Import bookmarks and settings from IE or Firefox

Do you have a lot of bookmarks, settings, or passwords set in Firefox or Internet Explorer that you simply do not want to replicate? No worries. Open the Tools menu and choose Import Bookmarks & Settings. Choose either Microsoft Internet Explorer or Mozilla Firefox in the From drop-down menu that appears. In the Select Items section of the dialog box, choose the items you want to download:

✔ Favorites/Bookmarks

✔ Search Engines

✔ Saved Passwords

✔ Browsing History

Search Effectively with Chrome's Omnibox

You can use the Omnibox in the same way you use the Google Search tool at www.google.com. And, there's no need to limit yourself to simple keyword searches. In this section, we give you a bunch of great ideas to help you find all the needles in all the haystacks in the world.

To refine your search queries, Table 9-1 offers a few tips.

Table 9-1	Search Box Queries	
Use Search as a	**Examples**	**Result**
Dictionary	define:word	Look up the definition of a word.
Calculator	2+2=, sqrt (3 x 42)/12	Enter formulas to have Google search work like a calculator.
Currency exchange rate calculator	100 USD to GBP	Calculate the value of currencies.
Stock quote and financial advisor	goog, msft, f, or ge	Look up stock quotes and information related to finance.
Synonym search tool	~food, ~facts	Search for information related to the words and synonyms of the keywords.
Domain search tool	admission site:www. uvu.edu	Search a specific domain for specific information.
Number range search tool	DVD player $50..$100, Willie Mays 1950..1960	Search a number range for information and products.
Area code locator	area code 973	Locate an area code.
Airport weather finder	weather SLC, weather EWR	Find the weather for any airport.
Flight status checker	United Airlines 1160, UA 1160	Find the status of a flight.

Everybody knows to visit www.google.com for the best universal searches in the Web world. What many don't know is that Google supports some specific search sites. Here's a list of some of Google's specific search resources that you can visit with Chrome. Use the tips in Chapter 2 to add them to your Omnibox and New Tab Page.

- ✔ **Blogsearch**.google.com. Narrow your search to only online blogs.

- ✔ **Books**.google.com. Search, read, and download scanned books.

- ✔ google.com/**patents**. Find patent filings and view archived inventions.

- ✔ google.com/**products**. Compare prices for products from multiple online stores, including Amazon.com and Target.com.

- ✔ **Groups**.google.com. Look for answers in discussion groups.

- ✔ **Images**.google.com. Search for images and graphics.

✔ **Local**.google.com. Find restaurants, dentists, libraries, and so on located in your home town.

✔ **Maps**.google.com. Get from point A to point B with directions, satellite imagery and cruise the streets in your neck of the woods or across the globe.

✔ **News**.google.com. Find information across major news headlines.

✔ **Scholar**.google.com. Look into academic journals and expert sources for backup to your research.

✔ **Video**.google.com. Keep your sights on YouTube and other online videos.

Chapter 10

Uncovering Chrome's Advanced Features

After you play with Chrome for a while, you'll notice a lot more tweaks and options than meet the eye. In this chapter, you find out everything you ever wanted to know about installing browser plug-ins, using Google Apps even when you're far away from an Internet connection, dealing with misbehaving tabs, and tweaking Chrome's options. We'd throw in the kitchen sink too, but you'll have to find another plumber for that one!

Dealing with Plug-Ins

Web 2.0 is made possible by a lot of cool technology, such as HTML, AJAX, Flash, and Java. Chrome is built to handle HTML and AJAX just fine on its own, but Flash and Java require special software to work properly. The plug-ins are provided by Adobe and Sun, respectively, and here we show you how to get these plug-ins working in a breeze.

Installing plug-ins automatically

When you open a page that requires a plug-in, such as Flash Player, a yellow bar slides in below the toolbar indicating that an additional plug-in is required, as shown in Figure 10-1.

Yellow bar

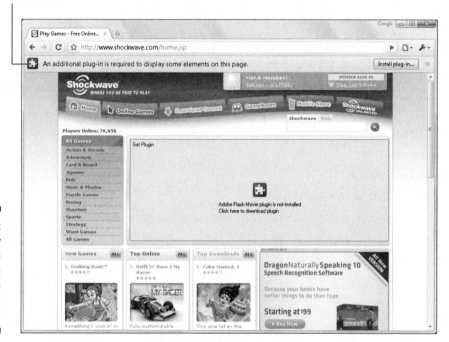

Figure 10-1:
A yellow
bar appears
when you
need to
install a
plug-in.

Click the Install Plug-In button on the right side of the bar to begin installation. A confirmation window appears. Click the Get Plugin button. The plug-in installer downloads and runs on your computer. You may have to click a few buttons to allow the installer to run.

After you run the plug-in installer, return to your Chrome tab and click the Reload button in the toolbar. The page should now show your added features.

Installing plug-ins manually

Some sites won't allow you to install plug-ins quite as easily as we describe above. You can still get them working, but it may take a few more steps, listed here:

1. **Navigate to the plug-in Web site.**

   We list a few essential ones below.

2. **Click the button(s) that say Download.**

   You may have to click through a few screens and accept a license agreement.

3. **Open the installer by clicking the icon in the Installer Bar at the bottom of your tab.**

   The plug-in installer opens in a new window.

4. **Click the Next and Accept buttons to install the plug-in, and then click Finish.**

   The installer closes.

5. **Switch back to Chrome and click the Reload button.**

   Your plug-in should load correctly and show your interactive content. In some cases, you may need to close Chrome completely and open a new tab.

Here's a list of plug-ins we can't live without and where you can download them:

✔ **Flash:** Enables you to watch YouTube videos and play online games. Many Web sites also use Flash for navigation menus and advertisements, as well. Go to www.adobe.com/go/getflash to download Flash.

✔ **Adobe Reader:** Opens any PDF file you come across. PDF files are digital replicas of paper documents, including manuals and eBooks. Download the reader at www.adobe.com/go/getreader.

✔ **Java:** This is used on shopping sites for 3D product views, for some online games, and other tools. Go to www.java.com for more info.

✔ **QuickTime:** View high definition streaming video and virtual tours. Find it at www.quicktime.com. If you've already installed iTunes, you already have QuickTime.

Enabling Offline Access to Google Docs

Although it's nice to have access to your Google Docs any time you're online, sometimes you're forced to work in the confines of an airplane or a room with lead-lined walls where the Internet is nowhere to be found. So how do you finish those last-minute changes on a document while you're taking the train to the city or give a presentation where a wi-fi connection is nonexistent? Easy . . . by using Chrome. Chrome, with the help of a built-in tool called Google Gears, keeps you in sync.

As we mention in Chapter 9, Google Gears adds functionality to Google Chrome. Basically, it creates space on your computer for your browser to store files offline, such as application shortcuts or your Google Docs. Google Gears is also available as an add-on to Firefox, Internet Explorer, and Safari. Navigate to http://gears.google.com and click the Install button. Then follow the on-screen directions to install the plug-in.

Here we show you how to sync your documents, spreadsheets, and presentations in a couple clicks and help you manage your Google Gears connections in the Options screen.

Going offline

Activating offline access is just a click away. The next time you log into Google Docs from your computer, look for the Offline link in the top-right corner of your screen. Here's how to enable Offline mode:

1. **Click the Offline link in the top-right corner of your Google Docs screen.**

   You see an Install Offline Access screen, similar to Figure 10-2.

Figure 10-2: Click the Offline link to enable offline access to Google Docs.

Install offline access for Google Docs

Google Docs Offline will give you access to your documents when there is no internet connection.

This feature will download your docs onto this computer. **Please make sure you are not using a public or shared computer.**

Learn more

[Enable offline access] [Cancel]

2. **Click the Enable Offline Access button.**

   The Google Gears window appears, asking you whether you want to create a shortcut to Google Docs on your computer.

3. **(Optional) Check the boxes next to where you want to create a shortcut and click the Yes button. Click No if you do not want any shortcuts.**

With Google Gears enabled, the Offline link is replaced by a green dot and your Docs begin to synchronize with your computer. From this point on, any new document, spreadsheet, or presentation you create will automatically sync to your computer.

To access your offline docs, open Chrome and navigate to your docs as you normally would or double-click the shortcut you create in Step 3 above. The next time you connect to the Internet, any changes you made while offline are synced to your online docs automatically.

If you decide to use Offline mode in multiple browsers, you'll need to enable offline access for each browser.

Turning Offline off

You may decide that Offline mode isn't for you or, more likely, you're ready to switch to a new computer. In either case, you can disable offline access very easily. Follow the steps below or see the "Fixing Pop-Ups and Google Gears" section later in this chapter.

If you have trouble with your offline access, click the Offline Help link in the top-right corner of the screen. This takes you to Google's Help Center and helps you troubleshoot your hiccup.

Follow these steps to turn off Offline mode:

1. **Click the green dot in the top-right corner of the screen and click the Settings link in the little window that appears.**

   The Offline Access Settings window appears.

2. **Click the Reset My Offline Access button.**

   Your offline documents are deleted and are no longer accessible without an Internet connection, and the green dot disappears from your Google Docs screen.

You can always reactivate offline access by clicking the Offline link on your Google Docs screen.

Managing Unruly Tabs

Sometimes the Web goes awry. Whether a Web site is misbehaving or a plug-in is getting greedy and hogging all of your computer's memory, on rare occasions you have to deal with a nonresponsive tab.

With other browsers, you have to close the whole program with some type of three-finger salute (Ctrl+Alt+Del on Windows and Cmd+Option+Esc on Mac). However, Chrome makes it easy to manage your unruly tabs without having to force quit the whole application, as we discuss in this section.

The Tab Task Manager, shown in Figure 10-3, keeps track of everything that's going on in Chrome. Because Chrome is built on advanced technology, each part of the browser, called a *process*, runs independently. This means that you can use the Tab Task Manager to stop a misbehaving tab or plug-in and the other tabs and plug-ins won't even notice that anything was wrong. Google calls these separate areas *sandboxes*.

Figure 10-3:
Use the
Tab Task
Manager to
shut down
misbehaving
tabs or
plug-ins.

Page	Memory	CPU	Network
Browser	53,524K	2	N/A
Tab: Gmail - Human Resources Weekly Diges...	52,600K	1	0
Tab: Google Docs - All items			0
Tab: Getting to know Google Docs : Welcom...			0
Tab: Chapter 8: Inviting Team Members - G...			0
Tab: Original text from authors (Google Sites ...	12,440K	0	0
Tab:			0
Plug-in: Shockwave Flash	25,008K	1	N/A
Tab: Verify Java Version	15,080K	2	0
Plug-in: Java(TM) Platform SE 6 U10	17,028K	0	0

Task Manager - Google Chrome

Stats for nerds   End process

To start the Tab Task Manager, press Shift+Esc on your keyboard or right-click the Chrome title bar and choose Task Manager from the list that appears. (Who said Google doesn't save you time; you only have to press two keys instead of three!)

In the Tab Task Manager, you notice three types of tasks and the amount of memory, CPU, and network that each is using. Here are the types of tabs to look for:

- **Browser:** This is the engine that runs Chrome. If stopping all the tabs and plug-ins fails, use a three-finger salute to force Chrome to shut down.

- **Tab:** Each of your tabs appears here. If a tab creates other tabs, they sometimes are grouped together in the same sandbox.

- **Plug-In:** Flash, Java, Google Gears, and more appear here. They sometimes get stuck and affect a bunch of tabs or cause Chrome to stop responding. Stopping a plug-in helps your tabs recover.

You can quickly identify which tab or plug-in is causing your computer all sorts of grief by looking for a very high percentage of CPU usage. Basically, your computer is trying really hard to make it work, but can't seem to get it right.

Click a task you want to stop and click the End Process button at the bottom of the Task Manager window. Then return to Chrome and close or reload the tab that was misbehaving.

Aw, snap!

As much as Chrome, or any browser for that matter, tries to be incredibly stable and secure, sometimes they are no match for the Internet. You have to realize that nearly 1.5 billion people around the world are connecting to roughly a trillion different Web pages. With all of those pages created by different people ranging from professional Web developers to hobbyists and junior-high students to governments, there's bound to be one or two that Chrome just can't handle.

Fortunately for you, when a Chrome tab does crash, it won't bring down your whole computer. Instead, you see a gray Dead Tab screen, as shown here. When this screen appears, you can either close the tab to keep working with your other tabs, or click the Reload button to have Chrome take another stab at the page.

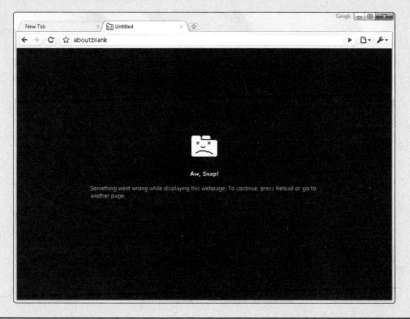

Adjusting Options

Like any good custom car, Chrome can be fine-tuned to run at peak performance and behave just how you want. Although the average person won't need to change most of the settings, we still want to take a moment in this section to pop the hood and show you how to tweak your browsing experience.

To access the Google Chrome Options window, click the Tools menu (the menu icon looks like a wrench), and then choose Options. The Google Chrome Options window appears, similar to Figure 10-4. The Options screen is divided into three tabs: Basics, Minor Tweaks, and Under the Hood. Unless you have some major adjustments to make, you should stick to the first two tabs, highlighted in this section. As a bonus, we throw in some common tasks from the Under the Hood tab, too, in case you're interested.

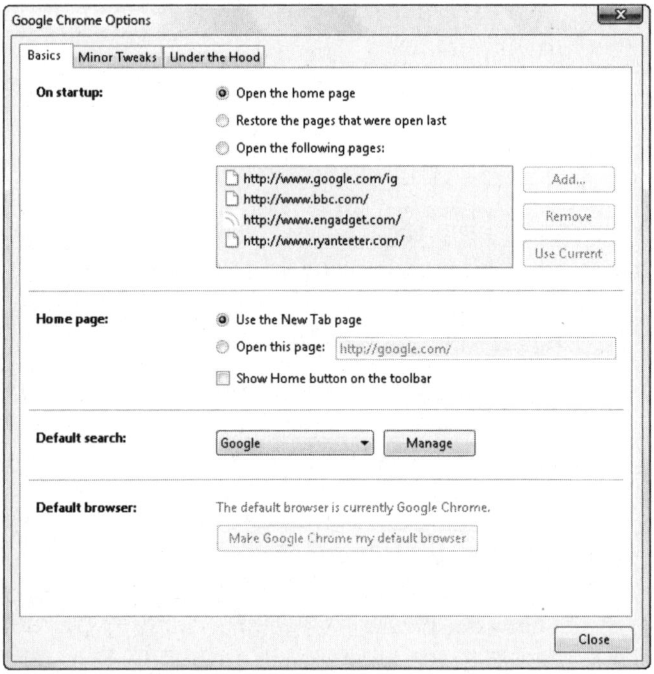

Figure 10-4:
Change
settings in
the Google
Chrome
Options
window.

Setting Basics

The Basics tab (refer to Figure 10-4) gives you control over how Chrome normally behaves, including

  ✔ On Startup

  ✔ Home Page

  ✔ Default Search

  ✔ Default Browser

Next, we explain what each option does and how to make adjustments. Any settings that you change take effect immediately.

Adjusting what Chrome shows on startup

Every time you launch Chrome, your choice of tab or tabs appears. The On Startup section of the Basics tab lets you decide which pages to load at startup. (Refer to Figure 10-4.) The options here include

- ✔ **Open the Home Page:** Click this bullet to open the Home page, which you select in the Home Page section. When your Home page is set to use the New Tab page, you see your favorite destinations when you start Chrome.

- ✔ **Restore the Pages That Were Open Last:** If you're the type of person who likes to take breaks in browsing, this option is for you. When this option is selected, all your tabs are saved when you exit Chrome. The next time you open the browser, you start browsing right where you left off.

- ✔ **Open the Following Pages:** Choose this option if you like to visit multiple pages when you start your browser. You can add more pages to the list or delete the pages you may have added by mistake:

  - • Click the Add button to return to the Add Page list. Pick a new page from the list or enter a new URL by hand.

  - • If you're already on the page that you want to appear on its own tab when you open Google Chrome, click the Use Current button.

  - • To remove a page, pick the page from the list and click the Remove button on the right.

Changing your Home page

Google Chrome doesn't normally start by displaying a default start page. With most new computers, the manufacturer's Home page appears, and most people don't know how to reset it. They often are stuck with the same Home page for a digital eternity. To prevent this problem, Chrome begins with the New Tab page to make it easy to pick exactly what you want to see.

Okay, okay. The New Tab page may not work for you. If you still need to see a traditional Home page as the first page you see, you can make it so. To start with a set Home page every time you start Chrome, follow these steps:

1. **Open your Chrome browser and navigate to the page you want to appear as your Home page or start page.**

2. **Copy the URL from the Omnibox.**

3. **Click Tools⇨Options.**

4. **In the Home Page section in the middle of the dialog box, select the Open This Page radio button and paste the URL (or type the URL) in the adjacent box.**

5. **(Optional) Check the Show Home Button on the Toolbar box to display a traditional Home icon on the Chrome toolbar.**

6. **When you're finished, click the Close button to save your changes and return to your browser.**

Quickly access your Home page by pressing Alt+Home on your keyboard.

Selecting your default search engine

Even though we think Google Search is the best (we're both slightly biased ex-Googlers), we realize that a bunch of other options are out there. If you find yourself going to Yahoo! or Windows Live often, and the search function of the Omnibox doesn't quite cut if for you (see Chapter 9 for more about Omnibox search), you can set any site with a search box as your default.

To set your default search, look for the Default Search option in the Google Chrome Options window. Click the drop-down list to reveal the major search providers and choose your favorite from the list.

If your preferred search engine doesn't appear in the list, you can still make it your default. Click the Manage button, and a screen similar to Figure 10-5 appears. Any site you've searched since you installed Chrome appears in this list. Click a site from this list and then click the Make Default button on the right side of the screen.

Figure 10-5: Choose an alternative search engine.

The easiest way to add a search engine that's not in the list is to navigate to that site in a new tab and perform a search. Chrome automatically adds that site to your Search Engines list.

If for some reason that doesn't work, you need to add your search engine manually. This is particularly helpful if you access your search engine through a proxy, such as for searching your university library. Here's how you do it:

1. **On the Search Engines screen, click the Add button.**

   The Add Search Engine window appears.

2. **Enter your search engine details:**

   • *Name:* Enter the name of your site.

   • *Keyword:* Choose a keyword for your search engine. When you type that keyword into the Omnibox and press Tab, it will search your site.

   • *URL:* Enter the URL for your search engine's results page. To find this, perform a search for *test* in your search engine. On the results page, copy the URL from the Omnibox. Return to the Search Engines window and paste the address here. Replace *test* in the URL with *%s*.

3. **Click OK.**

4. **Choose your new search engine and then click the Make Default button.**

5. **When you finish, click Close.**

   Now when you type words in the Omnibox, your preferred search engine is the one responsible for the results.

When you use other search engines, you may lose some functionality, but you can always search Google again by typing **Google.com** in the Omnibox, followed by the Tab key.

Making Chrome your default browser

While you're changing your settings, why not make Google Chrome your default browser? After all, do you really want to use any other browser? Do this from the exact same Options screen. Simply click the Make Google Chrome My Default Browser button in the Default Browser section. Now Chrome opens a new tab every time you open a Web link or go to browse.

After you choose Chrome as your default, the other browsers on your computer will get jealous. If you decide to fire up Internet Explorer or Firefox, they throw up a dialog box begging you to make them your favorite. Resist the temptation, but if you ever click OK on accident, start Google Chrome and return to the Options screen to make it your default once more.

Making Minor Tweaks

Although the Basics tab allows you to adjust how Chrome behaves normally, the Minor Tweaks tab in the Google Chrome Options window (shown in Figure 10-6) modifies some of the behind-the-scenes functions including:

- ✔ **Download Location:** Indicates where any file you download is saved locally on your computer.

- ✔ **Passwords:** Remembers your login and password information to sites you visit often, if you choose.

- ✔ **Fonts and Languages:** Chooses the language for your browser menus and options. Fonts can be adjusted to support Eastern languages, such as Japanese, and so on.

Figure 10-6:
The Minor Tweaks tab digs deeper into Chrome's options.

Relocating your Downloads folder

By default, your Downloads folder is located within your Documents folder. This keeps your desktop litter free — too bad it can't help you with all of your other random desktop files. But if you use Windows Vista or Mac OS X, you notice you already have a Downloads folder in your Home folder.

To start saving your downloaded files to a different folder, open the Minor Tweaks tab in the Google Chrome Options window. In the Download Location section, click the Browse button. In the dialog box that appears, navigate to your desired Downloads folder and click the OK or Open button, depending on your operating system.

If you're the type of person who likes to save each download into a different folder, check the box next to the Ask Where to Save Each File before Downloading option. This is very helpful when you download lots of e-mail attachments or other documents.

Remembering your passwords

The average person has hundreds of logins and passwords that they have to remember to log into Web sites. It would be easy to keep track of these if you could have just one login name and one password, but that's just not possible. Trying to keep track of them all is a daunting task, but Chrome can help you remember your login information, if you want it to.

By default, each time you successfully log into a Web site, you see a yellow bar along the top of the screen (just below the toolbar) asking you whether you want Chrome to keep the information you just entered. (See Figure 10-7.) Click the Save Password button to have Chrome remember your password. The next time you open that login page, your username and password are filled in automatically; all you have to do is click the Log In button.

Save Password bar

Figure 10-7: The Save Password bar appears when you successfully log into a site.

If you don't want Chrome to remember your password on a site, you can simply ignore the yellow bar by clicking the Close (X) button on the right side of the bar or by clicking the Never for This Site button.

To turn off the Password Manager completely, open the Google Chrome Options window, click the Minor Tweaks tab, and select the radio button next to Never Save Passwords. If you decide that you want to remember passwords later, return here and select the Offer to Save Passwords option.

Although saving passwords on your computer is convenient, you should never save your passwords on a computer that you share with others. Also, you should think twice about saving passwords to financial sites. If your laptop is stolen, for example, the thief could have access to more than just your personal files.

When you forget your password, which even people with the sharpest minds do, you can click the I Forgot My Password link on your sign-in page, or you can look in Chrome's options. Open the Google Chrome Options window, click the Minor Tweaks tab, and then click the Show Saved Passwords button. The Passwords window appears, revealing a list of sites where you've saved a password, along with your username for that site. Click the site you want to remember and click the Show Password button on the right side of the screen. Your password appears directly below that button.

Changing your fonts and languages

Most Web pages these days use a special file called a *style sheet* that tells the page which colors and fonts to use when it loads. This allows designers to create the amazing-looking pages you're used to. If a style sheet doesn't provide which font to use, however, your browser fills in the blank with your default font — usually Times New Roman or Arial. You wouldn't change these normally, but if you're feeling particularly keen to a specific font or, more likely, want to show larger or smaller fonts, you can tweak those as well.

On the Minor Tweaks tab in the Google Chrome Options window, click the Change Font and Language Settings button to choose your own fonts and select a different language. The Fonts and Languages window appears, as shown in Figure 10-8.

To adjust these fonts, click the Change button next to the font style you want to change. The Font window appears. Choose your font, font style, and size by highlighting an option in each respective column, and then click OK. The three font types are

- **Serif:** This font has little tails along the top and bottom of each letter, similar to the text you're reading in this book.

- **Sans-Serif:** This font is blocky and has rigid edges along the letters, just like the captions for the figures in this book.

- **Fixed-width:** This font uses the same width for each character. It is used primarily for logs or viewing HTML source code. In other words, you won't see it very often.

Sprechen sie Deutsch? ¿Hablas español? You can change your browser language on the Fonts and Languages screen as well. Simply click the Languages tab to see the language options available for Chrome, as shown in Figure 10-9.

Figure 10-8:
Set your
default font
for Web
pages.

Figure 10-9:
Set your
browser
language
and spell-
checker.

Some Web pages are available in multiple languages, and the box at the top
allows you to set your preferred language. To add Spanish, for example, click
the Add button on the right, choose Spanish - Español from the drop-down list
that appears, and then click OK. Spanish now appears in the list. Click Spanish
and click the Move Up button until it's at the top of the list. When Chrome
visits a page that has a Spanish language translation, the page will load the
Spanish version instead of the English one.

To change Chrome's language for tabs, menus, and so on, choose your preferred language from the Google Chrome Language list at the bottom. If you write most of your e-mails or blog entries in another language, Chrome has a built-in spell-checker for your language, too. Choose your main language from the Spell-Checker Language list. After you set your browser language, close all your Chrome windows and open a new Chrome tab to see the changes.

For languages that use different characters, such as Arabic or Japanese, changing the default encoding helps those letters display correctly (such as right-to-left). If you don't normally visit sites in foreign languages, this encoding setting doesn't need to be changed.

Getting under the hood

This last section discusses how to adjust more-technical stuff, such as turning features on and off and adjusting proxy settings if you connect to a work or school network. We cover the most important options here. To adjust your advanced settings, click Tools⇨Options to open the Google Chrome Options window. Then click the Under the Hood tab shown in Figure 10-10. Here are the basic categories on this screen:

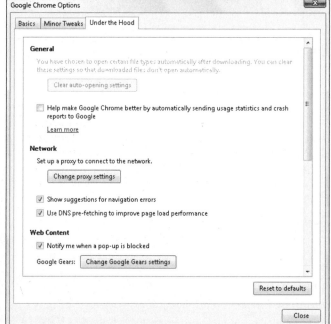

Figure 10-10:
Adjust advanced settings on the Under the Hood tab.

- ✔ **General:** Prevent downloaded files from opening automatically by clicking the Clear Auto-Opening Settings button. Help Google improve Chrome by sharing information with them by clicking the Help Make Google Chrome Better option.

- ✔ **Network:** Set your computer's proxy settings for connecting at work or school. Let Google help you find your way when you misstep with the Show Suggestions for Navigation Errors option. Enable Chrome to preload links to other pages so you can browse even faster with the Use DNS Pre-Fetching option.

- ✔ **Web Content:** Turn pop-up notifying on or off by checking the Notify Me When a Pop-Up Is Blocked option. Adjust your Google Gears settings by clicking the Change Google Gears Settings button.

- ✔ **Security:** Enable or disable phishing and malware protection, manage certificates for secure sites, adjust your SSL settings, and set cookie options in this section.

Using proxies and pre-fetching

Chrome uses your operating system's proxy settings to connect to the Internet. To change these, open the Google Chrome Options window, click the Under the Hood tab, and then click the Change Proxy Settings button. Your computer's Internet Properties or System Preferences window appears, depending on your operating system.

In Windows, click the LAN Settings button, and then enter the proxy server information you received from your network administrator. On a Mac, choose the network service you use, such as Airport or Ethernet. Click Advanced, and then click Proxies and enter your proxy server information.

Fixing pop-ups and Google Gears

Pop-up windows appear when you visit a site that wants you to see a special offer or load a separate page. They can be a pain, but they sometimes contain useful information. Normally, when a pop-up appears in Chrome, a blue "Blocked Pop-Up" bar appears along the bottom of the screen. (See Figure 10-11.) You can open the pop-up window by dragging the blue bar up and into view.

If you'd rather not see pop-up windows at all, open the Google Chrome Options window, click the Under the Hood tab, and uncheck the Notify Me When a Pop-Up Is Blocked option in the Web Content section.

Although most pop-ups are annoying, some sites will not work without pop-ups enabled, including some online testing and financial sites.

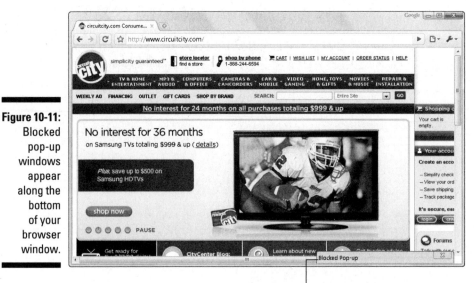

Figure 10-11:
Blocked
pop-up
windows
appear
along the
bottom
of your
browser
window.

Blocked pop-up window

When you need to adjust or disable sites that use Google Gears, click the Change Google Gears Settings button. The Google Gears window appears and lists all the sites for which you've given Chrome permission to save information on your computer. (See Figure 10-12.)

Figure 10-12:
Change
the Google
Gears
options to
view or
disable
offline apps.

From this window, you can allow, deny, or remove any site's access to Google Gears. The Allowed option is selected by default. Select the radio button next to Denied to disable the site from accessing Gears completely. Click the

Remove link to reset the site. If you choose the Remove option, you're given the opportunity to reenable access to Gears the next time you visit that site. When you finish changing your Gears settings, click the Apply button.

Staying secure online

Good Internet security is very important, especially if you do your banking and shopping online. Secure sites encrypt your personal information so that other people who may be watching your Internet activity can't make sense of it. Using the right security settings can help protect you while you surf and keep your information safe. To access security settings, open the Google Chrome Options window, click the Under the Hood tab, and scroll to the Security section, as shown in Figure 10-13. Here's what the options do:

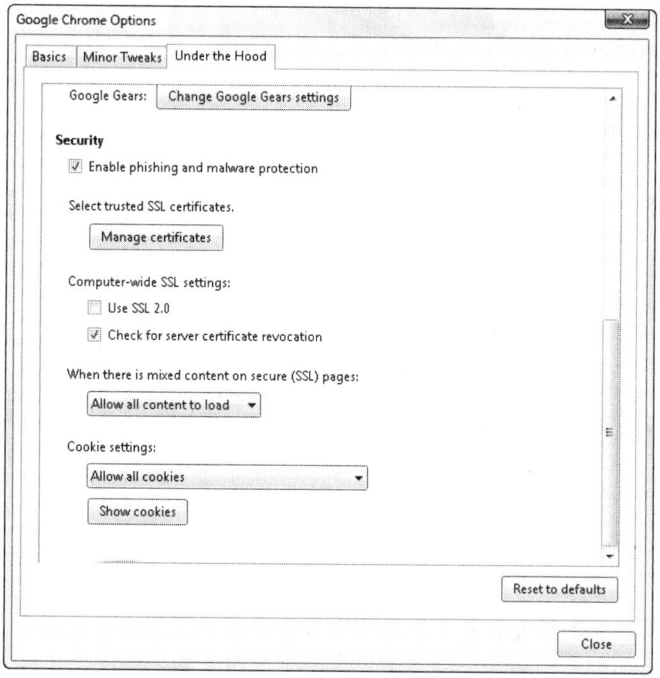

Figure 10-13: Adjusting security settings can make you safer online.

Google Chrome Options

Basics | Minor Tweaks | Under the Hood

Google Gears: Change Google Gears settings

Security

☑ Enable phishing and malware protection

Select trusted SSL certificates.

Manage certificates

Computer-wide SSL settings:

☐ Use SSL 2.0

☑ Check for server certificate revocation

When there is mixed content on secure (SSL) pages:

Allow all content to load ▾

Cookie settings:

Allow all cookies ▾

Show cookies

Reset to defaults

Close

✔ **Enable Phishing and Malware Protection:** Phishing sites imitate legitimate sites and try to trick you into giving your personal information, such as bank account numbers and PINs. Malware sites try to install viruses or other evil software that tracks your computer habits and keystrokes. Google keeps an updated list of known phishing and malware sites and checks to make sure that you're not visiting one of them. With this option checked, Chrome blocks access to bad sites.

Even though the phishing and malware filter work well, it's still a good idea to keep your information safe. Don't share any personal information, such as your Social Security Number or bank account information, on a site linked from your e-mail. When in doubt, visit the company's main page (type the *www.company.com* address) and call a customer service representative.

✔ **Manage Certificates:** Click this button to access your computer's certificates. Certificates are used to verify a site's identity. Browse through the Certificates window that appears and remove any certificates you don't want to keep.

✔ **Use SSL 2.0:** SSL 2.0 is an older security protocol that is less secure. Most sites use SSL 3.0 or newer, so you don't need this option normally. If you come across a site that only works with SSL 2.0, you can enable it here. However, we recommend you leave it unchecked.

✔ **Check for Server Certificate Revocation:** Certificates normally expire at a certain point, but some sites' certificates can be revoked before the expiration date. This option checks to make sure that your certificate is still valid before you access the site. If it is not valid, Chrome blocks access to that site.

✔ **Mixed Content on Secure (SSL) Pages:** Some secure pages show information found on insecure servers, such as images or text. Although it's usually fine to allow all content to load, you can protect yourself from sending information to insecure sites by only allowing images or blocking insecure content completely.

✔ **Cookie Settings:** Cookies are little files that store bits of information from Web sites, such as your login or location so those sites can quickly load your personalized content the next time you visit. Most cookies are safe, but some could potentially track the pages you browse or the links you click. Cookie settings in the Security section include Allow, Restrict, or Block. Cookies received in Incognito mode are deleted automatically when you close the window. Click the Show Cookies button to search for and delete any specific cookies you like.

Starting over

If you end up making more changes than you wanted, there is a quick and easy way to reset your browser settings to normal. You still have to clear your browser data, as we mention in Chapter 9, but at least your browser should behave normally again. Here's all you need to do:

1. **Open Chrome and choose Tools➪Options.**

   The Google Chrome Options window appears.

2. **Click the Under the Hood tab.**

3. **In the bottom-right corner of the screen, click the Reset to Defaults button.**

   A warning window appears, asking whether you really want to reset your settings.

4. **Click Reset to Defaults once again and then click Close.**

Part IV
Building Your Own Scheme

The 5th Wave   By Rich Tennant

"See? I created a little felon figure that runs around our Web site hiding behind banner ads. On the last page, our logo puts him in a non lethal choke hold and brings him back to the home page."

In this part . . .

Knowing the tools you need to build your own site is one thing, but coming up with ideas for one is completely different. This part shares some practical ideas for creating your own site. These samples, which we call *schemes*, build on some common themes: personal, school, and business.

Chapter 11

Proffering a Personal Scheme

. . . .

In This Chapter

▶ Going solo or keeping it all in the family

▶ Showing your face to the world

▶ Sharing your life experiences

▶ Entertaining your visitors with gadgets

. . . .

*N*ow that you have all of the tools that you need, it's time to put them to good use and create something that is truly indispensable. Remember that the Internet is all about sharing. This chapter helps you connect the many aspects of your online life in one place using a personal scheme. When you share your life with your friends and family and allow them to leave a comment or two, everyone benefits.

In this part of the book, we use the term *scheme* as a plan for your site. This chapter contains suggestions to help you build your own personal scheme, which might include pages for photos, phone numbers, announcements, and family trips. If you'd like some ideas for an educational or classroom scheme, check out Chapter 12. Chapter 13 also covers ideas for building a company scheme, complete with wiki and file sharing if that's what you're into.

Here you see some examples of what you can do with Google Sites, but feel free to go off on your own and make something uniquely yours. When you have some tidbits to share, invite friends, family, colleagues, and co-workers to visit and add their two cents.

Before you go on in this chapter, we thought you ought to know a thing or two about sharing personal information online. When you create a public site, anyone can search for you and find out a lot about you by what you post on your site. This includes parents, children, employers, and maybe even identity thieves. Be sure that you wouldn't mind these people seeing or reading about your party antics or antique abacus collection. And, you obviously shouldn't post any super personal info, like bank accounts, passwords, or ID numbers. You've been officially warned.

Going Solo or Keeping It All in the Family

The ideas that we contribute in this chapter can be used in two ways:

You can either use them to create a personal site that's your own space and that allows you to follow your own rules, or you can use them to get your family or friends involved to create a site where everyone can add their personal touches. Or, you can have a little of both.

Keeping your site to yourself

Think of it this way: In your own space, your main page will probably be a page about you, with links to more stuff about you, similar to Figure 11-1. Your site might include any of the following:

- A Profile page that describes who you are
- Your résumé
- A dashboard page
- A To-Do list
- An online backup of your important files

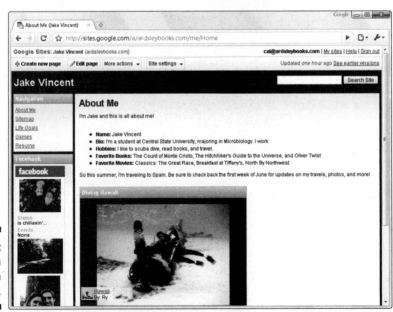

Figure 11-1:
Fly solo with your own site.

Gathering your family together

With a family site, you can create a main page for your family with a main dashboard that shows the family calendar and news, similar to Figure 11-2. You might also include pages for

- Family members
- Combined photo albums from individuals
- Holiday wish lists
- A family directory
- Interesting family folklore and other stories
- Shared recipes or scrapbooks

Figure 11-2: Keep your family on the same page.

The organization of the family site may be different from an individual's site, but the basics stay the same.

If you want to keep your family site on the down-low and not share it with everyone, be sure to invite only the people with whom you want to share it. To do so, click the Site Sharing button at the top of the screen, and then enter your family members' e-mail addresses. We assume you want everyone to collaborate, but you can always keep Uncle Joe from messing up the works by limiting him to "viewer only" status.

Staying in touch from far away

Because you only need Internet access to add or change pages on your site, it's really simple for family members to keep everyone in the loop. When Alex is in college across the country, he can post news of his adventures and find out whom his sister's dating this week. Mom can plan her well-deserved vacation on the family calendar and, while she's there, she can let the family know she's extended the vacation a week longer than she originally planned. And if Josey loses her phone, she can quickly look up her sibling's phone numbers in the family directory. After all, do you know anyone who still memorizes people's phone numbers?

Showing Your Face to the World: Adding Your Profile Info

Your personal page shouldn't require a lot of planning. Just start with your designated page (or sub-page) and add what you want. (For detailed information on the subject, see Chapter 4.) If you're not sure where you should begin, we suggest you create a profile or bio page. After you select a starting point, you can expand your site to include other pages. This section helps you get started with your new page.

Use a personal profile page to tell your family and friends about you. Here are a few suggestions of what to include, similar to what you see in Figure 11-3. We suggest using a bullet list or a table and fill in the items that make you cool, special, or freaking awesome.

- ✔ Your name
- ✔ A blurb about you
- ✔ Activities, hobbies, and interests
- ✔ Favorite movies, TV shows, and music

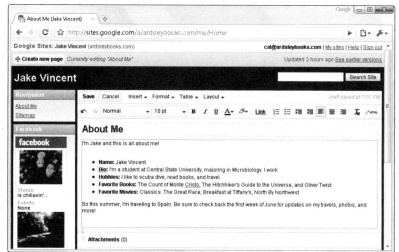

Figure 11-3: Create a site to tell the world about you.

You may already have profile information scattered throughout the Web. Rather than create it from scratch, link your site to your existing sources. For example, Facebook and MySpace allow you to add or embed your profile info to any site you want. Why not add it to yours?

Sharing Your Life Experiences

When it comes to your experiences, a picture is worth a thousand words and videos count for just about the same. The latest digital cameras can capture both pictures and videos, which makes sharing them on your site very easy. When you have a profile page in place, it's time to expand your virtual self by using the Google Sites Slideshow and YouTube gadgets, and create a multi-media page to act as your personal hub. This section helps you organize your gadgets. When you finish that, you can move on to lists and File Cabinets.

You can add your photo presentations, YouTube videos, or regular images anywhere on a page, which we discuss in Chapters 4 and 6. Add a gadget or create a new page with a Dashboard template and you'll be showing off in no time flat.

Adding a photo gadget or two

Start with your photos. As we cover in Chapter 6, you can show off photo presentations by using the Picasa Web Slideshow gadget, which connects to Google's free photo-hosting service.

Inserting badges from social networks

Many social networking sites allow you to display your profile information on your personal site. We don't cover all social networking sites, but here's an example of how to add a vertical Facebook profile badge to your site's Sidebar. Other sites may be similar.

1. Log into your Facebook account.

2. Click the Profile link in the blue bar at the top of the page.

3. Scroll to the bottom of the column on the left and click the Create a Profile Badge link.

4. On the Badges screen that appears, click the Blog Badge link.

   The Custom Badge screen loads, shown here:

5. Customize your badge by adding and removing different information. For the Format option, select the radio button next to Image. (The JavaScript doesn't work on Sites.)

6. Click the Save button.

   A screen appears, showing your completed badge with some HTML code.

7. Select the HTML code from the textbox and copy it (Ctrl+C).

8. Return to your site and click the Edit Sidebar link at the bottom of your Sidebar column.

9. On the Appearance screen, click the Add a Sidebar Item link.

10. Find the Text element in the list that appears and click the Add button.

11. Click the Edit link on your new Text Sidebar element.

12. On the Configure Textbox screen, click the HTML button.

13. Paste your code into the HTML textbox (Ctrl+V) and click the Update button to return to the Configure Textbox screen.

14. Click OK to return to the Appearance screen.

15. Click Save Changes in the top-right corner of the screen and then click the Return to Site link to return to your site.

When you complete these steps, your site's Sidebar looks similar to Figure 11-3.

Here's all you have to do to add your photos to your site:

1. **Start by uploading your photos to Picasa Web Albums.**

   You can find more about how to do that at `http://picasaweb.google.com`.

2. **Copy the address of the Picasa Web Album you want to share.**

3. **Return to your multimedia page and insert a Picasa Web Slideshow gadget or click one of the gadget placeholders and choose Picasa Web Slideshow from the list that appears.**

4. **Paste the album address you copied in Step 2, choose your gadget settings, and then click Save.**

Broadcasting yourself

Getting your videos online is fairly painless, too. And who doesn't want to see your latest undersea adventure? We talk about the YouTube gadget in Chapter 6, but here's the quick way to add your video to your site:

1. **Upload your video clip to YouTube.**

   If you've never uploaded a clip before, follow the helpful tutorials found at www.youtube.com.

2. **Open your video clip on YouTube and copy the Web address.**

3. **Return to your multimedia page and insert a YouTube Video gadget.**

4. **Paste the album address you copied in Step 2, select your gadget settings, and then click Save.**

Creating a virtual fridge

When it comes to sharing photos with your family, Google Sites allows you to create the ultimate refrigerator, like the one shown in Figure 11-4. Start with a dashboard page and different family members can simply edit the page and add their own Picasa Web Album or YouTube video. This page becomes your hub for family happenings. Just don't tell your real refrigerator . . . it might start feeling a little withdrawal.

Figure 11-4: See photos from everyone's adventures.

Keeping track of To-Do lists and digits

Your high school English teacher probably told you, "Goals that aren't written down are just wishes." Well now's your chance to take control and see what you can do with your life. With a List template, creating a To-Do list can help you get the motivation you need to go out and do stuff. If you're trying to decide what your list should look like, try some of these column header ideas:

- ✔ Goal
- ✔ Requirements
- ✔ Projected deadline
- ✔ Accomplished

Next, forget about the Rolodex or wipe-off board. Why not choose a more permanent place for everyone to connect? Creating a family directory is a great way to find addresses to send good old-fashioned holiday cards or thank you notes. Use a List template to keep track of phone numbers, as well. That way when you lose your phone (or get a new one) you can still find your important numbers easily. Here are some suggested column titles, as shown in Figure 11-5:

- ✔ Name
- ✔ Address
- ✔ Phone Number
- ✔ E-mail

Figure 11-5:
Create a list of family phone numbers.

Because lists allow links, you can link home addresses to Google Maps or set e-mail addresses to send new messages automatically when clicked. You may even find more useful information to keep track of.

Planning that trip of a lifetime

While we're on the subject of goals and coordinating info, we find that Google Sites helps us organize big family vacations or other events by sharing links, itineraries, and lists of people that are going, similar to the site shown in Figure 11-6.

On your vacation page, make changes to your itinerary in one place so everyone has the latest information. In a second column, add links to travel information, weather reports, or other useful sites that can help everyone have the best trip possible. Then insert a Spreadsheet Form gadget so everyone can RSVP if you don't know for sure who's planning to show.

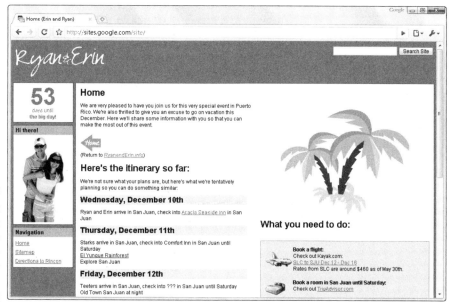

Figure 11-6: Work together to organize your family vacation.

Entertaining Your Visitors with Gadgets

As our final suggestion for a page to add to your personal scheme, think about your favorite gadgets. If you're like us, you may like to spend a few minutes each day keeping your mind fresh with word games or checking the local weather for your dream vacation destination. Plenty of Google Gadgets fit the bill. Group them all onto a single page to let other people know what you're checking out; similar to the Games page we created, as shown in Figure 11-7.

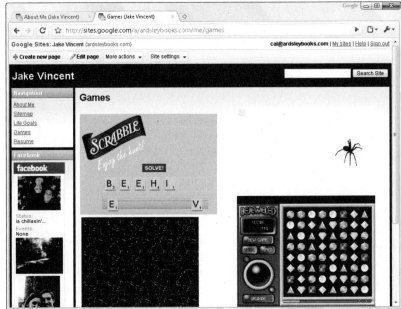

Figure 11-7:
Keep yourself and friends entertained with multiple games.

Chapter 12

Building a College Course Scheme

We believe that one of the best uses for Google Sites is to aid college courses or school classrooms by giving students and faculty alike a place to share ideas and keep on top of assignments and projects. Whether you're a researcher or leading a study group, you'll benefit from the arsenal of ideas in this chapter for getting the most out of Google Sites and, by extension, the other Google Apps.

In this chapter, we first help you identify your audience and then suggest some layouts for you to consider based on the needs of your course. Unlike the personal scheme in Chapter 11 or the business scheme in Chapter 13, the college course scheme focuses on the unique needs of a classroom.

When it comes to designing your college course scheme, we suggest you follow a few basic steps:

1. Analyze your audience.

2. Consider site elements and gather ideas.

3. Sketch your pages and diagram your sitemap.

4. Create.

Analyzing College Course Schemes

When designing a site scheme, everything starts with audience analysis. Take a few minutes to think about with whom you're communicating. For this example scheme, put yourself in the role of a college professor or a high-school teacher getting ready to teach several 11th or 12th grade college prep classes. In this role, you have several audiences: students, teaching peers, and supervisors. Knowing this, ask a few questions:

- ✔ What are your audiences' needs?
- ✔ What are their expectations?
- ✔ What are the benefits that can come from this site?

Supervisors are looking for a demonstration of professional competence. Teaching peers are looking to coordinate efforts and to share information. But for a college course, the needs of students matter most. Let's get the analysis rolling by examining Figure 12-1. Here you see a Google Site for a course in computer augmented accounting. This is an undergraduate course taught in a major university. Analyzing sites like this can help you plan Google Sites of your own.

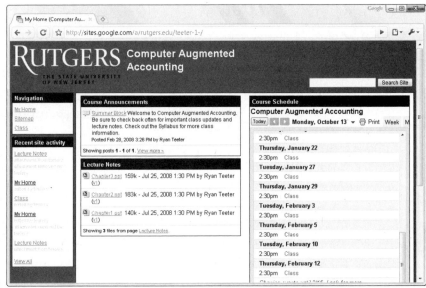

Figure 12-1:
A site page for a computer augmented accounting course.

Considering site elements and gathering ideas

The computer augmented accounting course in Figure 12-1 offers valuable elements to help students on just its first page, including:

✔ Course announcements

✔ Lecture notes

✔ Calendar with course schedule and deadlines

Additional site elements for college-level course sites usually include:

✔ A course outline or syllabus

✔ Links to course-related Web sites or test prep sites

✔ A page containing useful files, such as study guides or multimedia downloads

✔ Relevant gadgets and online tools

Lists, like those above, get you heading in the right direction and give you a pretty good idea of what your workload will be.

Looking at Web page, File Cabinet, and List page templates

The next step is to visualize what your course site can look like page by page. Again, the best place to go for ideas is online. Figure 12-2 shows a Web page prepared for a Political Science 1100 course taught in the fall of 2008 — the semester of the historic 2008 election. This page offers a few additional ideas, such as:

✔ Counter gadgets with countdowns to Election Day and the Democratic and Republican national conventions

✔ Links to the Web sites of the two nominees

✔ An Electoral College map

✔ Links to polling sites, political news sources, and other research sources for election analysis

✔ An RSS News Feed Gadget that gathers political news stories

The Web page template is just one of several alternatives. Two other styles, File Cabinet (see Figure 12-3) and List page (see Figure 12-4) have been applied to this college course site as well. The File Cabinet allows the uploading and downloading of files critical to a college course. In Figure 12-3, study guides for various exams have been posted for student download. They also have been organized into folders to correspond with upcoming exams.

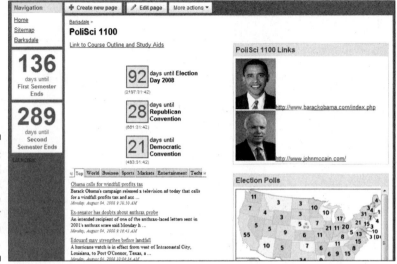

Figure 12-2:
The Political
Science
1100 Web
page prior
to an
election.

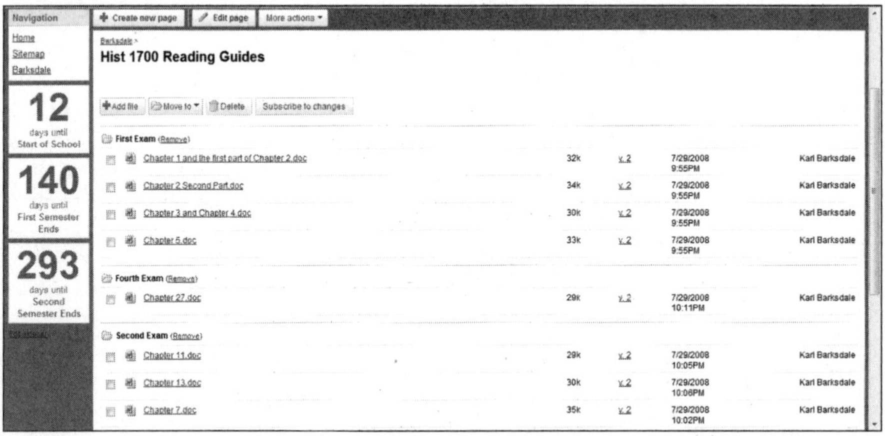

Figure 12-3:
A File
Cabinet
page.

The List page, seen in Figure 12-4, is a bit more obscure; however, in this case it solves a unique problem. A rather detailed list of reading assignments for two separate textbooks has been created so that students always know where they stand in regard to those assignments. This replaces a paper hand-out that many students lose or that becomes obsolete when assignments are modified.

Jump to the "Adding Web Page, File Cabinet, and List Page Elements" section near the end of this chapter to find out how to create pages using each of these template styles.

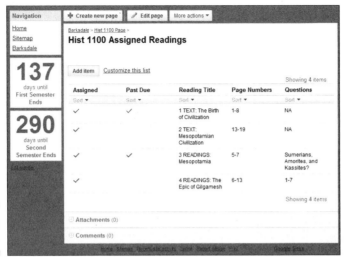

Figure 12-4:
A List page.

Sketching your pages and diagramming your sitemap

The Web page, File Cabinet, and List page sites depicted in Figures 12-2, 12-3, and 12-4 were sketched in advance on the back of napkins. (See Figure 12-5.) You can use paper or your PC drawing tools. However, because we do most of our design work at extended coffee breaks, napkins are our preferred Web site design media. (Why do we always draw on the "back of napkins" when both sides are pretty much the same?)

The minute your site spreads to more than one page, you need to diagram your site's navigation map. A *sitemap* shows the relationships between pages in a hierarchy. While you create pages, Google Sites keeps track of them in its own sitemap. In the sitemap shown in Figure 12-6, the instructor is teaching three courses. Each course has a unique starting page (History 1100, History 1700, and Political Science 1100) with one to four sub-pages. If you draw out and diagram the relationship between the pages, defining the navigation strategy for your site will be easier.

You can't possibly anticipate everything you'll need on a site in advance. Fortunately, Google Sites is very forgiving and you can modify things as you discover new needs and audience expectations.

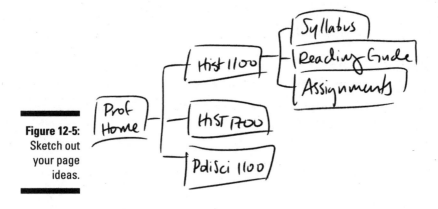

Figure 12-5:
Sketch out
your page
ideas.

Figure 12-6:
Diagram
your hier-
archy and
sitemap.

Sitemap

Hierarchy View   List View

Expand all   Collapse all

- UCAS Course Pages
- Barksdale
  - Hist 1100 Page
    - Hist 1100 Assigned Readings
    - Hist 1100 Course Outline
  - Hist 1700 Page
    - Hist 1700 Course Outline
    - Hist 1700 Reading Guides
  - PoliSci 1100
    - Hist 1700 Course Outline and Study Guides
    - PoliSci 1100 Course Outline and Study Aids
  - Home

Setting Site Settings

With your page designs and sitemap roughed out (at least in your head if not on paper or on your PC) it's time to develop the site. To begin, you need to set up the security rights for site participants. Then you apply appearance themes and navigation features. Finally, you create and flesh out your pages. The next few sections discuss these points in detail.

Setting up site rights and security

Each site needs a security plan. Normally, in a college scheme, anyone (including supervisors and other faculty members) is allowed access to view the site, but not to edit it, as shown in Figure 12-7. However, the site must be public so that students can access it online. For this reason, the Advanced Permissions settings are very important for a college course site. Here's how to set up the security to work for student access:

1. **Select Site Settings at the top of your Google Sites screen.**

2. **Click the Sharing tab shown in Figure 12-7.**

3. **(Optional) If you want to let specific people know that your site is available for them, select the As Viewers radio button and enter the e-mail addresses of any supervisors and peers you want to invite to view the site.**

4. **In the Advanced Permissions section, choose View from the Anyone at *Domain Name* May View/Edit This Site drop-down box.**

5. **(Optional) To make the site open to all students without requiring them to log in, select the Anyone in the World May View This Site (Make It Public) check box.**

6. **Click the Invite These People button to send an e-mail message inviting colleagues and supervisors to view your site.**

If you're a Google Apps user and find that you cannot make your site public, chances are good the problem is your security settings. Your Google Apps administrator will need to change a few settings for all users of the same Apps-supported domain. When a Google Apps administrator enables Google Sites for new users, he's able to define security settings. In the Service Settings section under the General tab, sharing options can be optimized. Normal users will not see this screen. Your Apps administrator must choose one of the Users Can Share options in the Sharing Options list, and then mark the box below the list stating that Users Can Make Sites Public. Of course, the administrator will need to save the settings.

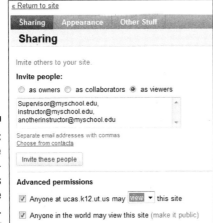

Figure 12-7: Pick the site's security settings from the Sharing tab.

Picking a name and defining your site settings

If you're creating a site from scratch, you're guided to name your site and choose key settings right off the bat. Start by logging into your Google Sites Home, as explained in Chapter 4, and then click the Create New Site button. At that point, you can name and describe your site, limit access if necessary by selecting the Only People I Specify Can View This Site option, and pick a site theme, as shown in Figure 12-8. After you pick your settings, save them, and your site is created automatically.

Don't worry about getting every setting right when you first create your site. You can always change your mind, as we show you in the pages that follow.

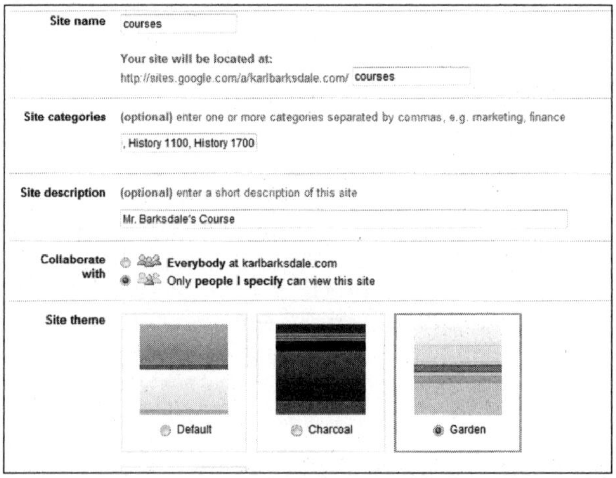

Figure 12-8:
Modify your
initial
settings.

Improving your site's appearance

After you create your initial site, you're free to make changes and to dig deeper into Google Sites' capabilities. For example, adjusting the color scheme and changing the Sidebar and Header elements is painless and quite fun. For a college scheme, most instructors pick school colors, so poke around and see whether any of the predesigned themes match your fabled institution's color palette. You can also tweak the colors for the background pages and individual design elements if you need to. Here's how to modify the appearance of a college scheme site:

1. **Log into your site and select Site Settings from the top of the Sites screen.**

2. **Click Appearance and choose the Themes tab, as shown in Figure 12-9.**

3. **Pick a new theme. (Click the Preview button to see what your pages will look like with the new theme.)**

4. **Choose the Site Elements tab.**

   The screen shown in Figure 12-10 lets you change Sidebar elements, add a logo or image to your header, and even change the layout of your pages.

5. **To change a logo on the top of your site, click the Change Logo link in the Header section.**

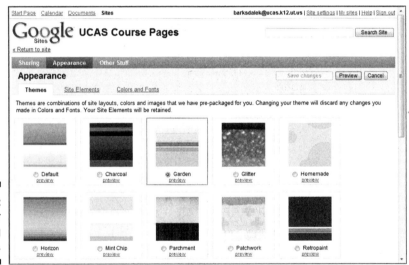

Figure 12-9: Change your overarching theme.

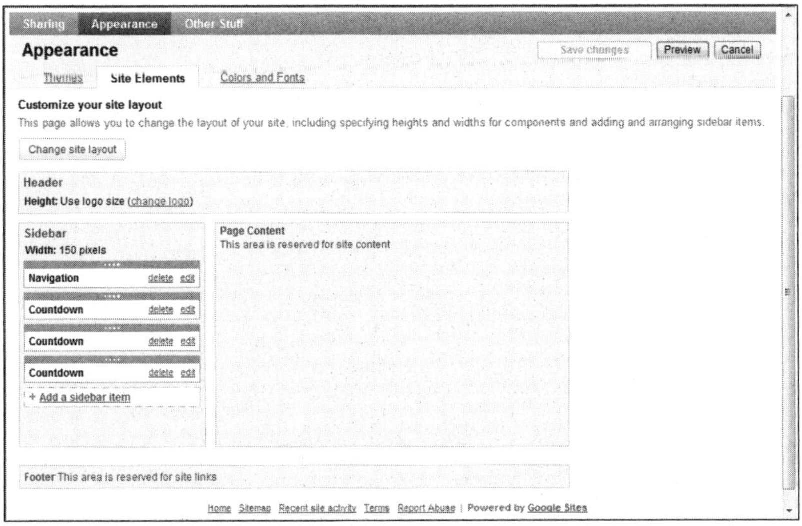

Figure 12-10: Add a logo and site elements to the Sidebar.

6. **Select the Custom Logo radio button, shown in Figure 12-11, and then browse to the image of your logo. Choose OK.**

   (If you decide your logo isn't exactly what you want, you can always repeat this process and go back to the Default Logo or select No Logo.)

7. **Add a gadget to the Sidebar by clicking the Add a Sidebar Item link. Scroll down the list of gadgets from the Choose a New Page Element dialog box. When you find a gadget you like, click Add.**

8. **Click the Edit link on any newly added gadgets and enter any information the gadget may require.**

   In a Countdown gadget, for example, you need to enter an Event name and a termination date.

9. **If you've created pages in your site that you want to access from the Sidebar navigation bar, click the Edit link in the Navigation gadget. In the Select Page to Add dialog box, select the page you want to appear in the Sidebar.**

10. **If you want to change the layout of your pages (by moving the Sidebar to the right or by making the header larger or smaller), click the Change site layout button and tweak the settings there.**

11. **To change the colors and fonts on your site, click the Colors and Fonts tab shown in Figure 12-12.**

12. **Select new colors for the various elements on your site by picking individual elements from the scroll-down list and then choosing a color from the color palette. (Don't forget to save your changes.)**

    If you need to get a more specific color, enter the hexadecimal code value in the box next to the color palette.

Figure 12-11:
Add a
custom logo
or remove
logos from
your site's
header.

13. To change your title or setup options, click the Other Stuff tab.

Change any settings that need changing from the original settings you picked in your first setup. (See Figure 12-13.)

Hexadecimal numbers (which are based on 16 digits) are used to represent over 16,000,000 colors that the human eye can see online. If you need to fine-tune your color choices, enter the hexadecimal code of the exact color you're looking for in your Colors and Fonts screen. For example, do you need a light, pastel green? Try #99FF99. Check out www.colorschemer.com/online.html to find the hex number of your favorite color.

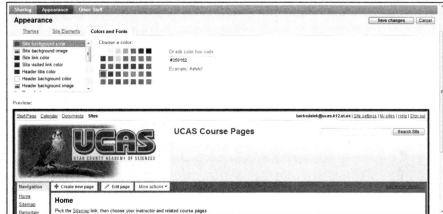

Figure 12-12:
Tweak your layout and colors.

Figure 12-13:
Modified titles and setup information.

Adding Web Page, File Cabinet, and List Page Elements

Google Sites gives you about a dozen different templates to start with. Not all of them will fit the site you're trying to create. (See Chapter 4 for more detail.) In this section, we give you ideas on how to use the options displayed in Figure 12-14 in a college scheme. The three most common templates are

- **Web Page:** The most versatile template. You can do almost anything with it.
- **File Cabinet:** The perfect template for sharing files.
- **List Page:** An obscure template, useful for, well, lists.

To start any one of these templates, follow these steps:

1. **Click the New Page button.**

   The Create New Page form appears. (See Figure 12-14.)

2. **Name the page in the Page Name textbox.**

3. **Select the radio button for your template.**

4. **Position the page, either at the "top level" or as a sub-page and subordinate to another page.**

   For example, several subordinate pages can be found under the HIST 1700 main page, such as a File Cabinet page and a List page.

5. **Click Create Page.**

Figure 12-14: Select a template, name the page, and position it.

Adding a gadget to a Web page

In this example, the Web page template — the most flexible template — was selected. We added graphics, gadgets, and an index to other course-related pages. Notice the sub-pages are listed automatically, making an index a bit redundant. Also, attachments (such as course-related files) and comments are designed into this flexible template.

To add a gadget, such as the RSS news feed shown in Figure 12-2, follow these steps:

1. **Click the Edit Page button.**

2. **Select the two-column setting by choosing Layout⇨Two Columns.**

3. **Click the column where you want the gadget to appear.**

4. **Click the Insert button and choose More from the menu that appears.**

5. **Browse the Add a Gadget to Your Page's topical index or use the search box to search for a gadget.**

6. **Click the link for the gadget you want and it's added to your page, as shown in Figure 12-15.**

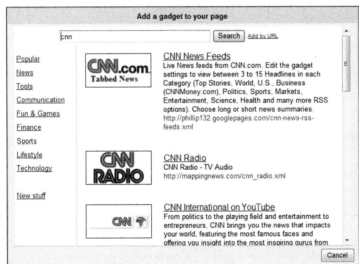

Figure 12-15:
Add a
gadget.

Adding images

Adding images is a snap, regardless if they are from your local hard drive or a link to a page on the Web. Let's touch on both. Here's how to add images:

1. **Open a Google Sites page and then click Edit Page.**

2. **Click the textbox where you want the picture to appear.**

3. **Choose Insert⊏⟩Image.**

4. **Now you can add an image. Images can come from either your computer or from the Web. Add the image as follows:**

   a. To upload a picture from your computer, select the Upload Images option and then click Choose File. After the file uploads, click the image and then click Add Image.

   b. To link to an image on the Web, select the Web Address (URL) radio button and enter the URL of the image you need. You can easily open a separate browser window and navigate to an image, copy the URL from the address bar, and paste it into the Insert Image URL box back on your site.

5. **Use the size and alignment options, shown in Figure 12-16, to adjust the image.**

Figure 12-16:
Size and align the image.

Align: L C R - Size: S M L Original - Wrap: on off - Remove ⊠

Adding a File Cabinet

A File Cabinet is an extremely useful tool, especially for college courses. Files need to be shared, and the File Cabinet has a lot to offer. Files of all types can be shared: Word, PowerPoint, Excel, JPG, and Google Apps can all be organized in the same File Cabinet. In this section, you see how Microsoft Office files from your hard drive are uploaded, as well as how Google Apps files, which reside online in the proverbial Internet cloud, can be shared.

Here's how to implement a File Cabinet (refer to Figure 12-3) and to upload files of all kinds:

1. **Click the Create New Page button.**

2. **Select the File Cabinet radio button and then click the Create Page button.**

3. **On the page that appears, click Add File.**

   The Add File dialog box appears. (See Figure 12-17.)

4. **Now you can add the files. Files can come from either your own computer or from the Web. Add the files as follows:**

   a. To upload a file from your PC, select the Your Computer radio button and then browse to your file and click Upload.

   b. To link to an online file, select The Web radio button and paste the URL or Web address in the box below. Enter a name for the linked file. Adding a discription is optional. Then click Upload.

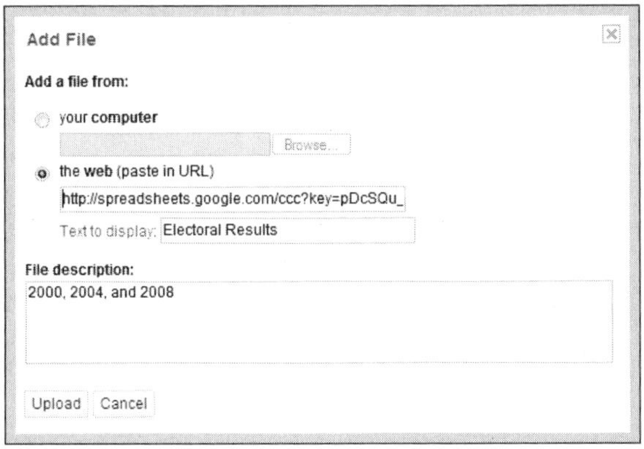

Figure 12-17:
Add a
new file.

Adding a List page

List pages can help solve unique problems. In this example, a long, complicated list of assignments is organized in a table format. When assignments are assigned, they are checked. Then when they are due, they are checked again. Details about each assignment are available 24/7 for students to look up.

To implement a List page, follow these steps:

1. **Click the Create New Page button and select the List radio button. (Refer to Figure 12-14.)**

2. **Choose Customize This List and define each column. In Figure 12-18, five categories are created.**

3. **Click the Add Item button.**

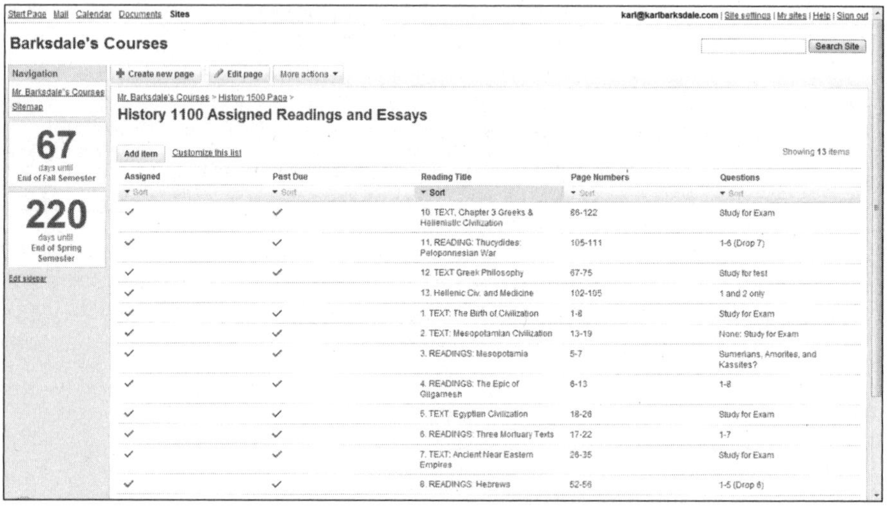

Figure 12-18:
Customize
the list and
add items.

4. **To modify an item, click it and make changes in the dialog box that appears.**

5. **Click Save after making your changes.**

Chapter 13

Building Business Schemes

*B*usinesses, large and small, require flexibility for their intranets. In this chapter, we present some practical ideas for corporate intranets and small business users alike. Perhaps this will trigger some valuable ideas for your business unit. While we reveal various Google Sites options, we also suggest how to integrate some of the other Google Apps and Google gadgets into your Sites scheme. (For specific how-to steps, review Part I of this book.)

Unlike a personal or educational scheme, your business scheme revolves around making your business better. Enabling workgroups and allowing your employees or co-workers to share their collective knowledge helps you make better decisions and get new employees up to speed quickly. It's no wonder that corporate wikis and blogs have become so popular in recent years. Add a splash of advertising and you've got an extra revenue stream besides. So get going and here's to more profitable quarters ahead!

Google's Advertising Tools

Google's profitable advertising tools, AdWords and AdSense, pay for just about everything else that Google does. AdWords — the system that feeds ads to Google Search queries and affiliated advertisers — provides most of Google's revenue. AdSense, also a moneymaker, allows Web sites to display AdWords ads at a profit. Then there is Google Analytics, which allows AdWords and AdSense users to track their ad traffic and the success of their advertising campaigns. When it comes to meeting the advertising needs of a business, Google's online solutions are unparalleled. (See Figure 13-1.)

Figure 13-1:
Google's
advertising
solutions
are the most
profitable in
the industry.

To find out more about AdWords and AdSense, read *AdWords For Dummies* by Howie Jacobson, *Google AdSense For Dummies* by Jerri L. Ledford, and *Building Your Business with Google For Dummies* by Brad Hill. Search for each at www.wiley.com.

Google's Other Business Tools for Intranets

Google has used its financial might to create new tools for internal business communications. The Google Apps program was created to bundle the communications software that businesses need to provide their employees. All the tools that can be offered to employees for free or at a nominal cost are as follows. (Each is explained in various chapters in this book.)

- ✔ Start Page
- ✔ Chat
- ✔ Web Pages
- ✔ Email
- ✔ Calendar

✔ Docs (Word processing, Spreadsheet, Presentations)

✔ Sites

Sites is just the latest tool added to the Google Apps solution suite. Businesses can make all of these tools available in a Sites-based intranet system. Figure 13-2 shows the Google Apps administrator's Dashboard where all of these tools are managed.

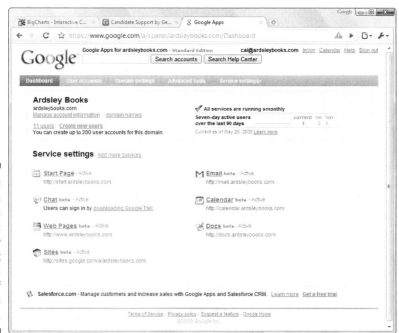

Figure 13-2: Google Apps provides a variety of intranet tools, the latest of which is Sites.

Using All of the Sites Template Options

Every business has very unique intranet needs. What works for a software company is likely not the same for a widget manufacturer or a small bookstore. Even departments within a business can have different requirements. This makes a one-size-fits-all approach as impractical as it sounds. Fortunately, Sites has the flexibility to meet most of your business's collaboration needs.

When creating your sites, consider what each of the five main template options can do for you.

✔ **Web page:** Great for most general intranet communcation needs

✔ **Announcements:** Perfect for, well, announcements

✔ **File Cabinet:** The best template for organizing, uploading, and downloading large numbers of files

✔ **List page:** Spot on for lists of things that neeed doing, such as a team project

✔ **Dashboard:** An effective way to organize gadgets for employees and team members

These options are discussed more fully in the next few sections.

The Web page template on an intranet

Figure 13-3 shows a Web Page template prepared as a starting point for employees at Ardsley Books. The page includes

✔ A calendar of events

✔ A link to the CEO's monthly message

✔ Key announcements

✔ A link to corporate dashboard containing helpful gadgets

✔ A link to each major department's intranet site within the company

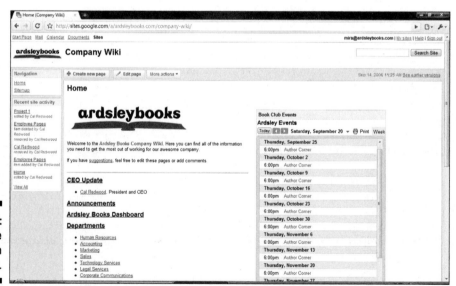

Figure 13-3:
A Web page template in action.

The Web page is easily the most flexible of all the Sites template options. It can be used by various departments, teams of employees, or even individual employees. For example, the Web page template offers each individual employee in the company their own professional business page. In another example, the HR department may create a page to provide necessary information for new employees.

Teams can create Sites pages for each of their projects, as shown in Figure 13-4. This project site has

- ✔ A secure team sign-in link
- ✔ A link to Google Talk, used for team communication
- ✔ A gadget that points to the team's List page of To Do items

If you scroll to the bottom of a typical Sites Web page, there is also a place for team comments and a place to upload files in a designated attachment section. (See Figure 13-5.) The attachment section provides a quick way to handle limited file transfers. (For more demanding file sharing, a File Cabinet would be a better choice. Also, a separate Announcements page can be created for heavy traffic needs. Both templates are discussed next.)

Figure 13-4: Team project and individual employee pages can use the Web page template.

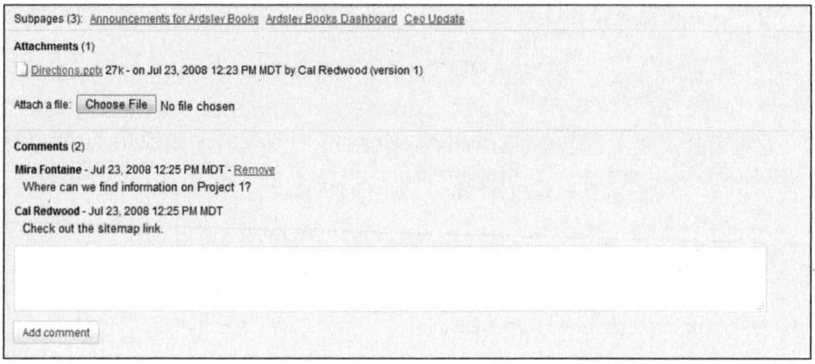

Figure 13-5:
Attachment
and
comment
options on
a Web page
template.

> Subpages (3): Announcements for Ardsley Books Ardsley Books Dashboard Ceo Update
>
> **Attachments (1)**
>
> ☐ Directions.pptx 27k - on Jul 23, 2008 12:23 PM MDT by Cal Redwood (version 1)
>
> Attach a file: [Choose File] No file chosen
>
> **Comments (2)**
>
> **Mira Fontaine** - Jul 23, 2008 12:25 PM MDT - Remove
>   Where can we find information on Project 1?
>
> **Cal Redwood** - Jul 23, 2008 12:25 PM MDT
>   Check out the sitemap link.
>
> [Add comment]

The Announcements template on an intranet

Early in the life of a site, businesses can place announcements at the bottom of a Web page template, but when the traffic increases, creating a specialized Announcements page will be warranted. Creating such a page is as easy as choosing New⇨Announcement. On the resulting page, announcements can be structured in chronological order. And one of the best features is the convenient Search tool.

The File Cabinet template on an intranet

The File Cabinet is one of the most important templates for teamwork and department sharing needs. Files of all types can be shared: PDF, Google Docs, Microsoft Office, images, and video.

When the number of files grows, they need to be organized by folders or labels. Creating folders is easy. Here's all you need to do:

1. **Choose Edit⇨Move To⇨New Folder.**

2. **Name the new folder.**

3. **Move related files into the folder by clicking the box next to the file's name, and then clicking Move To followed by the name of the new folder.**

Moving files from desktop PCs to a File Cabinet page is as easy as clicking Add File, browsing to the file, and clicking the Upload button. To add a file published on the Web, such as a Google Doc, spreadsheet, or presentation, follow these steps:

1. **Open the file you need in Google Docs.**

2. **Publish the document by clicking the Publish tab and then clicking the Publising link.**

3. **Copy the URL or Web address of the file, as shown in Figure 13-6.**

   Start by selecting the link first and then press the Ctrl+C keys to copy the link.

4. **Return to the File Cabinet page where you want the document to appear.**

5. **Click Add File.**

6. **In the Add File box, select the The Web (Paste in URL) radio button.**

7. **Paste the URL in the URL box**

   Press Ctrl+V to paste the link.

8. **Type in the name of the file (or what you want to call the document.)**

9. **(Optional) Add a description for the file.**

   This is helpful for both the users and for finding an obscure file with a search.

Select and copy the link

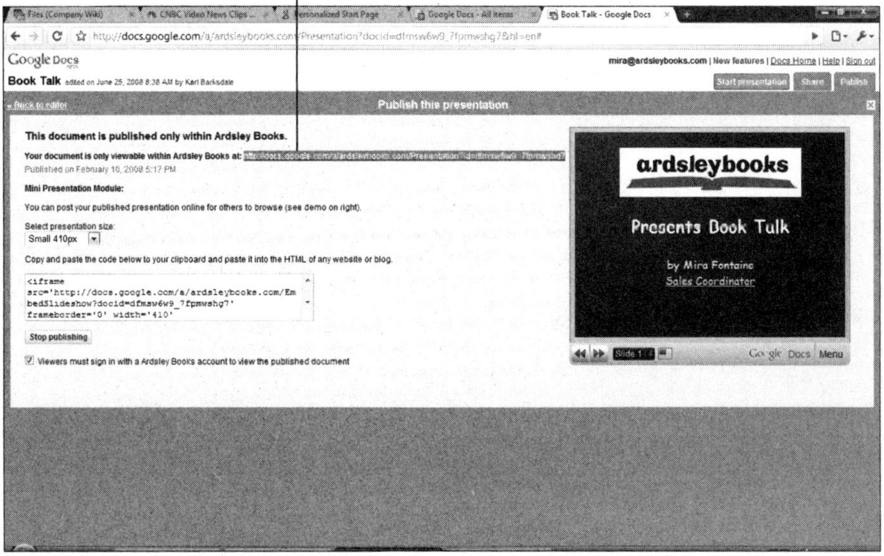

Figure 13-6:
Copy your published document's URL.

When you have many files, the one you need can be lost easily. Use the Search tool to find the exact file you need. The search box is located in the upper-right corner of each open Sites window. Enter a search word, which can include words in the file name or words in the document itself, and press the Search button. (Search also works on List, Announcements, Web site, and all other Sites pages.)

The List template on an intranet

The List template is the most obscure template. It is an ideal template for certain problems, like creating and tracking a list of team project steps or team activities. In the example shown in Figure 13-7, a rather detailed list of assignments due by team members can be created to track and check off upon completion.

One of the values of a List page is that the creators and collaborators can subscribe to changes. When people complete activities, other team members who have subscribed to changes are informed about those changes. After each change, an e-mail update of changes is sent to subscribers.

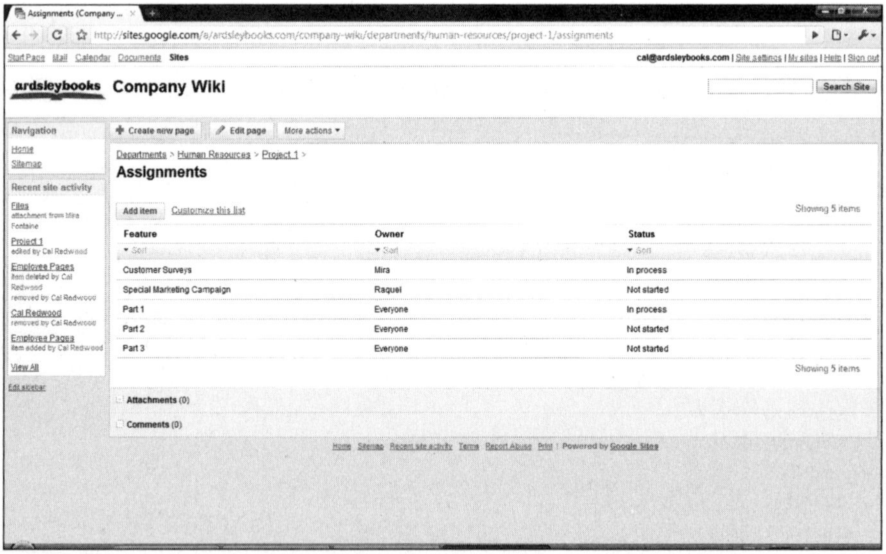

Figure 13-7:
A List template page.

The Dashboard template on an intranet

Dashboards allow the quick organization of gadgets. For instance, List or Announcements pages can be turned into gadgets. These gadgets can be placed on other pages that are more convenient to employees, such as on a start page or on a dashboard page. We explain how to do this with a List page in the next section. In fact, one has been placed on the dashboard page shown in Figure 13-8.

Many of these can be custom gadgets, coming straight from other intranet files or pages. For example, in Figure 13-8, you can see

- ✔ The Google Calendar gadget
- ✔ A Recent Announcements gadget
- ✔ A gadget listing recently uploaded files
- ✔ A gadget linking to a list or To Do page for teams

To add a list gadget to a dashboard (or any other page for that matter):

1. **Click the Edit Page button.**
2. **Click Insert and select the Recent List Items option.**
3. **Pick the desired page from the Show List Items From drop-down list.**
4. **Modify any features you want, and then name the gadget in the Include Title box.**

   The gadget then appears on the page you select, as shown in Figure 13-9.

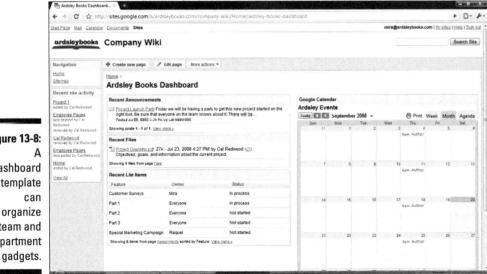

Figure 13-8: A Dashboard template can organize team and department gadgets.

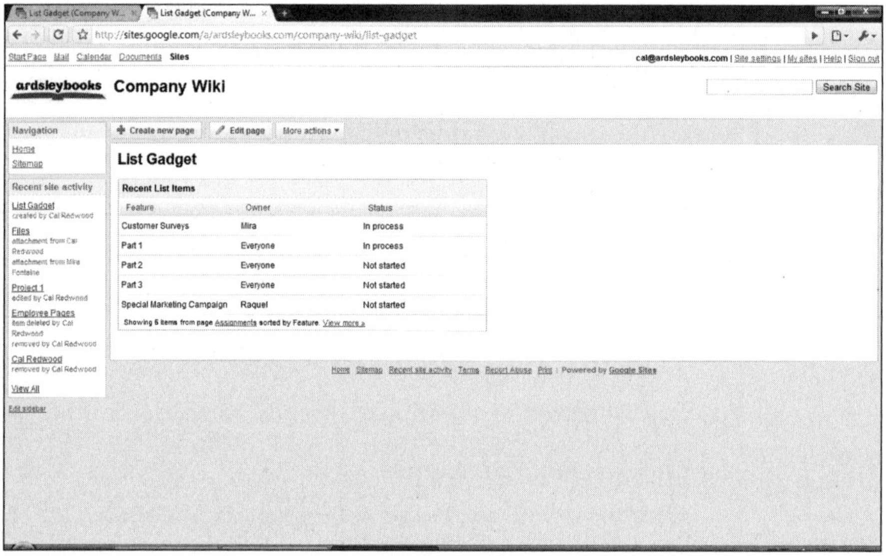

Figure 13-9:
How the
List gadget
can look
on another
page.

Creating a Common Start Page for Lost Souls

It's easy to get lost on corporate intranets. This is especially true for new employees. Create a portal, which we call a *start page,* to help them find their way around and get quickly up to speed. Start pages are readily available to all Google Apps users. A common corporate start page can direct novice users to all sorts of services, including high-value intranet Sites pages.

Analyzing a sample start page

Let's explain what's happening in the corporate start page shown in Figure 13-10. A start page has three columns. The first column can be defined by the company and can't be changed by the employee. The second and third columns can be filled with suggested gadgets, but individual employees can change them if they like. In our example, the first preset column has three necessary gadgets including:

- ✔ A gadget linking directly to intranet Sites pages of common interest. (More on that later.)
- ✔ A gadget linking to e-mail, which also gives access to contacts and chat apps.
- ✔ A gadget receiving a popular business and financial RSS news feed.

Figure 13-10:
A start page
in Google
Apps can
have a link
to gadgets
and intranet
Sites pages.

The company can define default gadgets for the second and third columns as
well. This helps new employees get the most from the start page right away.
Albeit, the gadgets in the second and third columns can be customized by
each employee to meet their needs over time.

New alternatives can be added by clicking the Google Add Stuff link. In brief,
the following gadgets have been used on this default start page:

- Link to Google Docs (word processing, spreadsheet, and presentation
  apps).
- General information news or RSS feeds.
- Link to corporate or team calendar.
- The local weather, (which can be customized to include the weather in
  each corporate office around the world).
- To Do list.
- Quote of the day.
- Fun site of the day.

Linking to Google Sites from a start page

The gadget linking the employee to the intranet Sites pages (refer to the
upper-left corner of Figure 13-10) was created by the Sites intranet administrator to give each employee one-click access to key intranet Sites pages.

To create a Sites navigation gadget, have the Google Apps administrator perform the following steps:

1. **Click the Manage This Site link.**

2. **Click Service Settings and then click Customize in the Start Page section.**

3. **Click the Content tab in the Start Page Editor.**

4. **Click the Add Stuff link.**

5. **Click the Custom Sections link, if necessary, and then click the Create Custom Content link.**

   The Update Custom Section dialog box appears. (See Figure 13-11.)

6. **Select the Static Text, Images, and Links radio button.**

7. **Enter the names of the links that are being targeted on the intranet's Sites pages in the box below the editing tools. Use the Link button to define the links.**

   It may be easier for experienced HTML users to create this gadget by clicking the Edit HTML link and entering the desired links in a text editor. (See Figure 13-12.) Click the Update button when you finish.

8. **Click the Update Section button after completing the data entry for your custom gadget.**

9. **Click the Ad It Now button under your newly created gadget.**

   If necessary, click the Custom Sections link again in the Add Stuff window.

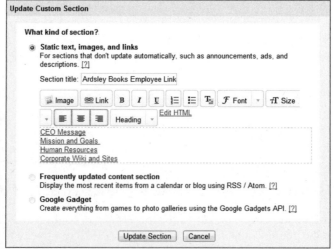

Figure 13-11:
Create a custom gadget to link to various Sites pages of corporate interest.

Figure 13-12:
Entering
the data in
HTML may
be easier for
some.

10. **Return to the Start Page content editor and position the gadget in the Locked section of the start page.**

View Your Sitemap and Link to Sub-Pages

The Web Page, File Cabinet, Dashboard, Announcements, and List Sites pages in this chapter can all fit into a broader site plan. This plan is automatically organized into a *sitemap*. A sitemap shows the relationship between pages on the site, as shown in Figure 13-13. Fortunately, Google Sites creates your sitemap for you automatically. Just click on Sitemap to see it. If a page is not in the correct position, you can just move it to where on the intranet that you want it.

To move a page around a site, follow these steps:

1. **Open the page you want to move.**

2. **Click More Actions.**

3. **Choose Move from the drop-down list.**

4. **Select the location from the Move Page window.**

5. **Click the Move button. (See Figure 13-14.)**

Figure 13-13:
View your
hierarchy in
a sitemap.

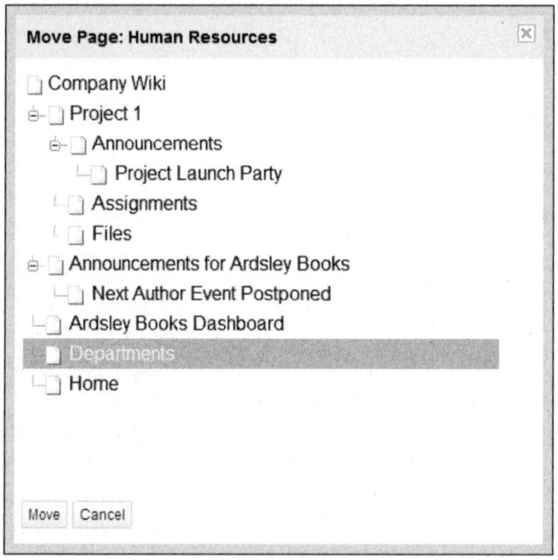

Figure 13-14:
Move Sites
pages
around an
intranet site.

Although employees can get to any page by clicking the sitemap, it may not always be convenient. Instead, some pages can be linked from the department or team page. To create links to sub-pages, follow these steps:

1. **Open a Sites page and click the Edit Page button.**

2. **In the Edit box, type in the words for the new link, select the words, and click the Link button.**

   The Create Link dialog box appears. (See Figure 13-15.)

3. **Pick the page from the list.**

   If the site is so large that you can't see the page by clicking the My Changes and the Recent Site Activity links, enter the page name in the search window and click Search Pages.

4. **Click OK.**

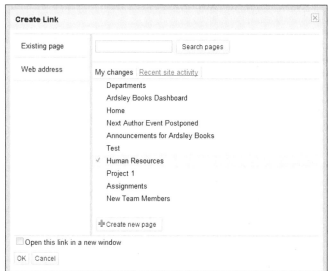

Create Link		☒
Existing page	[ ] Search pages	
Web address	My changes Recent site activity	
	Departments	
	Ardsley Books Dashboard	
	Home	
	Next Author Event Postponed	
	Announcements for Ardsley Books	
	Test	
	✓ Human Resources	
	Project 1	
	Assignments	
	New Team Members	
	✢ Create new page	

☐ Open this link in a new window

OK Cancel

Figure 13-15: Create links to other intranet Sites pages.

Setting Site Settings

Each intranet site needs a security plan. The Google Apps administrator needs to set up the security structure for the intranet site in accordance with company policy. Normally, in a business scheme, everything on the intranet is closed to the outside world. However, there may be a need to make some Sites pages public and open to other business partners. Administrators can control access in the Advanced Permissions settings. (For a more detailed example, read the discussion of site settings in Chapter 12.)

To set site settings for an intranet, follow these steps:

1. **Select Site Settings from the top of the Google Sites screen.**

2. **Click the Sharing tab.**

3. **Select the As Viewers radio button and enter the e-mail addresses of any supervisors and peers you want to invite to preview, view, and approve the site.**

4. **In the Advanced Permissions section, select View from the Anyone at _Domain Name_ May View/Edit This Site drop-down box.**

5. **Click the Invite These People button to send an e-mail message inviting colleagues and supervisors to view your Sites pages.**

More technical settings

When a Google Apps administrator enables Google Sites, they can change security settings in the Service Settings section under the General tab. Here, sharing options can be optimized. Normal users will not see this screen. (See Figure 13-16.) The first setting in the Advanced Permission settings allows anyone within a company to either view or edit a site. Allowing just anyone inside the company intranet wouldn't be prudent. However, flexibility needs to be given to teams and departments to edit their pages. Company leaders will need to come up with a policy involving who can make changes to certain pages and who can't.

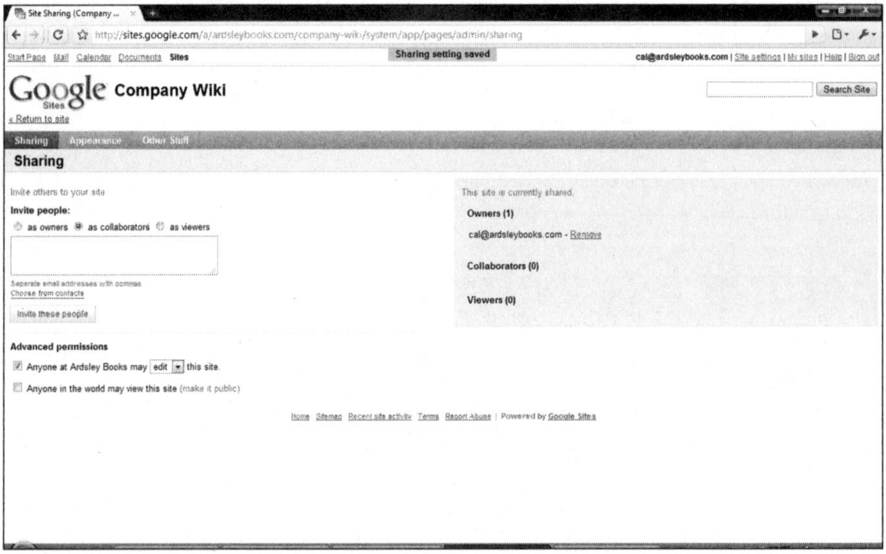

Figure 13-16: Administrative Settings need to match company policies.

Matching your site's appearance to your company brand

When you create your site, you want to customize the site to fit the corporate image and brand. You need to pinpoint your corporate color scheme and modify all the logos and branding messages. You can do this right out of the box or you can modify them later by clicking the Manage Settings link from the Admin login page. For some ideas, review the college scheme ideas in Chapter 12.

For example, you can adjust the color scheme and change the Sidebar and Header elements by performing the following steps:

1. **Log into your site and select the Site Settings from the top of the Sites screen.**

2. **Click Appearance and choose the Themes tab.**

3. **Pick a new theme.**

   Click Preview to see what your pages will look like with the new theme.

4. **Choose the Site Elements tab.**

   This screen lets you change Sidebar elements, add a logo or image to your header, and even change the layout of your pages.

5. **To change a logo on the top of your site, choose the Change Logo button in the Header section.**

6. **Select the Custom Logo radio button and then browse to the image of your logo. Click OK.**

7. **Add a gadget to the Sidebar by clicking the Add a Sidebar Item link.**

8. **Scroll down the list of gadgets in the Choose a New Page Element dialog box. When you find a gadget you like, click Add.**

9. **Edit the gadget's settings as needed.**

Part V

More Google Apps You Can't Do Without

The 5th Wave — By Rich Tennant

UBER-USER DWAYNE GRANTZ CHALKS UP BEFORE PUTTING GOOGLE SITES THROUGH ITS PACES.

In this part . . .

*R*emember that your site is only as good as the info you share on it. Rather than create everything from scratch, use some of the other Google Apps to do your work for you. Because you'll likely use Google Docs the most, we've got four chapters that help you begin sharing documents, spreadsheets, and presentations. Then you find tips for Google Calendar, Gmail, and Google Talk.

Chapter 14

Using Google Docs and the Docs Home

*G*oogle Docs is the name of Google's online productivity suite. The suite includes Google's word-processing, spreadsheet, andmultimedia-presentation apps. Powerful enough for most uses, the suite has one big advantage over popular desktop applications — you can use it for free. But we talk about many more advantages in this chapter, too.

Previewing Google Docs

Google Docs is a powerful online application suite that includes:

✔ **Documents (or docs):** An online word-processing software app, similar to Microsoft Word, Corel WordPerfect or StarOffice Writer. The Documents app is often called "Docs" for short. (Find out more in Chapter 15.)

✔ **Spreadsheets:** An online spreadsheet app, similar to Microsoft Excel, Quattro Pro, or Lotus 1-2-3. (Find out more in Chapter 16.)

✔ **Presentations:** A presentations app similar to Microsoft PowerPoint. (Find out more in Chapter 17.)

The Docs Home is the starting point for your docs. This is document central, a powerful management tool that keeps your files organized and at the ready. You can manage all your docs, spreadsheets, and presentations from a single Docs Home, as shown in Figure 14-1.

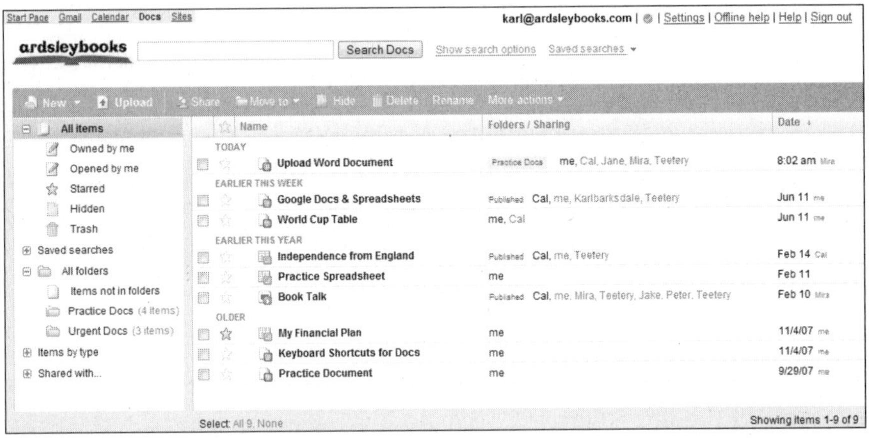

Figure 14-1:
Docs are
managed
from the
Docs Home.

Advantages of Docs

Using online apps has many advantages. First, you're never bound to your PC. Google gives access to your docs anytime you need them from any computer in the world through any Internet connection. Second, Google Docs is *platform independent,* which means you can work on a PC or Mac with equal ease. Third, there's no software to install because Google Docs works inside a Web browser. Google Chrome, Internet Explorer, Firefox, and Safari provide the support necessary to use Google Docs.

Here's a list of six additional advantages that we detail in the pages that follow:

✔ Docs are easy to launch, easy to use, and secure your files in Google's massive data centers.

✔ Innovative search and folder naming schemes in the Docs Home ensures that you'll never misplace a doc, spreadsheet, or presentation again.

✔ A single-document approach (that is, *singledocumindedness*) empowers superb sharing, team collaboration, and revision control.

✔ Online publishing to Sites and blogs makes docs a key part of your communications strategy.

✔ Seamless conversion and support for other file types throws docs into the mainstream.

✔ The ability to work offline presents you with powerful new ways to work. See Chapter 10 for more information about using Docs offline.

You can launch Docs Home in several ways:

✔ **Enter a Web address:** You can start your Google Docs directly from the Web by clicking the address bar and entering **docs** followed by your partnered domain name.

- *Google Account users:* Enter `http://docs.google.com` and log into your Google account.

- *Team, Standard, Preferred, and Education Edition Users:* Enter `http://docs.google.com/a/`*yourdomain.com* or `http://docs.`*yourdomain.com*. For example, `http://docs.google.com/a/ardsleybooks.com` or `http://docs.ardsleybooks.com`. Log into your Docs account.

✔ **Use a Start Page gadget:** You can launch Docs conveniently from a gadget on your Start Page. To add a gadget, follow these steps:

1. Click the Add Stuff link near the top left of the Start Page.

2. Click the Add It Now button below the Google Docs option, as shown in Figure 14-2. (While you're here, you may as well add a gadget for your Gmail and Calendar apps!)

3. To return to your Start page, click the Back to Homepage link on the top left of the Add Stuff screen.

After you add your gadget, click the Google Docs link at the top of the gadget. This takes you directly to the Docs Home screen. (See Figure 14-3.) The gadget gives you one-click access to a half dozen of your most-recently opened files in a short list. There's also a link to create new docs, which is activated in Figure 14-3. Look closely and you notice there's even a search box. (We talk about document search later in this chapter.) If the document you need does not appear in the list, click the All Docs link and go directly to the Docs Home.

✔ **Click the Documents link from other open Google Apps.** Regardless of which Google App you're using, if you peer at the upper-left corner, you can see a series of links. Click the Documents link to go straight to your Google Docs Home.

Figure 14-2:
Find the
Docs
gadget in
the Google
Apps
directory.

Figure 14-3:
Go to a file
or the Docs
Home with a
single click
on a gadget.

Your Docs account is protected by your login and password, just as they are on any other network. You can use the same login and password for all of your online Google Apps: Gmail, Sites, Calendar, Picasa, you name it. Click the Sign In link and input your secret password, as shown in Figure 14-4.

Figure 14-4:
Sign into
your Google
Apps, Sites,
and Docs.

If your computer crashes and your hard drive dies, your files are still safe online. As long as you have access to the Internet, you can access your files. You can even access your Google Docs from your smartphone browser as long as your phone account supports a higher-speed connection to the Internet.

If you can't use your computer, you can use any other computer that happens to be lying around and log into your private Google account online. Even if you login to your account from someone else's computer, you won't sacrifice your security if you sign out properly at the end of your session. However, you should beware of one thing when using a computer other than your own; never click the Remember Me on This Computer check box (refer to Figure 14-4). Save this convenience for your personal computer.

Google is constantly making improvements to Docs. The software is constantly being updated, but for the most part, you hardly notice. Because Google Docs is Web based, the most recent version of the software loads instantly. There's nothing for you to install. In fact, Docs is in a constant state of improvement; therefore, some of the screenshots you see in this chapter may be slightly different from the versions you see on your screen.

Using the Google Docs Home

The Docs Home is the hub where you can access all your files with ease. You can create new files; display, hide, sort, or delete files; import and export files; organize your files by folders or labels; and so on. The following sections describe how to do these tasks and more.

Creating, saving, naming, and renaming files

To create a new file, click the New button in your Docs Home andchoose either a word-processing document (doc), a spreadsheet, or a presentation from the drop-down list that appears. Wait a few seconds for the app to launch and you can start writing something deep and profound.

Google Docs wants you to save your files immediately so that nothing is lost. The saving and naming process is slightly different for each of the three apps, as follows:

- ✔ **For a word-processing document (or doc):** Whatever you type in the first line of your text becomes your default file name. Within a few seconds, the file is named or saved automatically. Choose File⇨Save or click the Save button to save manually. (For more details, review Chapter 15.)

- ✔ **For a spreadsheet:** As soon as you enter data into your first cell, a box appears begging you to save the file immediately. Click the Start Autosaving link, enter a file name, click OK, and then go about your work. (For more details, review Chapter 16.)

- ✔ **For a presentation:** As soon as you enter a title into the title field of the first slide, the name is adopted as the file name. (For more details, review Chapter 17.) Save manually by clicking the Save button.

For more information on various saving options, review the individual chapters on each app.

After you save a file, the file name appears in the header at the top of the screen. If you're not happy with the file name and need to make a change, you can return to your Docs Home, place a check mark next to the file name (as shown in Figure 14-5), and then click Rename on the Docs Home bar. (Other file renaming options are explained in Chapters 15, 16, and 17 for each individual app.)

Click Rename

Figure 14-5:
Rename in
the Docs
Home.

Searching for files

If you've ever lost a file before, you'll quickly appreciate Google's famous search abilities found in Docs. The Docs Home deploys Google's sophisticated search tools to quickly find any file on any topic in your personal Docs library, no matter how many files or folders you've generated or how fuzzy your memory of where you placed the file.

Google makes searching your entire Docs Home ridiculously easy. Search for any file by entering part or all of the file name or by typing keywords based on the content of the file. Simply enter a few keywords in the textbox. Google Search tries to help you as much as it can. For example, in Figure 14-6, just entering a few digits in the Search box displays a list of files starting with those letters.

Figure 14-6:
Enter
keywords or
phrases into
the Search
Docs
textbox.

Simple searches, like the one explained above, help you find most files. However, if you discover that a file has somehow been interred in a subterranean folder or hidden tomb, click the Show Search Options link next to the Search Docs button shown in Figure 14-6. This reveals the advanced search dialog box.

Fill in any and all information that you can remember about the file, as shown in Figure 14-7. For example, can you remember part of the file name? Can you remember the last time you made changes in the document? What type of file was it? Do you remember who originally owned the file? What about the names of other collaborators? Enter the e-mail addresses of these folks in the appropriate box.

After you make your most educated guesses, click the Search Docs button and see what appears. Chances are you'll find your document.

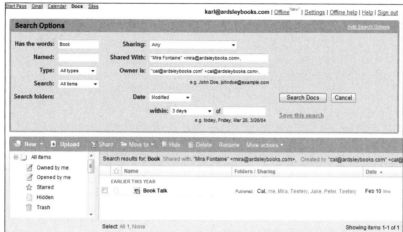

Figure 14-7:
Try an advanced search if you're desperate.

Viewing, sorting, hiding, and trashing files

Files appear in the Docs Home list with the most recent files appearing at the top. If you want to sort the files in another way, click the appropriate option (Name, Folders/Sharing, Date) on the column heading above the file list (refer to Figure 14-1):

- ✔ **Name:** Click Name to sort the docs alphabetically (A–Z). Click Name again to reverse the order (Z–A).

- ✔ **Folders /Sharing:** You can sort alphabetically by folder names by clicking this column heading.

- ✔ **Date:** Click Date to sort from the oldest to the newest file. Click Date again to sort from the newest to the oldest file.

Uncovering the Docs Home organization pane

The organization pane on the left side of your Docs Home holds a long list of valuable display options. Perhaps the list is too long for your liking. To roll up the options, click the minus sign (–) to the left of each major heading: All Items, Saved Searches, All Folders, Items by Type, and Shared With (shown on the left in Figure 14-8). To roll them out again, click the plus sign (+) to the left of each heading to reveal the options (shown on the right in Figure 14-8).

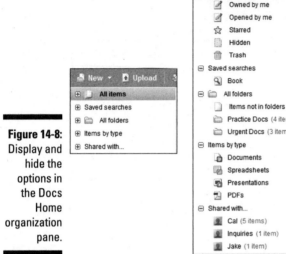

Figure 14-8:
Display and hide the options in the Docs Home organization pane.

Star struck

One of the most popular ways to sort files is with a star. (Yes, it's a gold star.) To mark a file, click the star icon to the left of the file name, as shown in Figure 14-9.

You can star files for any reason. They may be important, you may need to give them urgent attention, or you may want to jog your memory that you need to work on a particular file. To display starred files, click the starred item in the docs organization pane. (See Figure 14-9.)

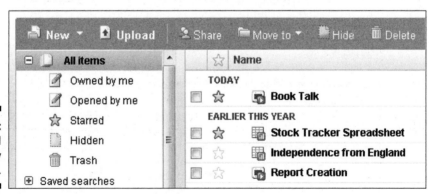

Figure 14-9:
Star and display key files.

Hide stuff

Docs allows users to hide files from view. You may want to hide old files so they don't clutter your Docs Home.

To hide a file, place a check mark to the left of each file name and click the Hide button. Choose the Hidden item in the docs organization pane to display all the hidden files again.

Show only your stuff

If you actively share files with others, and they start sharing with you, file names proliferate throughout your Docs Home list. If you want to see only your stuff and exclude files created by others, click the aptly named Owned by Me item in the organization pane.

Click All Items in the Docs Home organization pane if you've displayed just your own files, starred files, or hidden files and now need to see your complete list.

Empty the trash, or not

If you need to delete a file, select the check box to the file's left and then click the Delete button. Clicking this button sends the file to the Trash; but the file isn't lost forever, it still exists. Click the trashcan icon in the docs organization pane, select the check box to the left of the file name, and delete it permanently by clicking Empty Trash. (You can also trash multiple files by selecting a group of them before clicking the Empty Trash button.)

If you're trying to delete a shared document that you've created, you're faced with a warning box that asks whether you want to trash the document for everyone. (Not a good idea.) If you still want to trash this document, click Assign a New Owner. Follow the steps and hand the document off to someone else. Then you can trash it in your Docs Home without problems.

If you change your mind and want to restore a file, go to the Trash, select the check box to the left of the file that you want to recover, and click the Undelete button.

You really don't need to delete any items from the Trash — or, for that matter, to trash any files in the first place — because Google gives you plenty of space in which to save your files. However, if you find it helps to clear out a few files now and again, use the Hide feature. This places files out of sight but not out of mind and never trashed.

Uploading and converting your existing files

You can upload to Google Docs word-processing documents (docs), presentations, and spreadsheets that you've created with many different programs. Uploaded files show in your Docs Home where you can keep them safe, sound, and ready for editing.

Follow these steps to upload a file to the Docs Home:

1. **Sign into the Docs Home.**

   Refer to the earlier "Easy to launch, easy to use, and very secure" section.

2. **Click the Upload button.**

   The Upload a File screen appears.

   You can upload the following file types (see the left side of the Upload a File screen):

   • *Text and word-processing files:* `.doc`, `.docx`, `.rtf`, `.txt`, `.sxw`, `.htm`, `.html`

   • *Presentations:* `.ppt`, `.pptx`, `.pps`

   • *Spreadsheets:* `.csv`, `.xls`, `.xlsx`, `.ods`

   • *PDF:* `.pdf` files can now be uploaded and managed in the Docs Home

3. **Click the Browse button; in the Choose File dialog box that appears, select the file that you want to upload to Google Docs and then click the Open button.**

   Alternatively, you can enter the file path to the file (if you know it) in the Browse Your Computer to Select a File to Upload textbox. You can also enter a Web address in the Or Enter the URL of a File on the Web textbox.

4. **(Optional) Enter a new name for the file in the What Do You Want to Call It textbox.**

   If you don't name the file, it retains its current file name.

5. **Click the Upload File button.**

   The file that you upload converts, saves, and opens as a Google file.

6. **If you make any changes to your file, click the Save & Close button; otherwise, click the Docs Home link to return to the Docs Home.**

An alternative way to upload a file to your Docs Home is to e-mail it directly to your Google Docs. When you click the Upload button, your assigned e-mail address appears at the bottom of the open window. You may need to scroll down a bit to see it. Copy this e-mail address and use it to e-mail documents directly to your Docs Home.

Instead of using the upload feature, you can also copy and paste from an existing file to a new Google file. If you want to remove all the formatting from an existing file first, copy and paste the text into Notepad or another text editor, and then copy and paste the text into a Google Doc, spreadsheet, or presentation.

Singledocumindedness for Sharing, Collaboration, and Revision Tracking

Okay, we made up the word *singledocumindedness,* but we couldn't think of a real word that seemed to fit. The point is, you don't need to keep multiple versions of any file ever again — not for yourself, not for your collaborators, not for anyone else in the world with whom you want to share a Doc, spreadsheet, or presentation. Google's new single-file approach enhances collaboration, sharing, and revision control.

Revision History tracks changes by you and your collaborators

You need only one copy of each file, regardless of the number of collaborators because Docs catalogs and maintains changes within a single master file. The Revision History feature allows you to peek back in time to see what changes have been made at any point during the creation of that file — from start to finish. You can always revert to a time before certain changes were made to your file. You can also determine who among your contributors made specific changes because the names of the collaborators are recorded along with their changes. (See Figure 14-10.)

Launch the Revision History feature in a doc by choosing File➪Revision History. In the Spreadsheet and Presentation apps, click the Revision tab.

To go back to a prior revision, choose the hours, days, weeks, or months ago that you made a change. If you don't instantly land on the revision you need, click forward or backward until you find the version you're looking for.

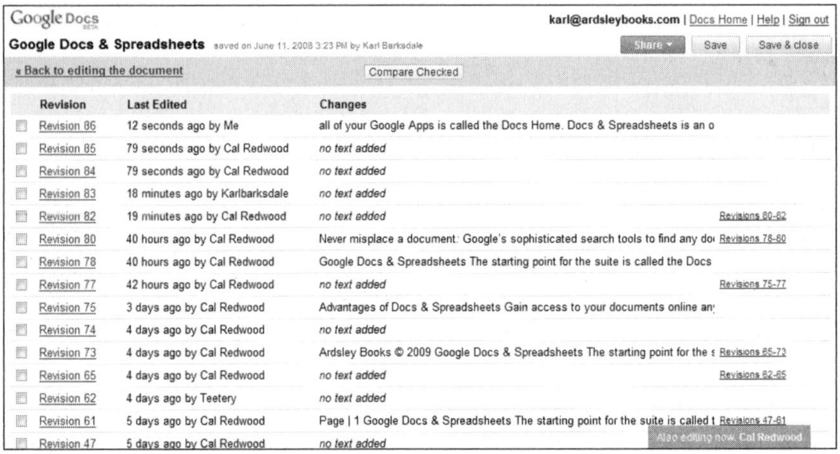

Figure 14-10:
Sharing
and version
tracking is
easy with a
single-file
approach.

Organizing your files by folders or labels

Folders provide a way to organize your files by categories. In thesingle-file approach, you don't physically move or copy a file into a new folder; rather, you attach a folder name or a label to the file itself.

You can label a file so that it appears in any number of folders without generating digital replicas. Instead, you can attach any number of folder names to a file. Each file appears with its folder label in the Docs Home. This way, the file appears like magic in any folder you pick.

This approach works like the files on an iPod or other digital media player. For example, the love song "Michelle," by the Beatles, has multiple labels, such as Beatles, 1960s, Love Songs, M, and My Playlist. Looking for any one of these different labels, you can quickly find and play the singular copy of the file you have on your iPod. (Singledocumindedness in action yet again.)

To create new folders and assign files to that folder, follow these steps:

1. **Choose New⇨Folder.**

2. **Name the folder and choose a color or other options if you want.**

3. **Select the check box to the left of any files that you want to label with your selected folder name.**

4. **Click the Move To drop-down list. In the menu that appears, choose the folder name. Then click the Move To Folder button. (Click Cancel if you change your mind.)**

5. To display only the files assigned to a folder, click the folder name in the organization pane.

6. You may need to expand the All Folders item to see all of your folders. Click All Items in the organization pane and look under the Folders/Sharing column heading to see the folder(s) assigned to a file.

With Google protecting your files, do you need to make backups anymore? Yes, of course. But backing up isn't the headache it used to be. When you save your Google files online in a Google data center, Google says that it creates backups just about as fast as you make changes to your file. However, it's still just a bunch of computers out there, so back up critical files on your hard drive at a minimum; you know, all the legal stuff or that report you can't do without, but don't lose any sleep over the rest of your files.

A quick way to create a backup copy of a file is to e-mail a copy of the converted file to yourself. More details are also provided for each individual application in Chapters 15, 16, and 17.

Sharing and collaborating

One of the pioneering features in Google Docs is the ability for people from anywhere in the world to work simultaneously on a file with very little fuss and bother. The only things required for collaborating is an e-mail address, an online connection, and the courage to know that everyone can be writing at the same time on the same file without the fear of losing anything or messing each other up.

Google Docs keeps track of the changes and shares the updated document every few seconds with everyone on the collaborating team — a good example of singledocumindedness in action. Your team is *not* working on separate files that you reconcile later, but on the exact same file at exactly the same time. So, don't worry if someone messes things up by adding something silly or deleting your perfect prose. You can always revert back to a previous version that Google saved several minutes, hours, days, or even months ago. (See the earlier "Revision Histories tracks changes by you and your collaborators" section.)

At the bottom of the screen, you see exactly who is actively collaborating at any one time. Changes made by others are tracked not just by name but by color as well, so you can quickly see who has been adding, what they added, and where they added the information. (See Figure 14-11.)

Figure 14-11:
You can
easily see
who is col-
laborating
with you.

View your active collaborators

About inviting collaborators

You will need to make a few decisions about your collaborators. First, you need to decide whether you want to invite people as collaborators — allowing them to make changes — or as viewers only. Viewers can only read the file itself but are not given the permission to make changes.

In Figure 14-12, we invited several collaborators. Inviting collaborators and viewers is as easy as entering in their e-mail addresses. This feature makes use of your contact list, so it's as easy to invite collaborators as it is to enter e-mail addresses into Gmail.

For the secretive among us, you may want to use some advanced permission features. For example, you can give or deny your collaborators the right to invite other collaborators or viewers. You can also allow or disallow the right for collaborators to broadcast the page to mailing lists. Generally, these first two options are both selected; however, if you want to keep everything private, simply remove the check mark from these two options. There's also a setting to only allow someone from within a company or organization to view a file online by requiring a login.

To start sharing with others, follow these steps:

1. **Click the Share button's drop-down arrow and choose Share with Others if necessary.**

2. **Choose one of the following options shown in Figure 14-12:**

   • Select the As Collaborators radio button to allow the people that you invite to make changes to the document.

   • Select the As Viewers radio button to restrict the people you invite so that they can read the doc but make no changes.

Figure 14-12:
Click the
Share
button and
start col-
laborating.

3. **Enter the e-mail addresses of the people with whom you want to share the document in the textbox in the Invite People section.**

4. **(Optional) Select any or all of the check boxes in the Advanced Permissions section.**

   • *Collaborators May Invite Others:* Give or deny your collaborators the right to invite other collaborators or viewers by selecting (to grant) or deselecting (to deny) the check box.

   • *Invitations May Be Used by Anyone:* Allow or disallow collaborators the right to broadcast the page to mailing lists by selecting (to allow) or deselecting (to disallow) this check box.

   • *Anyone from <your domain> May <selection> This Document at:* Allow only users from within a company or organization to view the document by requiring them to log in.

5. **Click the Invite Collaborators button.**

   An invitation screen appears. (See Figure 14-13.) Treat this screen exactly like an e-mail message. Your collaborators and viewers automatically appear in the To box. You also have the option to paste a copy of the document to the e-mail message after it has been sent.

6. **Click the Subject textbox and type a subject, and then click the Message textbox and type a message to your collaborators.**

7. **(Optional) If you want to paste a copy of the document into the e-mail message, do so by selecting the Paste the Document Itself into the Email Message check box.**

8. **Click the Send button to send the invitation.**

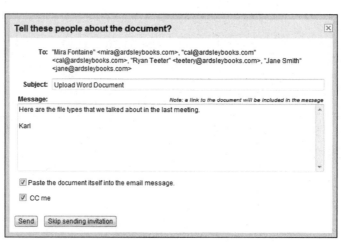

Multiple collaborators can enter data or change formatting on the same doc at the same time. Shared docs are saved every time you blink (or so it seems) to protect the changes collaborators are making. And don't worry if someone makes a mistake. All the changes are tracked to maintain quality control. You can always revert back to a previous reversion. To find out how, read more about Revision History in Chapter 15.

Editing your collaborators list

Click the Share button and choose Share With Others from the list that appears. You see a list of your collaborators and viewers in the right-hand pane of the Sharing window. (See Figure 14-14.) If you need to send additional e-mail messages or updates of your document to a team, you can do that from the Email Collaborators link. If you need to add or delete collaborators, you can do that from this panel also.

The documents you share are listed in the Docs Home page for all of your collaborators to open, see, and edit. Collaborators can then organize the documents in any way that suits them — by assigning labels or folders — just like they would for documents of their own creation. (See Chapter 11.) The list of all those collaborating on the document will also be available to them.

By getting the sharing and collaboration feature to work efficiently, Google Docs makes working in teams nearly hassle free. For app-specific details about sharing Docs, spreadsheets, and presentations, review the "Sharing and Collaboration" sections for each individual app in Chapters 15, 16, and 17.

Figure 14-14:
Update and communi-
cate with your collab-
orators from the Share screen.

Converting and exporting docs into other file formats

Google Docs may not give you all the options and settings that a high-end word-processing, desktop-publishing, spreadsheet, or presentation program can. You may need to download and convert a lot of files (a lot of work on your part) into a file format that a high-end application can handle.

You can make these conversions directly from the Docs Home. Start by clicking the box next to the file you want to convert and then click the More Actions drop-down list. From the menu that appears, choose the file format that you need.

A dialog box appears, asking whether you want to open or save the file. Click the Save button. In the Save As dialog box that appears, browse to where you want to save the file and click the Save button.

Changing your language settings

Many users will need to change the language settings for Google Docs. Change the language settings by clicking the Settings link in the header and making the necessary changes in the Settings window. For example, select a different language from the Language drop-down list. Click the Save button at the bottom of the screen to save your changes.

To change settings back to their original defaults, click the Settings link again. If you set the language to something other than English, you need to know the words for the options in that language. For example, *Settings* in Spanish is *Configuración*.

Google Docs is available to you anytime from any online computer anywhere in the world. And, if you're away from an Internet hotspot and need to work offline on a doc, Google Gears allows you to do just that by accessing the Offline link in the header. See Chapter 10 to find out more.

A dialog box appears that guides you through the process. There is a warning that you assume the responsibility for your own security after the files leave the friendly confines of Google's data centers. That being said, it's nice to have your documents safe on your PC for those times no Internet connection is handy. To make this happen, click the Enable Offline Access button and continue following the directions on the screen. If you need more help, click the Offline Help link.

You will be asked if you want to add a Shortcut to your desktop. That's probably a good idea so you can launch your documents without having to hunt around too hard for them.

Using Help and signing out of Google Docs

If you don't understand something (we can't describe every obscure detail in this book), click the Help link in the header to find out more.

When you're done for the day, click the Sign Out link and take the rest of the day off.

You're probably wondering, "Do I really need to sign out?" Not really, but it's still a good idea. Just closing your browser may close your file before the automatic backup has kicked in. You may lose some last-second changes to a file if you don't click the Save & Close button or sign out first. Even if you do exit quickly without signing out, though, you shouldn't lose much work because Google makes frequent automatic saves for you.

Chapter 15

Docs: Google's Word-Processing App

*T*he word-processing part of Google Docs, Documents, is often called *Docs* for short. Docs is exceedingly easy to use; experienced Word, WordPerfect, or OpenOffice.org Writer users will pick it up faster than it takes to do a Google search. And if someone has never used a word processor before, Docs is doubtless the most user-friendly word-processing app a beginner can have at her fingertips.

This chapter starts with the basics and moves with dispatch to the advanced features in Google Docs. We flag the beginner stuff with the word *simply* in the headings. We signal the power-user stuff with the words *power* or *powerful* to make it clear when you're stepping into the deep end of the word-processing pond.

Starting Simply with Google Docs

When you're ready to start writing, log into your Docs Home. There are two basic ways of logging in:

> ✔ **Google Account users:** Visit `http://docs.google.com` and log into your Docs account.
>
> ✔ **Team, Standard, Preferred, and Education Edition Users:** Visit `http://docs.google.com/a/yourdomain.com` and log into your Docs account.

Create a new document from the Google Docs Home by clicking the New button and picking Document. (Review Chapter 14 to find out about the Docs Home.)

Exploring the basic tools

Quickly — on to the basics of how to use Google Docs. The few-frills Google Docs workspace appears inside your Web browser and is divided into four main parts: header, menu bar, toolbar, and input area, as shown in Figure 15-1.

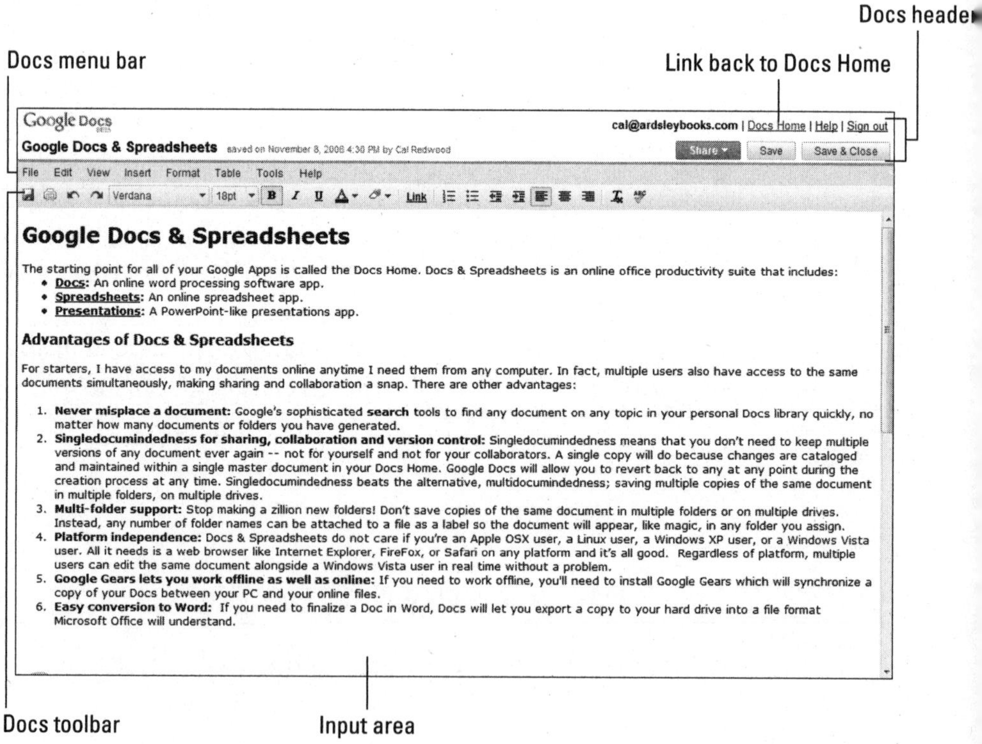

Docs header

Docs menu bar

Link back to Docs Home

Figure 15-1:
The Google
Docs work-
space.

Docs toolbar   Input area

Clearly, you enter your text into the Docs input area. Then you can apply formatting, such as italics, bold, bulleted or numbered lists, styles, and so on. After, saving and printing become necessary. All of these operations can be done by using the various elements of the workspace, as follows:

✔ **Docs Header:** The upper section of the Docs interface. It includes the name of your document, your login name, and a link back to your Docs Home. This header allows for sharing and superfast saving and closing. (Refer to Figure 15-1.)

✔ **Docs Menu Bar:** A traditional-looking menu bar. The menu bar's pull-down menus give you complete control of your word processor. When you need more depth and a few extra options, click one of the familiar menu names: File, Edit, View, Insert, Format, Table, Tools, and Help.

✔ **Docs Toolbar Buttons:** A traditional-looking toolbar. This toolbar gives you one-click access to the most frequently used word-processing commands and formatting features (highlighted in Table 15-1). Click the appropriate button on the Docs Toolbar when you're ready to save, print, or format.

✔ **Input Area:** A traditional blank space where you can enter your text, pictures, tables, and more.

✔ **Keyboard Shortcuts:** Fully supported keyboard commands. Addicted to your keyboard? Use the keyboard shortcuts. For example, press Ctrl+B for Bold and Ctrl+S for Save. Commonly used shortcuts appear in Table 15-1.

Watching the toolbar buttons

Take a look at the one-click toolbar buttons in Figure 15-2. Active buttons are highlighted. They appear with a thin blue line around them and are slightly darker. Just by looking at the toolbar in Figure 15-2, you can tell that a Verdana 10 point (10pt) font is being used. The text has been bolded and aligned to the left margin. Most people miss these details, which saddens the developers that spent ages adding these subtle complexities to the toolbar.

Figure 15-2:
The toolbar gives one-click access to word-processing actions.

The buttons on the toolbar are so traditional that you can probably guess what each one does just by looking at it. But if you need a quick review, Table 15-1 describes each option and gives you the corresponding keyboard shortcuts for each of the Docs Toolbar buttons.

Table 15-1	Editing Commands and Shortcuts		
Button	*Command*	*Keyboard Shortcut*	*What It Does*
💾	Save	Ctrl+S	Saves your document.
🖨	Print	Ctrl+P	Prints your document.
↰	Undo (Last Edit)	Ctrl+Z	Undoes the last change you made.
↱	Redo (Last Edit)	Ctrl+Y	Undoes the last undo.
Verdana ▼	Font		Changes the style of the font.
10pt ▼	Font Size		Increases or decreases the size of the font.
B	Bold	Ctrl+B	Applies bold formatting.
I	Italic	Ctrl+I	Applies italic formatting.
U	Underline	Ctrl+U	Underlines words.
A ▼	Text Color		Changes the color of your text.
✏ ▼	Text Background (Highlight) Color		Adds a color behind words just like a highlighter pen.

Button	Command	Keyboard Shortcut	What It Does
Link	Add or remove link	Ctrl+K	Creates a hyperlink in your document so that readers can click to view a related Web page or other resource.
	Numbered List		Creates a numbered list.
	Bullet List	Ctrl+Shift+L	Creates a bulleted list.
	Decrease Indent		Moves paragraphs or lists half an inch to the left.
	Increase Indent		Moves paragraphs or lists half an inch to the right.
	Left (Align Left)	Ctrl+L	Aligns text to the left margin of a document.
	Center (Align Center)	Ctrl+E	Aligns text to the center of a document.
	Right (Align Right)	Ctrl+R	Aligns text to the right margin of the document.
	Remove Formatting	Ctrl+Space	Strips any formatting, such as bold, underline, or font changes, from selected text.
	Check Spelling		Scans the document and highlights words that are possibly spelled incorrectly.

Google Docs is in a constant state of improvement. In Google-speak, it's a *perpetual beta*. You may notice slight differences between your version of Docs and a few of the screen images in this chapter. Don't panic. The basics don't change much and the improvements are usually well worth it.

Simply Saving, Renaming, and Printing Google Docs

The first two buttons on the toolbar are the Save and Print buttons, and we start there. As with most things in Google Docs, there are many ways to accomplish important tasks. For instance, you can save a document five different ways:

✔ Click the Save button on the Docs Toolbar.

✔ Click the Save button in the header.

✔ Click the Save and Close button on the header to both save and close the document in one convenient click.

✔ Choose the File menu and choose Save.

✔ Press Ctrl+S.

We know this is overkill, but it does make it user friendly! In another example of how easy Docs is to use, you can print several ways:

✔ Click the Print button on the Docs Toolbar.

✔ Choose the File menu and choose Print.

✔ Press Ctrl+P.

Google Docs is almost too eager to save your documents. Well-intentioned enough, Docs doesn't want you to lose anything, so it starts saving almost immediately. Docs doesn't save just a backup copy in case of a computer crash; it saves the actual document from any possible harm or eventuality. Documents are named automatically, based on whatever you enter in the first line of your text. Because of this, if you don't enter any text for a while, you may get stuck with "Untitled" as the document's name. This will never do. To rename a document:

1. **Choose File⇨Rename or click the file's name in the header.**

2. **If your browser gives you a prompt to allow scripts, follow the on-screen instructions and do so. Then choose File⇨Rename or click the temporary name in the Docs Header again.**

3. **Enter the new name in the dialog box.**

Simply Editing and Viewing Documents

Editing is the process of cleaning up a document. It includes proofreading, spell checking, and fixing mistakes. We start simply and put the power details off until later in the chapter.

Checking your spelling

Unless you were a finalist for the Scripps National Spelling Bee in your youth, face it, everyone is guilty of misspelling. To check spelling in your document, follow these steps:

1. **Click the Check Spelling button on the Docs Toolbar or choose Tools⇨Check Spelling from the menu bar.**

   Words that are potentially misspelled are highlighted.

2. **When you spot a misspelling, click the highlighted word and a list of alternatives appears.**

3. **Click the correct alternative from the list and the word will be corrected.**

Docs highlights all the words it thinks are misspelled. This includes words, names, or acronyms that are spelled correctly but aren't included in the Docs dictionary, such as a capitalized Vista or the acronyms XP and OS X. You can ignore these correctly spelled terms, but a better option may be to add unique words, names, and acronyms to the Docs dictionary by selecting each anomaly and clicking the Add to Dictionary button.

When you finish spell checking your document, just click on the Spell Check button again and spell checking discontinues.

Basic editing commands on the Edit menu

The Undo and Redo options are found on the Edit menu, along with some other important features like Cut, Copy, Paste, and Select All. The Select All command selects all the text in your Google Doc. Also, note that the keyboard shortcuts are listed under the Edit menu. If you forget a keystroke command, you can quickly look it up by choosing the Edit menu.

Undoing mistakes

When you make a mistake, you can restore your document to how it was before your mistake by clicking the Undo button on the Docs Toolbar or by choosing Edit⇨Undo. However, if you undo something unintentionally or if the Undo command creates more problems than it solves, you can reverse the operation by clicking the Redo button on the Docs Toolbar or by choosing Edit⇨Redo. (And don't forget the keystroke commands: Ctrl+Z for Undo and Ctrl+Y for Redo.)

Cutting, copying, and pasting

When you need to move or copy text, images, and tables, use the cut, copy, and paste functions. Make your selection and then choose Edit⇨Cut or Edit⇨Copy, followed by Edit⇨Paste to complete the action. You can also press the equivalent keyboard shortcut keys:

- ✔ Ctrl+X = Cut
- ✔ Ctrl+C = Copy
- ✔ Ctrl+V = Paste

With some operating systems, when you cut, copy, and paste, you need to permit access to the system *Clipboard,* which is a holding place in memory for cut and copied text and graphics, until you're ready to paste them. If a dialog box asking about access to the Clipboard appears, just click the button that allows access and paste away.

Finding and replacing words or phrases

At times, you may need to search and replace a specific word or phrase as you edit a doc. Do so by choosing Edit⇨Find and Replace or by pressing Ctrl+H. Enter the word or phrase you're looking for and its replacement. Press Enter or click the Replace/Find button to complete the action.

Viewing options

When you're working with Google Docs, you're working online — on an actual Web page. The default Normal (plain) view (available on the View menu) is used so you can see how the document will likely look online. Plus, the Normal view has the advantage of using all the available space on your screen to view your text while you edit it.

If you want to view how the pages will look when printed, click View⇨Fixed-Width Page View. Compare how this document view looks in Figure 15-3 with the Web page view shown in Figure 15-1. (***Note:*** We refer back to Figure 15-3 to help explain some other important features in the upcoming Simply Formatting Documents section, so keep your thumb on this page!)

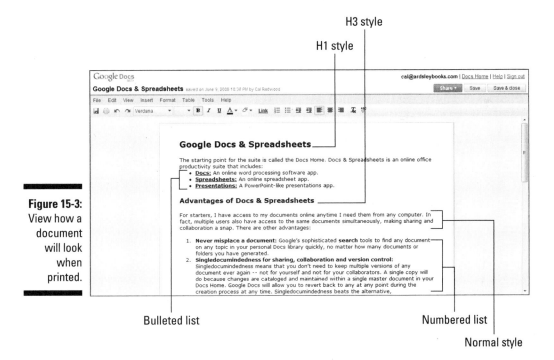

Figure 15-3:
View how a document will look when printed.

Simply Formatting Documents

Most of the buttons on the Docs Toolbar are used for formatting. Formatting makes documents more interesting visually and easier to read. You can apply formatting options two ways:

✔ Select any text you want to format and then click the desired toolbar button.

✔ Click a formatting button first to turn on the feature, enter your text, and then click the formatting button again to turn the option off.

Changing font size, style, text color, and highlight color

A new Google Doc starts out with a Verdana 10-point font as its default. Verdana is an easy-to-read font. The point size refers to how big or small a font appears on screen and in print. The higher the number, the larger the font. A 10-point (10pt) font is large enough for most readers.

If you don't like the default font, you can change it by clicking the Font drop-down list (click the little triangle) and choosing a different font — such as Georgia, Garamond, Tahoma, or Narrow. Similarly, to change the font's point size, click the Size drop-down list and choose a different point size, such as 12 or 14.

The same procedure applies for changing the color of your text or placing a highlight color around your words. To change the color of text, click the Text Color button and select a color from the color palette that appears. To add a highlight color around your words, click the Highlight Color button and choose the color you want from the palette. Be sure the highlight color contrasts with the color of your text so that it can be easily read.

Bold, italic, and underline

B *I* <u>U</u> There's nothing more basic than applying bold, italic, and underline formatting to your words. These three formats predate word processing. They are as follows:

- **Bold:** Has its origins in the very old typewriter ribbon days when important text was literally typed over two or three times to make the words appear **bolder** so they would **stand out** from the rest of the text.

- *Italic: Subtly slants a font onto its side to offset it from other text. Electric typewriters with removable typing balls made this formatting style very popular in the 1970s.*

- **Underline:** Another holdover from the typewriter days when important text, like side-headings and titles, were underlined by carefully spacing back over words and pressing the Shift+_ keys repeatedly until the words were underlined. Today, underlining words is discouraged because they appear to be hypertext links that people instinctively click to no avail.

Removing pesky formats

 Disappointed with some of your formatting choices? Remove them easily by choosing your text and clicking the Remove Formatting button. This removes bold, italic, and underline formats from text in one click. This is such an important command that you can implement it by either clicking the button from the Docs Toolbar or choosing Format⇨Clear Formatting.

Numbered and bulleted lists

 Numbered and bulleted list buttons work as advertised. A sample of both a numbered and a bulleted list appear in Figure 15-3. To begin a list, click either the Numbered or Bulleted list button, enter the first list item, and then press Enter. Each time you press the Enter key, a new bullet or the next number appears. You can also create the entire list first, select the list, and tap the appropriate button after the fact. Bulleted lists, like this one:

- ✔ Display information in no particular order or sequence.

- ✔ Provide an easy way to organize similar types of information.

- ✔ Make complicated lists of information easier to read and take in.

Numbered lists imply a sequence of events. You can start this kind of list by following these steps:

1. **Press the Numbered List button.**

2. **Enter your text.**

3. **Press Enter at the end of each paragraph.**

 To turn bulleting or numbering off, click the appropriate button again. You may need to press Enter after your list ends and also tap the Decrease Indent button a few times to realign your text to the left margin as explained below.

Understanding default margins

To understand alignment, you must first know about margins. The margin defines the unprinted space around the edge of the document. The defaults in Google Docs are set at 1 inch of unprinted space around the top, sides, and bottom of a Google Doc. (We explain how to change the margins in the "Power Converting, Saving, and Adjusting Doc Options" section of this chapter.)

Decrease or increase indentions

The Increase Indent button moves a selected paragraph ½ inch to the right of the current margin. This is often used for long quotes in reports. The Decrease Indent button does just the opposite by moving an entire paragraph ½ inch to the left. This button is often needed to correct paragraphs that may slip out of alignment. For example, if the bullets or numbers are removed from a list, oftentimes the paragraphs remain indented improperly. Simply select the misaligned paragraphs and then click the Decrease Indent button.

Aligning to the left, right, and center of a doc

The Docs Toolbar offers three one-click alignment possibilities:

- ✔ **Left Align:** By default, documents are aligned to the left margin. This means that the text appears straight on the left margin yet is ragged on the right-hand side, as a quick glance at the toolbar icons reveals. To move centered, right-aligned, or justified text back to the default left margin, reselect the text and click the Left Align button.

- ✔ **Center Align:** To center a title or an image, select your text or image and click the Center Align button. You can also click the Center Align button first and then enter your text.

- ✔ **Right Align:** Align your text straight on the right margin by clicking the Right Align button. This option is rarely used because it's often hard to read text that is ragged on the left side of a document.

The Format menu provides alternative ways of selecting the left-, right- and center-align commands. You can also align text straight on both margins by using the Justify command; choose Format➪Align➪Justified.

Power Formatting with Styles, Superscripts, Subscripts, and More

The most powerful commands on the Format menu are the styles found in its upper section. Styles allow you to apply consistent and professional-looking formats throughout the doc. To see examples of the H1, H3, and Normal styles, refer to Figure 15-3.

The following styles can be applied by selecting the target text and picking one of these options from the Format menu:

✔ **Normal Paragraph Text:** Apply the Normal paragraph style to remove other styles, such as H3 and H1.

✔ **Minor Heading (H3):** Apply the H3 heading, the smallest heading style. (Refer to Figure 15-3.)

✔ **Sub-Heading (H2):** Apply a larger heading style for sub-headings and section titles.

✔ **Heading (H1):** Apply the largest heading style for the most dominant titles. (Refer to Figure 15-3.)

In the lower section of the Format menu are some important, yet specialized, formatting commands:

✔ **Strikeout:** Draw a line through (or strike out) words.

✔ **Superscript:** Raise text above the line for footnote references and exponents such as $2^3=8$.

✔ **Subscript:** Apply this style to lower the text below the line such as in H_2O.

✔ **Block Quote:** Indent text on both the left and right margins by ½ inch like those used in long quotes in a report.

More Powerful Keyboard Shortcuts

Table 15-1 shows some of the most common editing and formatting shortcuts. If you're hooked on keyboard shortcuts, Google Docs doesn't disappoint. Table 15-2 gives you a few more powerful strokes.

Table 15-2   A Few More Powerful Keyboard Shortcuts for Docs

Keyboard Shortcut	Command	Use It To
Ctrl+A	Select All	Select all the text in a doc.
Ctrl+F	Find	Find words or phrases in a doc.
Ctrl+H	Replace	Find and replace words or phrases in a doc.

(continued)

Table 15-2 (continued)

Keyboard Shortcut	Command	Use It To
Ctrl+J	Justify	Align text (justify) on both the right and left margins.
Ctrl+M	Insert Comment	Add a comment to the text.
Ctrl+Shift+Space	Non-breaking Space	Insert a non-breaking space.
Tab		Insert a tab or move to the next cell in a table.
Shift+Tab		Move to the preceding cell in a table.
Ctrl+1	Heading (H1)	Insert the largest heading style used for titles.
Ctrl+2	Sub-heading (H2)	Insert a larger heading style. Apply to sub-headings and section titles.
Ctrl+3	Minor Heading (H3)	Insert the smallest heading style. Apply to side-headings.

Powerfully Inserting Elements

Many characterize Google Docs as an anemic product when compared to traditional desktop word processors, but as you see in this section, the gap has narrowed. Docs has enough bells and whistles to be a highly proficient tool for your word-processing needs. Most users will never need more word-processing features than those found in Docs. To see what we mean, click the Insert menu and look at the important options. This menu allows you to insert a host of elements: pictures, links, comments, tables, bookmarks, separators, and special characters.

Before we jump into this detailed list, it may be good to preview what some of these features actually do. Take a look at Figure 15-4. (We refer back to this figure a half-dozen times in the next few pages.)

Links

Header

Special character

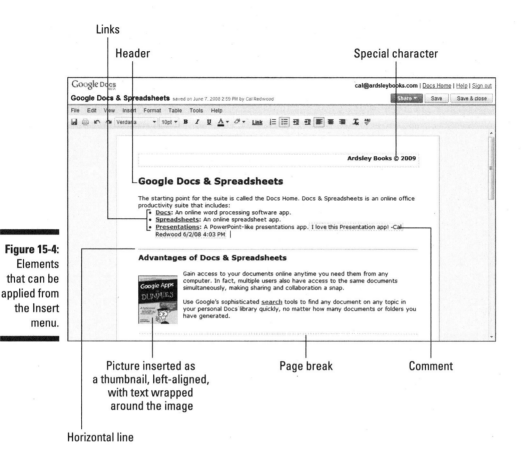

Figure 15-4:
Elements
that can be
applied from
the Insert
menu.

Picture inserted as
a thumbnail, left-aligned,
with text wrapped
around the image

Page break

Comment

Horizontal line

Inserting pictures

Adding images couldn't be easier. Just remember that you must upload
images before you can insert and view them, as explained in these steps:

1. **Position your insertion point where you want the image to appear in the document.**

2. **Choose the Insert menu and then select the Picture option.**

3. **Select either the From This Computer radio button or the From the Web (URL) radio button, as shown in Figure 15-5. Depending on which radio button you select, the steps change a bit.**

   a. If you select the From This Computer radio button, click the Browse button. In the File Upload dialog box that appears, browse to your file, select it, and click the Open button, which places the path to the file in the Browse box. In the Insert Image dialog box, click the Insert Image button.

   b. If you select the From the Web (URL) radio button, type or paste the URL into the Enter Image Web Address textbox. A preview of the image appears in the dialog box. Click the Insert Image button.

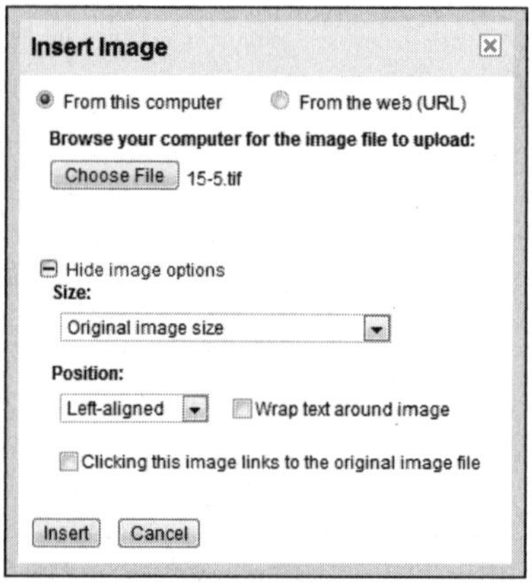

Figure 15-5:
Insert an
image by
uploading it
first.

4. **To make changes in the appearance of your image, select the More Image Options button. (The name of this button changes to Hide Image Options after you click it.)**

   This reveals the optional features of the Insert Image dialog box shown in Figure 15-5 including:

   • *Size:* Change the size of your image in the size drop-down menu.

   • *Position:* Align your image to the left, right, or center of the text adjacent to the image.

   • *Wrap Text around Image:* Allows the text to appear around or alongside the text, as shown in Figure 15-4. If you don't check this option, the text is pushed underneath the image.

5. **Click the Insert button to insert the image into your document or choose Cancel to abandon the process.**

Making links

One of the great strengths of Google Docs is its ability to link to other pages, such as to your Google Sites. (See the link samples in Figure 15-4.) To create a link (or *hyperlink*) in your Doc, select the text you want to turn into a link and click the Link button on the Docs Toolbar (or choose Insert⇨Link). The Change Link window appears, as shown in Figure 15-6.

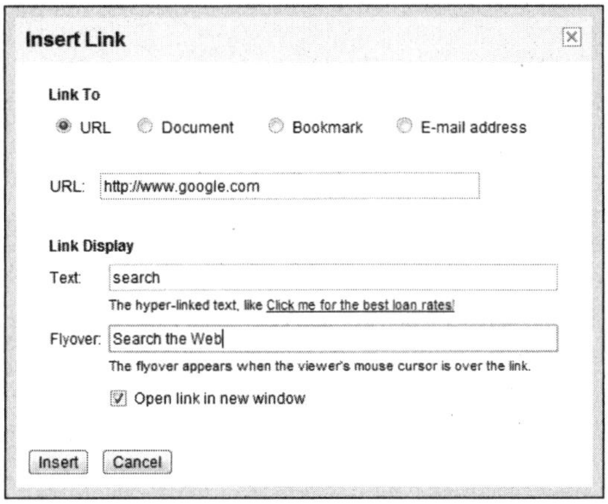

Figure 15-6:
Link to a
Web page,
e-mail
application,
bookmark,
or another
document.

Select the radio button that matches the resource to which you are linking. As you select a radio button, the textbox changes slightly so you can specify the correct type of linked data. Choose from the following options:

✔ **URL:** Links to a Web page. Enter the URL in the textbox that appears. In Figure 15-6, the Web address (URL) www.google.com has been entered. (Google Docs automatically adds the http:// for you.)

✔ **Document:** Links to another document that you've created in Docs. Choose the document from the drop-down list that appears.

✔ **Bookmark:** Links to a bookmark that you've made inside your document. (See the next section, "Sticking a bookmark in your document," for the steps required to create a bookmark.) Choose the bookmark from the drop-down list that appears.

✔ **E-Mail Address:** Creates a link that opens an e-mail application and pastes the target address in the To box.

✔ **Text:** Changes the text of your hyperlink in the Link Display section. This also changes the link text in your document.

> ✔ **Flyover:** Displays a word or phrase that you want to pop up when some-
> one hovers their mouse over the link.
>
> ✔ **Open Link in New Window:** Forces the link to open your destination page
> in a new browser window, which means your original document doesn't
> vanish from a reader's computer screen every time she clicks on your link.

If you need to change any of the settings above, right-click on the link and
choose Change Link from the contextual menu that appears. Remove the link
entirely by right-clicking and choosing Remove Link.

Sticking a bookmark in your document

Bookmarks allow you to create links from one part of a document to another.
You may find bookmarks useful in long documents so you can avoid paging
down endlessly to find the passage that you're looking for.

To create a bookmark, follow these steps:

1. **Click the location where you want the bookmark to go.**

   This is the *destination point* — where someone lands after clicking your
   bookmark.

2. **Click the Insert menu and choose the Bookmark command.**

   The Insert Bookmark dialog box appears.

3. **Click the New Bookmark textbox, type a name for your bookmark,
   and then click the Insert button.**

After you create your bookmark, you're only half done. The second half of the
process requires you to create a link to your bookmark that readers can click to
go to the bookmark's location. For example, you can create a table of contents at
the top of a document that links to bookmarks to each section within the document. We describe how to create a link in the earlier "Making links" section.

If you need to edit or manage your bookmarks, choose Tools➪Manage
Bookmarks. You can delete or add bookmarks as needed from the dialog box
that appears.

Inserting comments

Comments are a valuable tool for tracking edits or for discussing issues about
a document with team members. They appear in multicolored boxes following the selected text. Several people can comment, and each has a different
colored comment box. Comments are dated and contain the name of the
person commenting. To add a comment, follow these steps:

1. **Place your insertion point where you want a comment to appear and then choose Insert➪Comment.**

   A box with your name, the date, and the time appears.

2. **Start typing in the comment box. When you finish typing the comment, click elsewhere in the document.**

   Your comment appears as shaded text; refer to Figure 15-4.

3. **To edit your comment or to change its color, click your comment.**

   A menu appears giving you the following options: Close This Menu, Delete Comment, and Insert Comment Text into Document. You can also select a color to change the color box around your comment from this menu.

4. **Ignore the menu and start typing to enter your thoughts into the comment.**

Inserting special characters

Now and again, you need a character that isn't found on your keyboard. These *special characters* can include anything from a copyright symbol (©), a registered trademark (®), or an Albanian schwa (ë). (See the copyright symbol at the top of Figure 15-4.)

To insert a special character, click the spot where you want to place the character and choose Insert➪Special Characters. The Insert Special Character dialog box appears, shown in Figure 15-7, giving you hundreds of choices. If you don't see the character you need, select the Asian Characters, Wingdings, or Advanced options.

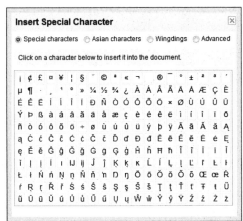

Figure 15-7:
Pick your
favorite
symbols and
umlauts.

The Advanced option enables you to pick the Unicode value for nearly any character in the world in every major language. Unicode values assign numbers for every character in every major, and some minor, alphabets throughout the world. Many special characters also have their own Unicode values. There are literally tens of thousands of options.

If you need help with Unicode values, click Advanced and then click the Help question mark in the Advanced dialog box. From there, you can search for your language (even Bengali or Syriac) and find the numerical code for any special character that you may need.

Inserting horizontal lines and page breaks

Horizontal lines can be placed in a document as a separator between sections or paragraphs. It's like drawing a line with a pencil horizontally across a piece of paper. (Refer to Figure 15-4.) Create a horizontal line by simply choosing Insert⇨Horizontal Line.

A *page break* is used to separate pages for printing. When you insert a page break, you force the printer to start printing on a new page. Create a page break by choosing Insert⇨Page Break (For Printing). The page break appears as a faded double broken line, as shown at the bottom of Figure 15-4. Use this option to control the amount of text on a single page, pushing the remaining text to the next page. Don't worry; the broken double line doesn't appear in your printed document. To delete a page break, just select and delete the faded double line from the document.

Inserting headers and footers

Headers create a space at the top of a document for information. (Refer to Figure 15-4.) *Footers* leave space for information at the bottom of a document. In traditional school reports, headers and footers often contain such things as page numbers, author names, the name of the instructor, or the course name. In business reports, the name of the company often appears in either the footer or the header on every page, as shown in the example of Ardsley Books in Figure 15-4. After they're entered, both headers and footers appear on every page when the document is printed. To create one, open the Insert menu and choose Header or Footer.

Building Powerful Tables

Tables create little boxes in a grid pattern inside a document. These make up rows and columns that can be used to organize information in a valuable and visual way. (See Figure 15-8.) For example, you can organize data about events, people, objects, and places.

Figure 15-8: The Table menu and a table with six columns and three rows.

Follow these steps to create a table:

1. **Click Insert Table from the Table menu.**

   The Insert Table dialog box opens, as shown in Figure 15-9.

2. **Define the rows and columns for your table.**

   Tables are calculated by the number of its columns and rows. Figure 15-9 shows a 3-x-6 table being created — three rows, six columns, and 18 cells.

3. **To create a basic table, click Insert.**

   To discover how to design a more interesting table by changing its settings, review the "Optional table settings" section that follows.

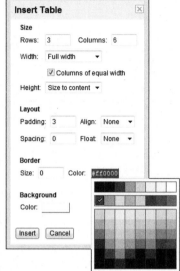

Figure 15-9:
Calculate
the size
and look of
your table in
advance.

Optional table settings

The Insert Table dialog box shown in Figure 15-9 offers a host of features to customize your tables. All the features are optional, and are as follows:

✔ **Width and Height settings:** *Width* refers to the size of cells horizontally. *Height* refers to the size of cells vertically. The four possibilities are

- *Full Width/Height:* Fits the table, using all the available width between the margins of a page. Height is set on the default setting.

- *Size to Content:* Adjusts the width and height of a table's cells to the size of the words or graphics within the cells.

- *Pixels:* Defines the width and height of the cell to a specific number of pixels.

- *Percent:* Adjusts cell width and height based on a percentage of the available space found between the margins.

✔ **Columns of Equal Width:** Selecting this check box creates a table with columns of equal size.

✔ **Layout settings:** Changes the spacing between cells or around words, and then aligns or floats the text to the left, right, or center of the cell.

- *Padding:* Refers to the width of the space between the words and the outside line of the cells; measured in pixels.

- *Spacing:* Refers to the space between cells; measured in pixels.

- *Align:* Defines the horizontal position of the words within a cell (Left, Center, Right, or None).

- *Float:* Floats the text within a cell. The Left, Right, or None options are available from the Float drop-down list.

✔ **Border Size and Color:** To add a border, enter a number in the Size text-box — the larger the number, the wider the border. To change the color of the border, click the Color box and select a color from the palette that appears; refer to Figure 15-9.

✔ **Background Color:** To change the background color in the cells, click the Color box below Background and select a color from the palette that appears.

Editing tables

After you create your table, you can format the text from the toolbar and then insert images, links, or anything else from the Insert menu. For example, in Figure 15-8, columns 2–6 have been centered with color and graphics inserted. Titles are bold and the font has been changed. And that's just a few of the possibilities.

The Table menu (refer to Figure 15-8) gives you further control over your table. From the menu, you can modify, move, insert, or delete an entire table, or one or more columns, rows, and cells. The options available are as follows:

✔ **Modify Tables, Rows, Columns or Cells:** After your table is created, the Modify options allow you to apply all of the features explained in the "Optional table settings" section. Start by selecting the cells, rows, or columns you want to alter and choose the appropriate Table menu options shown in Figure 15-8. Choose the Table menu followed by Modify Table Properties, Modify Row Properties, Modify Column Properties, or Modify Cell Properties.

✔ **Moving Rows:** Select the row you want to move and then choose Table⇨Move Row Up or Table⇨Move Row Down. (Refer to Figure 15-8.)

✔ **Inserting Rows and Columns:** Place your insertion point in the column or row where you want the new row or column to appear. Choose Table menu followed by Insert Row Up, Insert Row Down, Insert Column on the Left, or Insert Column on the Right, as shown in Figure 15-8.

✔ **Deleting Rows and Columns:** Select the column or row you want to delete. Choose the Table menu followed by Delete Table, Delete Row, or Delete the Column. (Refer to Figure 15-8.)

Moving existing columns is more problematic than moving rows. Start by inserting a new column as explained above. Select and copy the column you want to move and paste the information into the new column. Only then should you delete the original column of information.

Power Converting, Saving, and Adjusting Doc Options

The Edit and File menus make it possible for you to change print and document settings, review revision histories, and convert your documents into other document types. Google has dramatically improved the compatibility of Google Apps, making it work well with mainline desktop software products.

The next few sections discuss these actions in greater detail.

Downloading and converting Google Docs into other types of files

Converting a document to another file type is as easy as picking the document or file type you need from the File menu's Download option and following the on-screen instructions. The instructions are self-explanatory. Choose a folder on your hard drive in which to place the converted file, and there you have it.

Google Docs converts files into key application file types:

- **PDF:** Adobe's PDF format, which is used by Acrobat reader, a very popular online file type that restricts a reader's ability to make changes.

- **Word:** Microsoft's Word format; the most universal file type available for word-processing documents.

- **HTML (Zipped):** A compressed Web-compatible file type.

- **RTF:** A rich text file type that can be read by most word-processing applications.

- **Text:** A simple text file type that removes all additional formatting and images, leaving just the words.

- **OpenOffice:** Open source products; very comparable to Microsoft Office.

The process of converting and downloading does not harm your Google Doc. Your original Google copy of your document is unchanged. It's still safe and ready for you to use from your Docs Home.

Saving new copies, reviewing revisions, and deleting

Beyond the basics, several File menu commands require brief mention:

- ✔ **Save as a New Copy:** This feature allows you to retain a copy of a document under its original name while creating a duplicate copy that you can change without messing up the original.

- ✔ **Revision History:** This option allows you to look at all of the updates made in the history of a Google Doc. Revisions are recorded instead of creating multiple copies of revised documents (also known as *single-documindedness*). If you need to look at changes that you made, do so by choosing approximately how many hours, days, weeks, or months you made a change. Click forward or backward to get to the exact revision you need. Review Chapter 14 to find more about the Revision History feature, shared by all of the apps in Google Docs.

- ✔ **Delete:** Although this command pretends to delete the current document, it doesn't work that way in practice. Nothing is ever deleted in Google Apps until you go to the Docs Home and delete the document by empting the digital Trash. (For more, see Chapter 14.)

Print Settings: Orientation, margins, paper size, and page numbering

When you choose Print Settings from the File menu, the Print Settings dialog box appears and gives several key settings from which to choose. (See Figure 15-10.) After you make your selections, as explained later in this section, click OK to make the settings part of your document. Click Print to print your document with your new settings or choose Cancel to forget the whole thing ever happened.

Figure 15-10: The Print Settings dialog box.

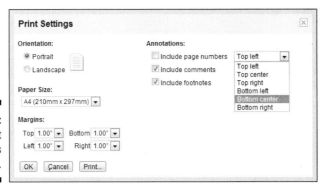

✔ **Orientation:** Orientation changes the direction of the printed pages, typically from 8.5 x 11 for *Portrait* to 11 x 8.5 for *Landscape*. Portrait documents are longer than they are wide. Landscape documents are wider than they are long. While most documents are printed in portrait orientation, landscape is handy for Web-style documents, wide tables, and spreadsheets.

By default, documents will print with a 1-inch margin in portrait mode. However, if you want the file to print like a Web page in landscape mode, choose File➪Print as a Web Page. If you want to see how this document will look before you print, which is always a good idea, choose File➪View as a Web Page.

✔ **Margins:** Margins are set at 1 inch along the top, bottom, left, and right margins of a document. You may need to increase those defaults. For example, if you're going to bind a document along its left margin, you may want to increase the width of the left margin to 1.5 inches. If you're having trouble fitting your document on a single page, you may want to reduce the margins, say to .75 inch, to allow more words on a printed page.

✔ **Paper Size:** The default paper size for most documents is 8.5 x 11, as shown in the Print Settings dialog box in Figure 15-10. If you need to print on legal-size paper or another paper size, change the Paper Size settings by clicking the drop-down menu and choosing the correct paper size.

✔ **Annotations/Include Page Numbers:** Adding page numbers to a document is as easy as choosing the down arrow in the Include Page Numbers box and choosing the location of the page number from the list that appears. In Figure 15-10, the page number has been placed in the bottom center of a printed page.

Changing document settings

If you want to change the default fonts and spacing settings permanently for every document you create, choose Edit➪Document Styles. This opens the Document Styles dialog box, as shown in Figure 15-11.

Try these steps to change your document styles:

1. **Change your font style from the default (Verdana) to another font, like Narrow or Tahoma.**

   The preview shows you what the font will look like.

2. **Change the line spacing from Single Spaced to Double Spaced or another line spacing option.**

3. **Don't select the Right-to-Left orientation unless you are writing in Hebrew or Arabic.**

Document styles ☒

● Use my font and line spacing settings, below   ○ Turn Off All Styles

Font:

| Narrow ▼ | 12pt ▼ | Text without formatting will be in this font and size. |

Line-spacing:

Double spaced ▼

Right-to-left:

☐ Make the page text align right-to-left
(for Hebrew and Arabic documents)

Document Background Color:

#ffffff

Preview:

The quick brown fox jumps over the lazy dog. The quick brown

☑ Make these the default styles for all new documents

OK   Cancel

Figure 15-11: Change the document's settings.

4. **Choose the Make These the Default Styles for All New Documents box to apply your new style settings to all new documents. (If you change your mind, you can come back and redo the settings or choose Turn Off All Styles.)**

5. **Choose Document Background Color if you want a color other than white for your on-screen Docs word processor.**

The Tools and Help menus

The Tools menu can be used to start and stop your spell checking, count the words in your document, review your revision history (as explained in Chapter 14), and edit your bookmarks. The Tools menu also provides multilingual support for spell checking. The spell checker inside Docs and Spreadsheets defaults to Auto, picking the language currently in use by the browser. If you're using your browser in English, the English vocabulary spell checker will be auto-selected. However, if you need to switch the spell checker to another language, such as Spanish, Arabic, French, or Dansk, do so by clicking Tools⇨Language and choosing the target language.

If you need answers to your questions, which should be a lot fewer after reading this chapter, click the Help menu. As you'd expect from Google, all of its Help files are found online. Access the Google Docs Help Center, participate in an online forum with other Google Docs users, or watch YouTube videos of tips and tricks by choosing Help⇨Watch a Video Introduction. You can also click a link that takes you to all of the available keyboarding shortcuts — a typist's delight.

Publishing to Sites and Other Places

The Publish as a Web Page feature allows you to post online versions of your documents, upload copies to one of your Sites, or post copies to a company or personal blog. Click the Share tab's down arrow and choose Publish as a Web Page to explore the options. Immediately, you see two choices: Publish Document and Post to Blog. We talk about both choices in separate sections.

Publish a document online

Publishing is as easy as clicking the Publish Document button. As soon as you do, you're taken to the Publish This Document screen, shown in Figure 15-12, which displays the Web address where your document can be viewed. You can select and copy the link, and share it with anyone you want via your e-mail or instant messaging clients. You can also post the link on any of your Google Sites or Web pages. Clicking the link takes you straight to your published page for a quick preview.

Figure 15-12:
Set the publishing settings.

You need to know about four additional publishing options:

- ✔ **Re-Published Document:** If you make changes to your document, press the Re-Publish Document button to upload the latest copy to the publishing site.

- ✔ **Automatically Re-Publish When Changes Are Made:** If you get tired of updating the published document every time you make a change, click this option and the latest copy is re-published for you every time you alter something.

✔ **Viewers Must Sign In with Their Account to View the Published Document:** To limit viewership to just those within your immediate intranet or domain, place a check mark in this box.

✔ **Stop Publishing:** If you need to stop publishing a document for any reason, say the information is outdated or you're being sued for copyright infringement, click the Stop Publishing button. It's the modern day equivalent of the call to "Stop the Press."

Publishing to a blog

To publish a document to a specific blog location, follow these steps:

1. **Choose Share⇨Publish as a Web Page⇨Post to Blog.**

   The Blog Site Settings dialog box appears, as shown in Figure 15-13.

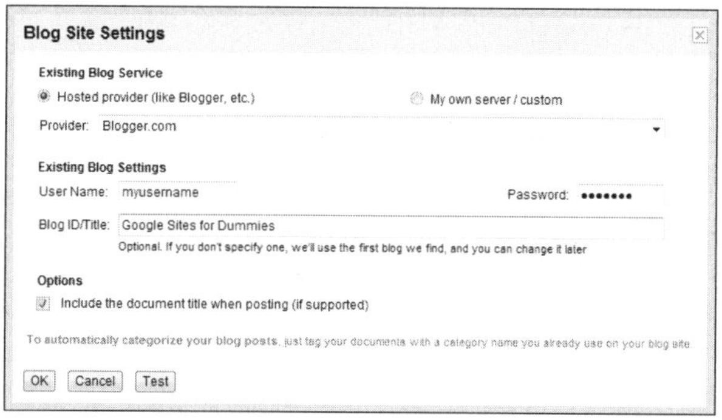

Figure 15-13: Enter the settings for your blog.

Blog Site Settings

Existing Blog Service
● Hosted provider (like Blogger, etc.)   ○ My own server / custom
Provider: Blogger.com

Existing Blog Settings
User Name: myusername   Password: •••••••
Blog ID/Title: Google Sites for Dummies
   Optional. If you don't specify one, we'll use the first blog we find, and you can change it later

Options
☑ Include the document title when posting (if supported)

To automatically categorize your blog posts, just tag your documents with a category name you already use on your blog site.

OK   Cancel   Test

2. **Select the Hosted Provider radio button if your blog is on a major blogging service, and then choose the name of the service from the Provider drop-down list. If you host your own blog, select the My Own Server/Custom radio button.**

   If you select the My Own Server/Custom radio button, you can enter all the data necessary to upload directly to your personal, corporate, or organization Web site or the blog associated with it. Be sure to complete each field in the detailed sign-in options, as shown in Figure 15-14. If you don't know the information, ask your system administrator for advice.

3. **Enter your username and password in the User Name and Password textbox to sync with the site.**

4. **(Optional) Enter the name of your blog in the Blog ID/Title textbox.**

5. **Click OK when you're ready to post the document to your blog.**

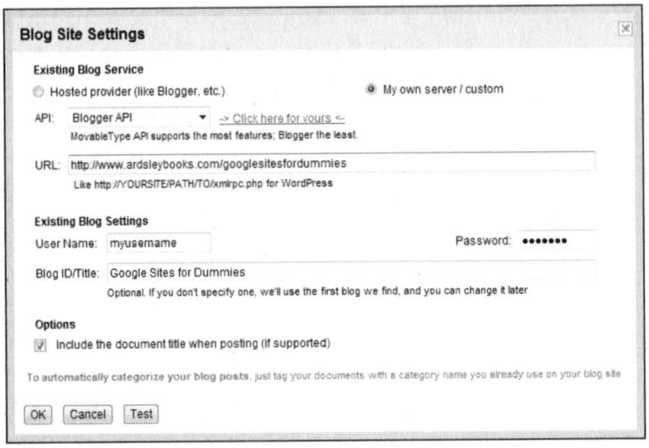

Blog Site Settings

Existing Blog Service

○ Hosted provider (like Blogger, etc.)   ● My own server / custom

API: Blogger API   ▾   -> Click here for yours <-
MovableType API supports the most features; Blogger the least.

URL: http://www.ardsleybooks.com/googlesitesfordummies
Like http://YOURSITE/PATH/TO/xmlrpc.php for WordPress

Existing Blog Settings

User Name: myusername   Password: •••••••

Blog ID/Title: Google Sites for Dummies
Optional. If you don't specify one, we'll use the first blog we find, and you can change it later

Options

☑ Include the document title when posting (if supported)

To automatically categorize your blog posts, just tag your documents with a category name you already use on your blog site

[OK] [Cancel] [Test]

Figure 15-14:
Enter your custom Web server or blog address.

The Post to Blog feature works extremely well with Blogger, Google's free blogging software (check out `www.blogger.com`). You can also publish directly to a start page or Sites gadget, which you may find extremely valuable for team or company announcements. Of course, you need to know the various passwords and login names for whatever online site you're publishing to.

If you need to peek under the hood and edit the actual HTML code that displays your published online document, you can do so by choosing Edit⇨Edit HTML. The same applies to those publishing CSS, or Cascading Style Sheets. This feature is available for Google Docs, Spreadsheets, and Presentations. For more information, review this topic in Chapter 14.

Sharing, Collaborating, and Working Offline

If you haven't tried sharing and collaborating, you're in for a treat. This section gives you the bare-bones essentials for sharing Google word-processing documents. This is a shared feature between all Google Docs and Spreadsheet apps, so if you need more details, refer to Chapter 14.)

Sharing gives recipients access to the document in their Docs Home. When they have a copy, they can open it and make changes simultaneously with you and other recipients. All changes are monitored so you can return to earlier revisions if someone makes a mistake.

A quick way to share a document is to just e-mail it! To do so, click the Share tab's down arrow and choose Email as Attachment. An e-mail screen appears that you can use to pen a note to your recipients.

Another way to share is with the Share with Others feature. After selecting this option, add the e-mail addresses for all participants. A notification is generated so they will know they have access and can begin working on the document.

To start sharing with others, follow these steps:

1. **Click the Share tab's down arrow and then choose Share with Others.**

2. **Choose one of the following options:**

   - Select the As Collaborators radio button to allow the people that you invite to make changes to the document.

   - Select the As Viewers radio button to restrict the people you invite so that they can read the document but not make changes.

3. **In the Invite People section textbox, enter the e-mail addresses of the people with whom you want to share the document.**

4. **(Optional) Select any or all of the check boxes in the Advanced Permissions section.**

   - *Collaborators May Invite Others:* Give or deny your collaborators the right to invite other collaborators or viewers by selecting (to grant) or deselecting (to deny) the check box.

   - *Invitations May Be Used by Anyone:* Allow or disallow collaborators the right to broadcast the page to mailing lists by selecting (to allow) or deselecting (to disallow) this check box.

   - *Anyone from <your domain> May <selection> This Document at:* Allow only users within a company or organization to view the document by requiring them to log in.

5. **Click the Invite Collaborators button.**

   An invitation screen appears. Treat this screen exactly like an e-mail message. Your collaborators and viewers automatically appear in the To box.

6. **Click the Subject textbox and type a subject. Then click the Message textbox and type a message to your collaborators.**

7. **(Optional) If you want to paste a copy of the document into the e-mail message, do so by selecting the Paste the Document Itself into the Email Message check box.**

8. **Click the Send button to send the invitation.**

Multiple collaborators can enter data or change formatting on the same document at the same time. Shared documents are saved every time you blink (or so it seems) to protect the changes collaborators are making. And don't worry if someone makes a mistake. All the changes are tracked to maintain quality control. You can always revert to a previous version. To find out how, read more about revision histories in Chapter 14.

Your Google Docs are available to you anytime from any online computer anywhere in the world. And, if you're away from an Internet hotspot and you need to work offline on a document, Google Gears allows you to do just that by accessing a link in the Header section. For more, see Chapter 14.

Chapter 16

Calculating with Google Spreadsheets

*S*preadsheets perform calculations and organize data, especially numeric data. Sounds like a snoozer, but the more people know about spreadsheets, the more they wake up to their value. And regardless of whether someone's number-crunching needs are lightweight or heavy duty, Google Spreadsheets makes an impression and gets the job done. Google Spreadsheets can help you:

✔ Juggle a bundle of numbers for a family budget.

✔ "Number crunch" mountains of data with colleagues.

✔ Create clever charts, graphs and gadgets for an upcoming report.

✔ Create a spreadsheet with fiendishly complex formulas.

✔ Publish a spreadsheet online to impress a client with your digital acumen.

Starting Up a Spreadsheet

When you're ready to create a new spreadsheet, log into your Google Docs Home by launching it from a Google gadget, clicking the Documents link atop an open Google app (see Chapter 15), or launching it directly from a Web browser. Next, you have to sign in, which you can do one of two ways:

✔ **Google Account users:** Go to `http://docs.google.com` and enter your login name and password in the Sign In box on the right side of the screen. Then click the Sign In button.

✔ **Google Apps users:** Go to `http://docs.google.com/a/your domain.com` and enter your username and password in the Sign In box on the left side of the screen. Then click Sign In.

Create a new spreadsheet from the Docs Home page by clicking New ➪ Spreadsheet from the menu that appears. Google Spreadsheets opens a new, blank spreadsheet, as shown in Figure 16-1.

Figure 16-1:
A new, unsaved spread- sheet.

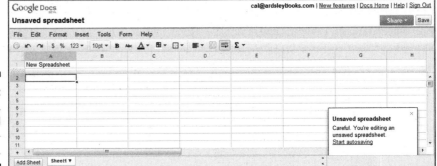

Start autosaving immediately

Google Spreadsheets wants to start autosaving immediately so that you don't lose any important cell entries. Enabling autosaving means that Spreadsheets will begin automatically saving your spreadsheet. A few moments after you create a new spreadsheet, a popup message appears, encouraging you to turn on autosaving. Click the Start Autosaving link (refer to Figure 16-1); a dialog box appears in which you can name your spreadsheet.

Note: The sample spreadsheet that you see in the figures in this chapter organizes statistics about five former British Colonies and the order in which they received independence. Incidentally, we want to visit all these places — no offense to the Falkland Islands or the 50 other members of the Commonwealth.

After you save, the file name appears in the header at the top of the screen. If you're not happy with the file name and need to make a change, here's how you do it:

Cells, rows, and columns

Like all spreadsheets, Google's online version is a grid. Each rectangle in the grid is a *cell*. The cells are organized horizontally in *rows* and vertically in *columns:*

✔ **Rows:** Numbered 1, 2, 3, and so on.

✔ **Columns:** Lettered A, B, C, and so on. When the spreadsheet runs out of letters in the alphabet, it doubles up the letters and starts using AA, AB, AC, and so on; then BA, BB, BC, and on and on it goes.

✔ **Cells:** Identified by the intersection of a row and column. This is the *cell address*. For instance, cell D8 is located at the intersection of column D and row 8.

---

1. **Click the file's current name in the header or Choose File⇨Rename.**

2. **If your browser prompts you to allow scripts, follow the on-screen instructions to do so. Then choose File⇨Rename or click the temporary name in the Docs Header again.**

3. **Enter the new name in the dialog box.**

Getting familiar with Spreadsheets' header, menus, and tabs

Atop the Google Spreadsheet App are the header, menus, and tabs: the power center of spreadsheet activities. In the header, you see the familiar Docs Home, Help, and Sign Out links. (See Figure 16-2.) Your login name, the file's name, and the date the spreadsheet was last saved appears in the header.

Figure 16-2:
The header, menu bar, and toolbar in the Spreadsheets app.

Below the header, the File menu and several tabs power the spreadsheet. In this list, we briefly describe each key menu and tab.

- ✔ **File menu:** Contains familiar File menu features, such as New, Import, Open, Create a copy, Rename, Print, and Save & Close. It also includes a Revision History and an Export function.If you need to export a spreadsheet to another file type, this is the menu you need.

- ✔ **Edit menu:** Allows editing options like Undo/Redo, and Cut, Copy, and Paste. The Find and Replace and Search the Web features are helpful. In a spreadsheet, important functions include deleting rows and columns, past formats and values, defining ranges of numerical values, and clearing selections.

- ✔ **Format Menu:** Lets you apply typical formatting elements like bold, italic, underline, strikethrough, and color options. You can also clear styles with this option.

- ✔ **Insert Menu:** Allows you and your collaborators to insert rows above or below a selected row or to add a column to the left or right of selected columns. You can also insert formulas, charts, comments, gadgets, or images from this powerful menu.

- ✔ **Tools Menu:** Allows users to sort columns and rows alphabetically and numerically. An important link allows you to freeze the top few rows or columns so they never disappear no matter what.

- ✔ **Form Menu:** Allows you to create a form using Spreadsheets that make data entry easy and consistent for you and other users with whom you share your spreadsheet forms.

- ✔ **Help Menu:** Google's Help Center is available from the Help menu. There is also a helpful video introduction and a list of keyboard shortcuts. One of the most helpful features is the Formula builder, which lets you choose from hundreds of precreated formulas so that you don't need to figure them out for yourself.

- ✔ **Share Button:** Permits the sharing of spreadsheets to whomever you like. Allows you to restrict changes that viewers can make.

Entering values and moving around

Any data entered into a cell is a *value*. The most common values are

- ✔ **Numbers or numerical values:** Used for calculations. Numerical values include both numbers and a few symbols, such as +, –, the comma as a separator, and the percent sign (%).

- ✔ **Text values:** Letters or words.

- ✔ **Labels:** Text values that act like headings or titles to identify columns or rows of values.

You can enter values only into an active cell. Make a cell active by clicking it or by using the keyboard as described in Table 16-1. Active cells are highlighted by darkened lines around its four sides. In Figure 16-3, cell A2 is active. After you make a cell active, you can enter values directly into that slightly expanded cell.

Figure 16-3:
Enter values
directly into
an active
cell.

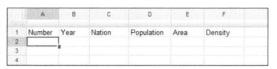

After you enter a value into the cell, you must activate another cell for the values to update in the spreadsheet. (You need to take this step in all spreadsheets.) For example, in Figure 16-3, we added six text labels and made cell A2 active. You can update values in a cell in several ways. Start by clicking a cell and entering the values, and then

✔ Press Enter, Tab, or any of the arrow keys.

✔ Click a different cell.

Table 16-1 lists the keystrokes you can use to navigate around a spreadsheet, allowing you to move from cell to cell.

Table 16-1	Keystrokes for Spreadsheet Navigation		
Press	*Action*	*Press*	*Action*
Tab	Move one cell to the right	Shift+Tab	Move one cell to the left
Enter or Return	Move down one cell*	Shift+Enter or Shift+Return	Move up one cell*
Left arrow	Move left one cell	Right arrow	Move right one cell
Up arrow	Move up one cell	Down arrow	Move down one cell
Ctrl+Home	Go to first cell	Ctrl+End	Go to last cell
Ctrl+down arrow	Go to bottom-most cell in the current column	Ctrl+up arrow	Go to topmost cell in the current column

(continued)

Table 16-1 *(continued)*

Press	*Action*	*Press*	*Action*
Ctrl+left arrow	Go to left-most cell in the current row	Ctrl+right arrow	Go to right-most cell in the current row
F2	Edit active cell	Esc	Cancel cell entry
Ctrl+spacebar	Select entire column	Shift+spacebar	Select entire row
Shift+Page Up/ Page Down	Extend the selection up/ down one screen	Shift+down, up, left, or right-arrow key	Manual select
Ctrl+D	Copy down (used with Shift+down arrow)	Ctrl+R	Copy right (used with Shift+down arrow)
Page Up	Move up one screen	Page Down	Move down one screen
Ctrl+Page Down	Move to following sheet	Ctrl+Page Up	Move to preceding sheet

*(May need to press twice to both accept data first, then move cells.)

Selecting multiple cells

You can select a single cell by clicking it. You can also move to a cell using the navigation keys described in Table 16-1. To select a range of cells, either

- ✔ **Use the mouse:** Click a cell and drag to highlight all the cells you want to select.
- ✔ **Use the keyboard:** Navigate to a cell and then hold Shift as you use the arrow keys to highlight the cells you want to select.

You can select an entire row by clicking the row header, or select an entire column by clicking the column header. Alternatively, press Ctrl+Shift+right arrow to pick a row or Ctrl+Shift+down arrow to pick a row.

Formatting multiple cells

You can put information in a spreadsheet as simply as clicking a cell and typing. Generally, text values are short — most often, just a few words in any given cell. Spreadsheets aren't the place for longwinded ramblings — save that for Blogger.

Figure 16-3 shows a portion of a spreadsheet comparing a few former British Colonies in the order of their independence. To start the worksheet, we entered the words Number, Year (for the year of independence), Nation, Population, Area (for land area), and Density (for population density) into the first six columns of the first row.

You can format all six text values at the same time by selecting the six cells (or selecting the entire row by clicking the 1 at the beginning of the row). Then start clicking the formatting buttons: Bold, Italic, Font style, and so on. In Figure 16-4, we selected cells A1 to F1 as a group. We made the labels bold and shaded, applied a different color, and increased to an 18-point font.

Figure 16-4:
Format values in multiple cells by using the Edit toolbar.

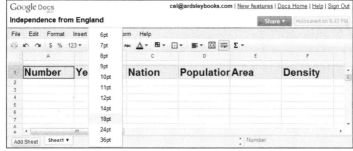

Changing the column width or row height

In Figure 16-4, the label *Population* is too long for the width of the column. The word is simply too big, so you can't see all of it. You can resolve this issue quickly — just adjust the width of the column. Hover your mouse pointer directly over the line between the column headers. A thick blue line with a double-sided arrow appears over it — this line is called the *Column Width slider*. Click and drag the line to the left or right to resize the entire column. (You can also double-click on the line between columns or rows to resize the column or row to the left of the line.)

The same technique works for resizing rows, too — hover the mouse pointer over the line between row headers until the two-sided arrow appears, and then click and drag up or down to resize the height of a row.

Entering sequences quickly with the Fill Handle

One of the important features in any spreadsheet is its ability to automatically anticipate patterns and increment values in adjacent cells. For example, say we need to create a list of numbers from 1 to 5. When we enter 1 in Cell A2 and 2 in Cell A3, Spreadsheets recognizes a pattern and can fill in the rest of the numbers in the sequence.

To use the Fill Handle to complete a sequence quickly, follow these steps:

1. **Enter the first few values in the sequence into their cells.**

   For example, enter **5** in one cell and **10** in another cell if you want to make Spreadsheets count by fives. (***Note:*** The cells must be touching — in either the same row or the same column, such as cells B1 and B2, or cells A6 and B6.)

2. **Select the cells as described in the "Selecting multiple cells" section.**

   In the bottom-right corner of the selected cells, a little dark square appears. This square is the *Fill Handle.*

3. **Click the Fill Handle and drag it down (to fill in a sequence within a column) or right (to fill in a sequence within a row). You can also fill cells by dragging up or to the left.**

   Google Spreadsheets fills in the pattern to all selected cells.

The same technique works for almost any sequence or pattern, such as:

- ✔ Days of the week
- ✔ Months of the year
- ✔ Multiple years
- ✔ Formulas (see the section, "Formula Fixin'," later in this chapter)
- ✔ Other types of data in which a pattern is obvious, such as counting by threes, fives, or tens

Changing values and undoing mistakes

To change or edit an existing value in any cell, double-click the offending cell to make it active and then make the desired change. Press Enter or click a different cell to make Spreadsheets accept the new value.

If you make a mistake (and we all make mistakes), click the Undo button on the Edit toolbar or press Ctrl+Z. If you make a mistake with your undo, click the Redo button or press Ctrl+Y to undo the Undo you just undid (*phew!*).

Inserting new rows or columns

You need to plan spreadsheets, but you can't anticipate everything. Fortunately, you can insert rows and columns anywhere you need them. To add a row or column, follow these steps:

1. **To add a row, highlight the entire row by clicking the number at the beginning of the row; to add a column, highlight the entire column by clicking the letter at the top of the column.**

2. **Click the Insert menu and choose the appropriate command from the menu's drop-down list.**

   • If you select a row in Step 1, choose either Row Above or Row Below from the menu.

   • If you select a column in Step 1, choose either Column Left or Column Right from the menu.

Merging and aligning cells

When you enter text that's too long to appear in its entirety in a cell, you can adjust the column width. But sometimes you don't want a column to be that wide — for example, if you have a long title for a spreadsheet. In that case, use the Merge Across button to merge two or more cells together.

To merge cells, follow these steps:

1. **Click a cell and enter text.**

2. **Select the cells that you want to merge.**

3. **Click the Merge Across button from the toolbar.**

   Google Spreadsheets merges the cells together, and any text that you enter in the cell in Step 1 spreads across the newly merged cell.

 If you want to break a merged cell back into separate cells, select the merged cell and click the Break Apart button on the Toolbar. (The Merge Across and Break Apart button are in the same position on the toolbar.)

You probably want to center align the text in a merged cell. To align text (or numbers), select the cell(s), row(s), or column(s) that you want to align, and then click the Align button on the Edit toolbar. Choose the alignment that you want from the menu that appears, as shown in Figure 16-5.

For example, in Figure 16-5, we

✔ Centered the title in row 1

✔ Aligned Column B's text values to the right

✔ Aligned the values in column C to the left

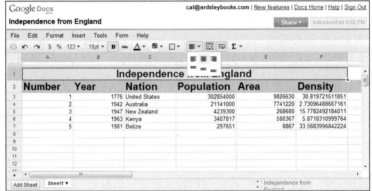

Figure 16-5: Select entire rows or columns and then apply alignments or formats.

Deleting rows and columns

Delete rows and columns much like you insert rows and columns. If you have an extra column or row that you don't want, simply select the entire row or column by clicking its number or letter, respectively, and then click the Edit menu followed by Delete Row or Delete Column.

Formatting numbers

Number values can take many forms. Google Spreadsheets can represent numbers as digits, percentages, and currency values with or without decimals and commas. You can change these forms, called *number formats*, by clicking the More Formats button on the Toolbar. For example, by clicking More Currencies in the menu that appears under the More Formats button, you can see a list of supported currencies.

Even dates and times have their unique formats. You can use a 24-hour clock or a 12-hour clock; you can use an American month/day/year format or the day/month/year format most other countries use.

To apply a number format, follow these steps:

1. **Select the columns, rows, or cells that you want to change.**

2. **Click the More Formats button on the toolbar and choose the number or date formats that you need from the menu that appears.**

Freezing rows and columns

You will need to freeze certain cells at the top and on the left-hand side of certain spreadsheets. *Freezing* locks cells in position so that when you scroll down the spreadsheet, those rows remain at the top of the screen no matter how long the spreadsheet gets. For example, if we expand our sample spreadsheet to include 50 new rows for the current members of the British Commonwealth, we need to freeze the top two rows. By freezing the labels in the topmost rows, you can scroll down to row 20, row 50, or row 5,000 and still read the labels at the top of each column.

You can freeze rows in two ways:

✔ Click the Tools menu followed by Freeze Rows or Freeze Columns as needed. From the menu that appears, select how many rows or columns you want to freeze. In Figure 16-6, we selected Freeze 2 Rows from the menu.

✔ Click and drag the Freeze/Sort bar (shown above or below Row 1) down a couple of rows, as indicated in Figure 16-6.

Selected from the menu...

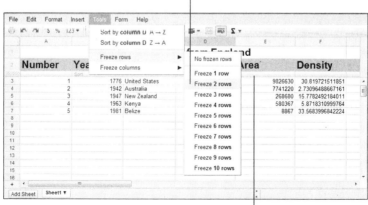

Figure 16-6:
Freeze the labels on the top of the spread-sheet.

...or click here and drag to freeze rows

To unfreeze rows, click the Sort tab, click the Frozen Rows or Frozen Columns button, and select No Frozen Headers or No Frozen Columns, respectively, from the menu that appears. You can also drag the Freeze/Sort bar to the top of the spreadsheet.

Sorting from A to Z and Z to A

Sorting text and numbers is one of the essential power-user features of Google Spreadsheets. You can sort in two ways:

- **A to Z:** Sort alphabetically from A to Z or numerically from one to infinity.
- **Z to A:** Sort alphabetically from Z to A or numerically from infinity to one.

Google Spreadsheets gives you two sorting options. You can sort by any column that you want by using either the Freeze/Sort bar or the Sort tab. For example, to sort data alphabetically (or numerically) you can

- Click the Freeze/Sort bar above the column you want to sort, and select A→Z.
- Highlight the column that you want to sort by, click the Tools menu, and click the Sort By Column A→Z button.

Either way you choose, Spreadsheets sorts all the data in the adjacent rows to reflect your sort. (In Figure 16-7, the country with the lowest population would move to the top of the list.)

If you want to reverse the sort order (for example, place the country with the greatest population at the top), repeat the sort process, but this time, click Z→A.

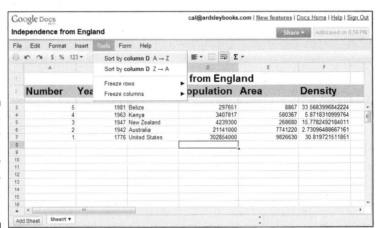

Figure 16-7: Sort your data from the Freeze/ Sort bar or from the Tools tab.

Using Charts, Graphs, and Diagrams

 If you are graphically deprived, you can easily overcome this ailment by creating charts and graphs with Google Spreadsheets. To create a chart, simply select labels and the related numbers (called a *range*), and then click the Add Chart button on the Edit toolbar.

Google Spreadsheets lets you display information by using many different charting and graphing styles, including:

- ✔ Column charts
- ✔ Bar charts
- ✔ Line graphs
- ✔ Pie charts
- ✔ Scatter diagrams

The next few sections discuss how to create and manage your charts.

Defining a range of data for your chart

Before you create a chart, a graph, or even some gadgets, you must define your data range. When creating a chart, it's helpful to select labels (at either the top of columns or the beginning of rows) and then choose data that corresponds with your labels. For example, in Figure 16-8, we chose three former British Colonies, their populations, and their land areas by selecting a range of cells from C5 to E7.

You define a range by clicking a beginning cell in the upper-left corner of the data set and extending down to the lower-right cell in the data set. Spreadsheets typically separate a range with a colon (:). For example, C5:E7 means, "Look at cells C5, E7, and everything in between." Spreadsheets will add the colon (:) automatically in most cases, but if it doesn't, you can add it manually.

Figure 16-8:
Select your
data range.

	A	B	C	D	E	F
1			Independence from England			
2	Number	Year	Nation	Population	Area	Density
3	5	1981	Belize	297,651	8,867	33.5683996842224
4	3	1947	New Zealand	4,239,300	268,680	15.7782492184011
5	2	1942	Australia	21,141,000	7,741,220	2.73096488667161
6	4	1963	Kenya	34,707,817	580,367	59.8032227883391
7	1	1776	United States	302,854,000	9,826,630	30.819721511851

Creating a chart

After you decide what range you want, follow these steps to create a chart:

1. **Select the range by clicking and dragging over the desired cells.**

2. **Select Chart from the Insert menu.**

   The Create Chart dialog box appears, as shown in Figure 16-9.

3. **Select the charting options according to how you want your chart to look.**

   You can select different options in the following areas:

   - *What Type:* Click one of the icons in the What Type section — Columns, Bars, Lines, Pie, or Scatter. You can refine your choice by clicking one of the Sub Type icons, which includes variations on the chart type selected.

     You need to decide which type of chart can represent your data in the best possible way. For instance, you could compare the population of the United States with that of Australia and Kenya (refer to the data range in Figure 16-8) in a visually appealing pie chart. However, the selection of cells in Figure 16-8 includes Population and Area. Pie charts are not effective with multiple comparisons and may not represent this type of data properly; you might find a column or bar chart to be better choices in this example.

   - *What Data:* The cell range that you select in Step 1 appears in the What Data textbox. You can also choose how to group the data by selecting either the Rows or the Columns radio button. Select one of the check boxes (Use Row X as Labels or Use Column X as Labels) to tell Google Spreadsheets where to find the labels for the chart.

   - *Labels:* Click the Chart Title, Horizontal Axis, and Vertical Axis textboxes, and enter labels for those parts of the chart. Choose where you want the legend to appear on your chart from the Legend drop-down list — you can choose No Legend, On Right, On Left, On Top, or On Bottom.

     If you set your spreadsheet up by attaching either column or row labels to a range of numerical data, the labels automatically appear as a legend in the chart. (See Figure 16-9.)

     Depending on the chart type, you can add a title and place subtitles on the horizontal and vertical axes. You may find labeling the horizontal and vertical axes especially helpful when you create a column, bar, or line chart.

- *Preview:* Look at the Preview window to see how your changes affect the chart.

4. **Click the Save Chart button in the bottom-right corner of the Create Chart dialog box.**

   Your chart appears at the top of your spreadsheet.

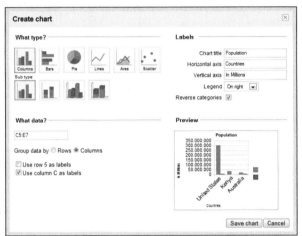

Figure 16-9: Select your data range and chart options in the Create Chart dialog box.

Managing charts

After you place a chart in your spreadsheet, you're not finished! You can do more. Just click the chart to activate it, and then click the down arrow at the top of the chart window. From the Chart menu that appears, you have the following options:

- ✔ **Edit Chart:** Change the look or data range of your chart.

- ✔ **Delete Chart:** Get rid of the chart and start over. Careful, after it's gone, it's gone for good.

- ✔ **Save Image:** Save your chart as a graphic file to use in other documents.

- ✔ **Publish Chart:** Publish your chart online for others to view easily. (For more on publishing, see the "Publishing and Printing Spreadsheets" section, later in this chapter.)

- ✔ **Move to Own Sheet:** Move your chart to its own browser Web page apart from the spreadsheet data that created it. This makes your chart much bigger and easier to view.

Creating gadgets and maps

In the online world, where Google resides, gadgets are popping up faster than housing subdivisions during the baby boom. Gadgets go from the fun to the functional, and range from the powerful to the perfunctory.

You insert gadgets in a spreadsheet the same way you insert graphics in a document or video in a presentation. So many new gadgets are created each month, however, that you'll want to preview your options. To view some possible gadgets, choose Insert⇨Gadget. This opens the Add a Gadget dialog box, as shown in Figure 16-10.

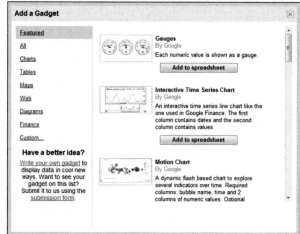

Figure 16-10: Find your Gadget favorites.

Most gadgets require a value from the spreadsheet. For example, the Gauges gadget (see Figure 16-10) requires numeric values. The Maps gadget requires a place value. In Figure 16-11, we chose Belize for the Map gadget created for that country.

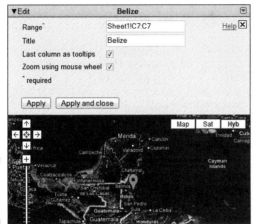

Figure 16-11:
Inserting a
map.

Formula Fixin'

Formulas are mathematical expressions that solve numeric problems. Don't
let this technical definition deter you from using formulas — Google has
made them easy to use and understand. Formulas use familiar operators,
such as those shown in Table 16-2.

Table 16-2	Mathematical Operators	
Operator	*Meaning*	*Used To*
+	Addition or plus sign	Adds two or more numbers together
–	Subtraction or negative sign	Subtracts numbers or indicate a negative number
*	Multiplication sign	Multiplies two or more numbers together
/	Division sign	Divides numbers or indicate a fraction
^	Exponential notation sign	Indicates that the number following the caret (^) is an exponent
( )	Parentheses	Groups part of a formula to indicate that operation should be performed first

You can write formulas that use these operators directly into any cell to perform simple mathematical calculations. To enter a formula into a cell, follow these steps:

1. **Select the cell and enter =.**

   A formula starts with an = (equal) sign. The = sign is a trigger that tells the spreadsheet to start calculating.

2. **Type the formula.**

   You can use rather simple formulas, involving a single operator, or much more complicated formulas, involving multiple operators, multiple cell references, and the order of operations.

3. **Press Enter to enter the formula in the cell.**

   After you enter a formula, that formula disappears, and you see only the answer to that formula.

To view or change the formula itself, you must double-click the cell again to make the formula reappear. You can now change the formula the same way you change any value.

Take a peek at a few sample formulas in Table 16-3.

Table 16-3	Simple Cell Formulas
Cell Formula	*Answer Returned*
=2+3	5
=2–3	–1
=2*3	6
=2/3	0.666667
=2^3 or =2*2*2	8
=(2*3)–(2/3)	5.333333

Using cell references and selecting a range

When performing your magical spreadsheet wizardry, save time by using *cell references* (you remember — cell addresses like A1 or E5). Any formula can reference any numerical value in any cell. If the numerical values change, the formulas automatically update their calculations.

You can perform calculations on a bunch of numbers in a row or column by defining a cell range inside a formula. For example, C5:D7 means that all the numbers from cell C5 down to cell D7 are included as part of the range. When you use a cell range in a formula, the beginning and ending cells are separated with a colon and are enclosed in parentheses, such as (A1:F15). (See the section "Defining a range of data for your chart," earlier in this chapter, for an explanation of cell ranges.)

To select a range, click the top-left cell and drag to the bottom-right cell. Using this method, you can add the entire range automatically to your formula and the colon (:) will be added automatically.

Built-in functions

Functions define the type of operation that a spreadsheet will perform. Functions are built into Google Spreadsheets. You, as the spreadsheet user, can choose from hundreds of functions. A few of the more commonly used functions appear when you select Formula from the Insert menu, providing you one-click access. We explain these functions in Table 16-4.

Table 16-4	A Few Built-in Functions	
Function	*How It's Written into a Formula*	*What It Does*
Sum	=Sum(range)	Adds all the numbers in a range to find a sum total
Min	=Min(range)	Finds the lowest number in a range
Max	=Max(range)	Finds the highest number in a range
Count	=Count(range)	Counts how many cells contain numbers in the range
Average	=Average(range)	Averages all the numbers in a range

You can see how functions work inside formulas by looking at a few examples. We applied the Sum, Min, Max, Count, and Average functions in our sample colonial spreadsheet, as shown in Figure 16-12. We used each function in a formula that has a range, applied from the Population column. Each formula and function uses the same range, (D3:D7); for example, =Sum(D3:D7) and =Average(D3:D7). Also in Figure 16-12, we added a label for each function in column D to show how the functions calculate.

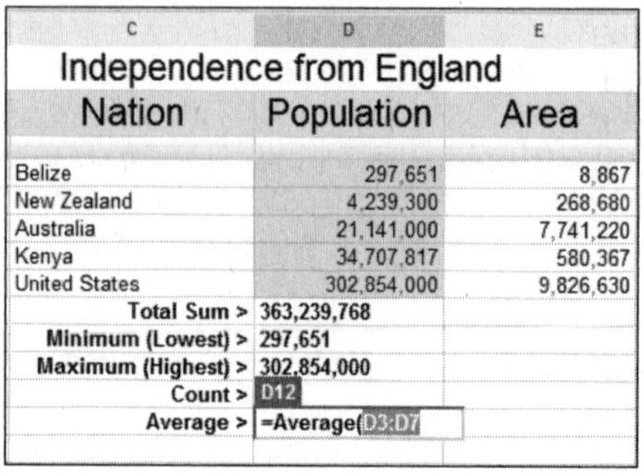

Figure 16-12:
You can apply basic functions to a range of data.

	C	D	E
		Independence from England	
	Nation	Population	Area
	Belize	297,651	8,867
	New Zealand	4,239,300	268,680
	Australia	21,141,000	7,741,220
	Kenya	34,707,817	580,367
	United States	302,854,000	9,826,630
Total Sum >		363,239,768	
Minimum (Lowest) >		297,651	
Maximum (Highest) >		302,854,000	
Count >		D12	
Average >		=Average(D3:D7	

Follow these steps to use a function in a formula:

1. **Click the Formulas tab.**

2. **Click the cell in which you want the formula and function to reside.**

3. **Click the function link that you need in the upper-right corner of the Formulas tab (for example, Sum, Max, or Product).**

   The Average link was clicked in Figure 16-12.

4. **Click and drag over the range of numbers that you want to calculate.**

5. **Press Enter.**

   You don't need to type the parenthesis if you follow the steps in the right order. If a mistake is made, click Undo and try again, or enter the formula by hand.

Filling and incrementing formulas

To apply the same functions and formulas from one column to another column (or columns), select the cells containing the formulas, click the Fill Handle that appears in the corner of the cell, drag it across the columns you want to include, and then release the mouse button.

Presto! You've created multiple formulas. Also, the spreadsheet applies to the range of cells listed in the formula the incremental concept explained in the "Entering sequences quickly with the Fill Handle" section. For example, instead of applying the formulas by hand to adjacent columns or rows, select the cell containing the formula you want first and drag it over to the new colomns or rows. You can also use the Copy and Paste commands to copy formulas to new cells. How's that for convenience?

If you don't want cells to automatically increment when you use the Fill Handle, you can add $ to cell references to fix their positions in your formulas. For example, using the cell reference ($D$2) prevents the data from cells D2 from incrementing when copied to other cells. The same applies to a range of cells to be copied ($D$2:$D$7).

Advanced and creative online formulas

If you need to apply more advanced functions into your formulas, click the Insert menu, choose Formula, and then select the More Formulas option. The Insert a Formula dialog box appears. This dialog box stores every possible function you should ever need; at least, Google hopes they've accounted for everything you might want to do! (See Figure 16-13.) The dialog box divides the functions into nine categories to make them easier to scour: Math, Financial, Logical, Date, Lookup, Statistical, Text, Info, and Google. (In Figure 16-13, you can see the Math category on the left side and the Google category on the right side.)

Google has supplied some creative, beyond-the-normal spreadsheet functionality that allows you to integrate and update data directly from the Internet into a spreadsheet. For example, you can insert stock quotes into a spreadsheet (see the sidebar, "Inserting a stock quote," later in this chapter, for the steps).

Figure 16-13: Access advanced built-in functions by category in the Insert a Function dialog box.

Insert a Function	
Math	ABS
Financial	ACOS
	ACOSH
Logical	ASIN
Date	ASINH
	ATAN
Lookup	ATAN2
Statistical	ATANH
	CEILING
Text	COMBIN
Info	COS
	COSH
Google	COUNT

=ABS(number)

more»

Double-click to insert into spreadsheet

Insert a Function	
Math	GoogleFinance
	GoogleLookup
Financial	ImportHtml
Logical	ImportXML
Date	ImportData
	ImportFeed
Lookup	
Statistical	
Text	
Info	
Google	

more»

Double-click to insert into spreadsheet

Creating multiple sheets

Google Spreadsheets allows you to create multiple sheets in the same spreadsheet. (Microsoft Excel calls these sheets *worksheets.*) You may find using multiple sheets extremely helpful. Say you're working on the company budget; you can create a separate sheet for each department or each team.

Sheets can interact with each other. You can use numbers and calculations from one sheet in formulas or results on another sheet. For example, if you're calculating multiple expenses from three separate departments, the total expenses for multiple departments can appear on a summary balance sheet for every sheet in the spreadsheet.

To create a new sheet, simply click the Add Sheet button at the bottom of the Google Spreadsheets screen. To make sheets easier to find, you can give each sheet a unique name by right-clicking the tab at the bottom of the sheet and choosing Rename. You can even rearrange the order of the sheets, if you want, by right-clicking the tab at the bottom of the sheet again and choosing Move Left or Move Right.

Inserting a stock quote

If you want the current, updated price of a stock displayed in a spreadsheet, click the Insert menu, choose Formula and select the More option. Click the Google category in the Insert a Formula dialog box, and select the `GoogleFinance` stock ticker function (refer to the right side of Figure 16-13). After your spreadsheet inserts the formula, Google updates the stock price every few seconds.

The `GoogleFinance` function requires both a ticker symbol and an attribute. For example, `=GoogleFinance("GOOG"; "price")`. Quotation marks appear around the ticker symbol and the attribute, and a semicolon is placed between them. These symbols and words, and how they're organized, is called the *syntax* of the formula. You can easily find ticker symbols on the `http://finance.google.com` Web site. Here are a few examples:

- ✔ GOOG for Google
- ✔ MSFT for Microsoft
- ✔ APPL for Apple

Attributes, such as volume and price, are important stock information. To find out more about attributes of any formula, click the More link to the right of the function description at the bottom of the Insert a Function dialog box to view a Web page that describes all the attributes that a function uses.

Sharing and Collaborating with Spreadsheets

In Chapter 15, we share with you the what-you-need-to-know-basics for sharing Google Docs & Spreadsheets. The instructions are the same for all the Google word-processing, spreadsheet and presentations apps. If you need more details about sharing, check Chapter 15.

Multiple collaborators can enter data or change formatting on the same spreadsheet at the same time. Shared spreadsheets are saved every time you blink (or so it seems) to protect the changes collaborators are making. And don't worry if someone makes a mistake. All the changes are tracked to maintain quality control. You can always revert to a previous version. To find out how, jump ahead in this chapter and read the "Revisions and version control" section, or reread more about revision histories in Chapter 15.

Keeping a single version of a spreadsheet, while maintaining a record of all the changes made to it, is much more efficient than keeping multiple versions of the same sheet and trying to reconcile all the changes after the fact. And Google Spreadsheets always lets you know who's currently contributing to the spreadsheet by listing the names of collaborators at the bottom of the screen.

Discuss while you work

The discuss panel offers another great feature for spreadsheet collaborators. Click on the down arrows next to the name of any participant that appears below the Toolbar to activate the discussion feature. This opens the discussion panel, as shown in Figure 16-14. If you're working with others, you can chat about the spreadsheet while you work on it. And, because you can chat about almost anything you want, we bet that after a few minutes, chatting about the spreadsheet will fall to a low priority.

Figure 16-14:
Discuss the
spreadsheet
while you
work on it.

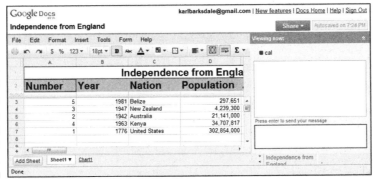

Revisions and version control

To view changes to a spreadsheet or to revert to an earlier spreadsheet, click the File menu followed by the Revision History option and then click the Older or Newer buttons to view the various versions. If you decide that you want to revert to an earlier version, click the Revert to This One button. A dialog box appears, asking you to verify your decision. See Chapter 15 for more details on the Revision History feature.

Converting and Exporting to Other File Formats

You may need to convert a Google spreadsheet to a file format that desktop spreadsheet applications use (think Microsoft Excel, StarOffice Calc, or Lotus 1-2-3). You can make these conversions by clicking the File menu and selecting Export from the menu that appears. Then choose the spreadsheet format that you need from the menu that appears to the right of Export. (We explain these formats in Table 16-5.) When you select an option, a dialog box appears that allows you to set options and parameters for exporting your spreadsheet. If you're even remotely familiar with these formats, the screens should be self-explanatory.

Table 16-5	Spreadsheet Conversions
Format	*Explanation of Format*
.html	A format that displays the data in a Web page format.
.csv	A comma-separated values format in which you can transfer data to another spreadsheet application or to a database.
.txt	This text format simply preserves the data but loses all the formulas that you may have applied.
.ods	An open document format that applies to a universal set of applications. An ideal format for those using StarOffice, OpenOffice, or another open source application.
.pdf	The portable document format that captures a picture of the data. Use this format if you want to lock the data down to protect it from changes.
.xls	The Microsoft Excel spreadsheet format.

Publishing and Printing Spreadsheets

The Publish on the Web feature posts an online HTML version of your spreadsheet and uploads a copy to your Web site or blog. You may find this a nice advantage if you want to share the spreadsheet with audiences beyond your collaborators. You access the publishing features by clicking the Share button and then clicking the Publish as Web Page.

After you publish your spreadsheet, you can still make changes or upload fixes to the spreadsheet publication by clicking the Publish tab again. From the update screen that appears, you can republish changes to your document, stop publishing altogether, select just the parts that you want to share, or select the Automatically Re-Publish When Changes Are Made check box.

You have several ways to print your spreadsheet:

✔ Click the File menu and choose Print from the menu that appears.

✔ Press Ctrl+P.

All these options open the Print settings dialog box. For the most part, stick with the defaults. Unless you have multiple sheets, stick with the current sheet. Also, most spreadsheets look better when you print them in Landscape (11.5/8.5) with the Fit to Width selection. (See Figure 16-15.)

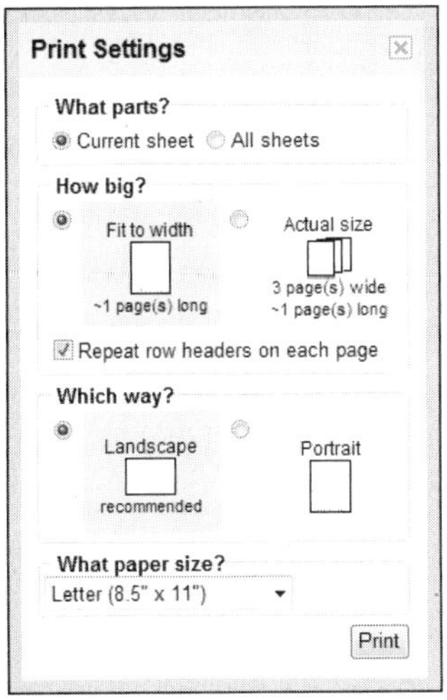

Figure 16-15:
Republish
changes
to your
spreadsheet
publication.

After you select your print options, the spreadsheet is converted into a PDF (Portable Document Format) document for printing. PDF is a great way to capture a spreadsheet for permanent storage. You may want to save the PDF version of the file to capture the exact document you just printed in an electronic format. Your PDF files can also be uploaded to your Docs Home.

Chapter 17

Creating Amazing Google Presentations

. . . .

. . . .

Need a quality presentation in a hurry and don't have the time (or the patience) for a complicated, ultra-sophisticated, über-difficult desktop presentation program? Then you'll enjoy Google Presentations.

Google Presentations is totally portable. You can access and run your presentations from any computer with a 'Net connection — which means you don't need to store gigabytes of presentations on your PC or USB flash drive. You'll glide through airport security on your way to your conference unencumbered by a laptop, confident that your presentation is safe on a Google server, ready for you to log into your account and start the show.

Starting Up Presentations

Google Presentations is the third jewel in the crown of Google's online productivity suite. When you're ready to create a new Presentation, log into your Google Docs Home by launching it from a Google gadget, clicking the Documents link atop an open Google app (see Chapter 15), or launching it directly from a Web browser. You can sign in one of two ways:

- ✔ **Google Account users:** Go to `http://docs.google.com` and enter your login name and password in the Sign In box on the right side of the screen. Click the Sign In button.

- ✔ **Google Apps users:** Go to `http://docs.google.com/a/`*yourdomain.com* and enter your username and password in the Sign In box on the left side of the screen. Click Sign In.

Create a new presentation from the Docs Home page by choosing New⇨Presentation from the menu that appears. A new, blank presentation opens, as shown in Figure 17-1.

Header

Formatting toolb

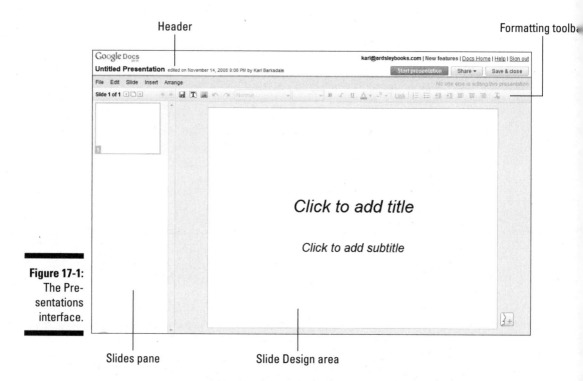

Figure 17-1: The Presentations interface.

Slides pane

Slide Design area

Getting familiar with the header, menus, and tabs

The header and its menus, tabs and its toolbar form the nerve center of the Google Presentations app. In the header, you see links to Docs Home, Help, and Sign Out. (Refer to Figure 17-1.) Your e-mail login name, the file's name, the date the presentation was last updated, and a link to start your presentation also appear in the header. Below the header you find the menu bar, various tabs, and the Toolbar power Presentations. In this list, we briefly describe each key menu:

✔ **File menu:** Contains typical File menu features, such as Save, Rename, Print, and create a New Presentation. If you need to convert a presentation to another file type, such as PowerPoint (.ppt), this is the menu you need.

✔ **Edit menu:** A typical edit menu, it allows you to Undo, Redo, Cut, Copy, Paste, and Select All.

✔ **Slide menu:** Permits you to add, duplicate, and delete slides and zoom in and out on slide elements.

✔ **Insert menu:** Makes it easy for you to insert textboxes, images, and video. You can also add shapes like arrows, circles, triangles, and rectangles. Most important, if you have slides you want to add from an existing PowerPoint on your computer, you can do that from this menu.

✔ **Arrange menu:** Lets you arrange objects, such as shapes, textboxes and images by bringing them in front of or behind other elements. You can also flip objects upside down and backwards.

✔ **Share tab:** The most important menu in the arsenal; it permits the sharing of presentations to whomever you like. It also allows you to restrict the changes that viewers can make.

The all-important Toolbar

The Toolbar gives you all the basics you need to create a presentation — formatting text; inserting images, videos, and shapes; and so on. The Toolbar is divided into two subsections containing the most frequently used icons or buttons described here going from left to right. (Refer to Figure 17-1.)

✔ **Slide Pane section:** Contains icons to help organize slides:

• **New Slide:** Add a new slide to your presentation and choose from a variety of slide layouts for each slide.

• **Duplicate Slide:** Select a slide and then use this link to make an exact duplicate of the existing slide.

• **Delete Slide:** Remove a slide completely.

• **Previous/Next Slide:** Navigate between slides in the Slide Page which brings them up in the Slide Design area.

✔ **Slide Design section:** Contains all of the editing and saving buttons seen on a traditional toolbar described in Table 17-1.

Table 17-1 **Slide Design Toolbar Commands and Shortcuts**

Command	Keyboard Shortcut	What It Does
Save	Ctrl+S	Saves your document
Insert Text Box		Insert a new textbox
Insert Image		Insert a picture into your presentation
Undo (Last Edit)	Ctrl+Z	Undoes the last change you made
Redo (Last Edit)	Ctrl+Y	Undoes the last undo
Font		Changes the style of the font
Font Size		Increases or decreases the size of the font
Bold	Ctrl+B	Applies bold formatting
Italic	Ctrl+I	Applies italic formatting
Underline	Ctrl+U	Underlines words
Text Color		Changes the color of your text
Text Background (Highlight) Color		Adds a color behind words just like a highlighter pen
Add or remove link	Ctrl+K	Creates a hyperlink in your document so that readers can click to view a related Web page or other resource
Numbered List		Creates a numbered list
Bullet List	Ctrl+Shift+ L	Creates a bulleted list
Decrease Indent		Moves paragraphs or lists half an inch to the left
Increase Indent		Moves paragraphs or lists half an inch to the right
Left (Align Left)	Ctrl+L	Aligns text to the left margin of a document
Center (Align Center)	Ctrl+E	Aligns text to the center of a document
Right (Align Right)	Ctrl+R	Aligns text to the right margin of the document
Remove Formatting	Ctrl+Space	Strips any formatting, such as bold, underline, or font changes, from selected text

Adding Text, Themes, Shapes, Video, and Images to Slides

If you're a beginner, let Presentations make the font size and style decisions for you until you get to know the app fairly well. Presentations can make your slideshow presentation look good without you having to think too much about its design, leaving you free to focus on your message.

Making a new slide

To build your presentation, you need to create new slides. After all, a one-slide presentation isn't very interesting — and it's really short!

To create a new slide, follow these steps:

1. **Click the New Slide button on the Toolbar or pick New followed by Presentation from the Edit menu.**

   The Choose a Slide Layout dialog box appears. In this dialog box, you choose among a variety of predefined slide layout options, as shown in Figure 17-2.

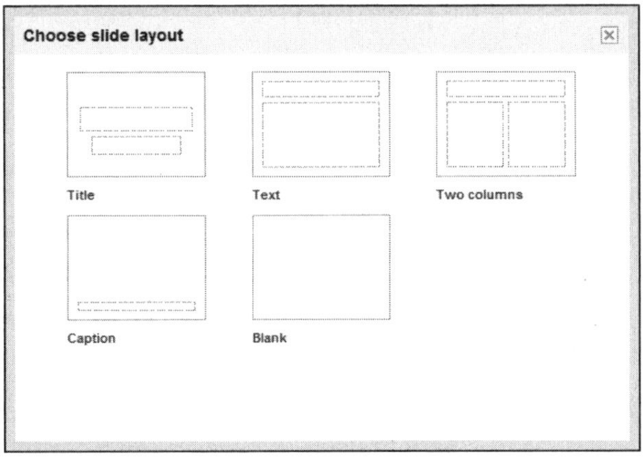

Figure 17-2:
Select a slide layout in the Choose a Slide Layout dialog box.

Choose slide layout

Title   Text   Two columns

Caption   Blank

2. **Click the slide layout that you want.**

   The new slide appears in the slide design area. Unless you choose the Blank slide layout, placeholder text appears in the textboxes defined by the slide's layout.

For most slides, the Text or Two Columns layouts work well. But choose whichever layout fits your content. In our example, we used the Two Columns layout. This template places two textboxes side by side, as illustrated by the dotted marquees (see Figure 17-2). Additionally, another textbox appears at the top that you can use as a title or caption. To enter a caption or a column of text, simply click any of the three textboxes and start typing. (See the section, "Inserting textboxes and formatting text," later in this chapter, for details.)

Changing the placeholder text

Each new slide you create positions textboxes and placeholder text where you can enter your text, shapes, video, and images. For example, as soon as you start a new presentation, Presentations creates a title slide (refer to Figure 17-1). Here's all you have to do to change the text in that slide:

1. **On the slide, click the Click to Add Title placeholder text.**

   A textbox appears in its place.

2. **Click this textbox and type a new title.**

3. **(Optional) You can add a subtitle (such as your name) by clicking the Click to Add Subtitle placeholder text, clicking the textbox that appears, and typing a subtitle, as shown in Figure 17-3.**

   After you change the placeholder text, the tiny preview slide in the slide pane on the left updates its image.

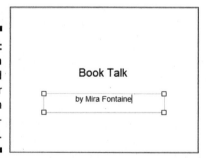

Figure 17-3:
Enter a title and subtitle for your slide in the placeholders.

Changing themes

Themes bring together color schemes, templates, and font choices that are designed to work well together. Some artistic person somewhere created the themes so that the rest of us can just click and type, and still create a great-looking presentation.

Pick an attractive theme by clicking the Edit menu's Change Theme command (refer to Figure 17-1). The Choose Theme dialog box appears, shown in Figure 17-4, giving you many premade themes to select.

Presentations offers some great options and avoids any obnoxious color schemes. Remember to keep your audience in mind when choosing a theme for your presentation. For example, Pink n' Pretty is very, well, pretty — but you should probably avoid it unless you're Elle Woods (you know, from the *Legally Blonde* movies). For the sample presentation shown in the figures throughout this chapter, we use the Chalkboard theme; it's a stark choice, but it shows up well on the black-and-white pages of this book.

Figure 17-4: Select a theme from the Choose Theme dialog box.

Some old-school presenters say that you should enter all of your content into a blank slideshow first, and then select a theme and color scheme later. However, we prefer to select a colorful theme right off the bat, and then add content. It's much more fun that way. Colors, stripes, images, fades, and textures get the creative juices flowing. After all, presentations are a visual medium, so why be boring at the start?

Another value of picking your theme early is that each one has its own unique characteristics. You may need to tweak your words and pictures a bit so that everything looks readable and balanced for a given theme. And, if you suddenly decide that a particular theme isn't right, you can always change it by clicking the Change Theme button and selecting a new theme entirely. You're never stuck with a boring theme.

Inserting textboxes and formatting text

If you're using a theme, a few default textboxes appear in the slides. To create a textbox that doesn't fit inside the normal template, follow these steps:

1. **Click the Insert Text button or select the Insert menu and choose the Text command.**

   A new textbox appears with the placeholder text Click to Add Content.

2. **Click the textbox and type away.**

   You can also paste text that you cut or copy from elsewhere.

   You can type, format, and edit text in the textbox. When you finish typing, click outside the textbox.

3. **Move the textbox or resize it as needed to accommodate the text you add (you may need to click the textbox to select it), as follows:**

   - *Move:* Hover your cursor on the side of the textbox; when the cursor changes into a cross with four arrows, click and drag to move the textbox where you need it.

   - *Resize:* Click and drag a corner handle any direction you want to reshape and resize a textbox. If you have text inside the textbox, the text adjusts to fit the new dimensions.

All the formatting tools available in Presentations work the same way in Presentations as they do in Docs or Spreadsheets (click the formatting button and type, or select text and click a button to apply that formatting to the selected text). They also share the same keyboard shortcuts (if applicable).

Table 17-2 shows the keyboard shortcuts specific to Presentations. (For more keyboard shortcuts, see Chapter 15.)

Table 17-2	Keyboard Shortcuts for Google Presentations
Keyboard Shortcut	*What It Does*
Ctrl+A	Selects all text in a textbox
Ctrl+spacebar	Removes formatting
Page Down	Moves to the bottom of a textbox
Page Up	Moves to the top of a textbox
Ctrl+Home	Goes to the top of a textbox
Ctrl+End	Goes to the bottom of a textbox
Ctrl+M	Inserts a new slide
Ctrl+S	Saves
Ctrl+P	Prints
Esc	Closes a live presentation
Ctrl+F5	Starts a presentation

Keyboard Shortcut	What It Does
F11	Displays your browser in full-screen mode or returns to the browser window from full-screen mode. (When using the Chrome browser, use the Maximize button instead of pressing the F11 button.)

Inserting links

You can add links in your presentation. Placing a hypertext link into your presentation has advantages. For instance, you can create a list to one of your Google Sites pages that lists Web sites or online articles that support your presentation. Also, you can put a link to your company or school Web page somewhere convenient (such as on the title slide) so that you can link to it quickly. To create a link, follow these steps:

1. **Click the Link button from the Toolbar.**

   The Edit Link dialog box appears. (See Figure 17-5.) You can choose to enter a Web address or an Email address.

2. **Enter your link information.**

   In the example at the top of Figure 17-5, we entered the URL `www.ardsleybooks.com`. (The http:// is added automatically.)

3. **Click OK.**

Figure 17-5: Create, change, or remove a hyperlink to a Web page or e-mail address.

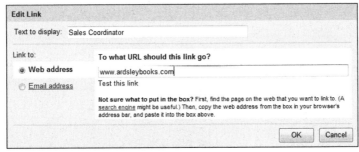

On your presentation, you can click any hyperlink text to edit or remove the hyperlink. (See the bottom of Figure 17-5.)

Clean up with Cut, Copy, and Paste

If you need to clean up your presentation, you can cut, copy, and paste text, shapes, and graphics by using the keyboard shortcuts Ctrl+X, Ctrl+C, and Ctrl+V (Windows) or ⌘+X, ⌘+C, and ⌘+V (Mac). You can also select your text and then right-click to open these options in a contextual menu.

With some browsers and operating systems, when you cut, copy, and paste, a warning dialog box appears, asking whether you want to allow the Web page to have access to the system Clipboard. Click the Allow Access button to allow temporary access, and then try your operation again.

Inserting shapes

You can add simple shapes to your presentation, such as squares, circles, speech bubbles, starbursts, and arrows. For example, you can add arrow shapes to create a simple flowchart.

Follow these steps to insert a shape:

1. **Click the Insert menu and select the Shape command.**

2. **From the pop-out menu that appears, choose the shape that you want to insert.**

   The shape appears in the middle of your slide.

3. **Move, resize, and recolor the shape, as needed, as follows:**

   • *Move:* Click and drag the shape to move it into position.

   • *Resize:* Click a corner handle (you may need to click the shape first to select it), and then drag to resize or reshape the image.

   • *Add color:* Click the Paint Bucket or Line Color buttons that appear in the top-left corner (you may need to click the shape first to select it), and then pick a color square from the menu that appears.

Inserting images

A presentation can be boring if it's all text (even with a theme applied). You can add images to your slides to make your presentation more visually appealing to the audience. You can also insert images that you create in Google Spreadsheets, such as charts or graphs.

To insert an image into a slide, follow these steps:

1. **Click the Insert Image button from the Toolbar or select the Insert menu and choose the Image command.**

   The Insert Image dialog box appears.

2. **Click the Browse button.**

3. **In the Insert Image dialog box that appears, select Browse Your Computer for the Image File to Upload to snag a picture from your PC. (If you want to link to a Web image, select Specify an Image URL and enter the URL to the image.)**

4. **Browse to your picture file, select it, and then click the Open button to return to the Insert Image dialog box.**

   You can use only Web-compatible image files: `.jpg`, `.gif`, or `.png`. (Presentations can't load other types of image files, such as `.tif`.)

   You can insert a chart or graph that you create in Google Spreadsheets. (See Chapter 16 for steps to create a chart.) In the Spreadsheet app, create your chart or open an existing chart. Click the chart to select it, and then click the Chart menu at the top of the chart. Choose Save Image from the menu, and click the Save button in the dialog box that appears to save the file to your computer. In Presentations, follow Steps 1 through 3 in this list and select the chart's image file in the Choose File dialog box.

5. **Click OK in the Insert Image dialog box.**

   Presentations uploads and inserts a copy of the image file into your slide.

6. **Move and resize the image, as needed.**

   The default placement of the image, dead center in your slide, is probably not the right spot. The image is probably too large, as well. You can adjust your image as follows.

   - *Move:* Click and drag the image to move it into position.

   - *Resize:* Click a corner handle (you may need to click the image first to select it), and then drag to resize or reshape the image. (Hold the Shift key down to enlarge or shrink and retain the same ratio of height to width.)

If you right-click an image or a shape, a contextual menu appears that allows you to delete, cut, or copy the image. You can also choose to make the image look like it's in front of or behind text or another image by right-clicking and choosing Bring to Front or Send to Back, respectively. You can use this feature to make your presentation more visually appealing.

Inserting video clips

You can add video to your presentation. Adding video is similar to adding a graphic or image. Follow these steps to insert a video:

1. **Click the Insert menu and choose the Insert Video command.**

2. **From the dialog box that appears, search for the video that you want to insert.**

   You can do a YouTube search for a video that works with your presentation.

3. **Move and resize as needed:**

   • *Move:* Click and drag the video to move it into position.

   • *Resize:* Click a corner handle (you may need to click the video first to select it), and then drag to resize or reshape the video window.

Organizing Slides

When you have a presentation with several (maybe several dozen) slides, you may need to duplicate slides (to make the first and last slides identical, or to start a new slide based on a previous slide), delete unneeded slides, and even change the order of slides. The following sections show you how to create new slides and keep them organized.

The *slide pane* (sometimes called the *slide navigator*) is on the left side of the Presentations screen. This pane displays thumbnails listing the slide order and a caption for each slide. Additionally, you can keep your slides organized by deleting, duplicating, reordering, and so on in this pane.

 Use the Previous and Next buttons or drag the scroll bar in the slide pane to navigate through the slide thumbnails. You can also use the Page Up and Page Down keys on your keyboard. You find this pane helpful when you have more than five slides and need to skip to a particular slide quickly.

You can rearrange your presentation in the slide pane two ways. You can click and drag a slide to change its order. Or, if you right-click any slide in the slide pane, a contextual menu appears. This menu allows you to

✔ **Start presentation from this slide:** Pick this option if you want to start your presentation from any slide other than the first one. This is a great option if you are editing because it allows you to quickly view a slide in the middle of the stack without having to start at the beginning.

- ✔ **Change the order of the slides:** Choose Move Slide Up or Move Slide Down. (Remember, you can also click and drag a slide in the slide pane to change its order.)

- ✔ **Create a new slide:** Select New Slide. (See the previous section for more information on creating a new slide.)

- ✔ **Duplicate an existing slide:** Select Duplicate Slide. When you duplicate a slide, you make an exact copy, including all the text, images, shapes, and layout of the existing slide. The duplicate slide appears below the original slide in the slide pane. (You can also click and drag a slide while holding the Ctrl key on your keyboard to create a duplicate.)

- ✔ **Inport slides:** Use this feature if you have precreated slides in another presentation or PowerPoint file and want to copy and paste them into a Google Presentation.

- ✔ **Delete a slide:** Select Delete Slide. If you accidentally delete a slide, press Ctrl+Z (Windows) or ⌘+Z (Mac) or click the Undo link in the toolbar to restore your slide. You can't retrieve it after you make any other edits.

- ✔ **Copy and paste an existing slide:** Select Copy Slide. Place the mouse cursor where you want the copied slide to appear in the slide pane, right-click, and then choose Paste Slide from the menu that appears. Your slide appears immediately below the slide you clicked.

Of course, if you need to edit a slide, select it in the slide pane first to make it appear in the slide design area.

This simple idea can save you time: If you've worked hard on a slide and intend to use some of the same elements (caption, image, or text) in the following slide, click the Duplicate Slide button on the Toolbar, choose Duplicate Slide from the right-click menu or select Delete Slide from the Slide menu. Then you can edit and change just a few elements, leaving the rest of the slide intact.

Using the File Menu to Full Advantage

One of the most important tools in Google Presentations likes to hang out inconspicuously in the top-left corner of the screen. Don't underestimate its power, though. While you create your presentations, you absolutely need to understand the Presentations File menu.

The File menu allows you to do many tasks, such as creating a new file; opening a file; uploading or importing a presentation; saving, printing, renaming, and deleting a presentation;.

Renaming a presentation

You may initially be stuck with a name like "Untitled Presentation." To rename a presentation, click the File menu and choose Rename from the menu. Alternatively, you can click the title itself to rename the presentation. A dialog box opens and you can type a new presentation name in the textbox that appears.

A warning about scripted dialog boxes may appear in your browser when you try to rename a file — just click the warning bar and choose Temporarily Allow Scripted Windows from the menu that appears. The browser then allows the dialog box to appear when you choose File➪Rename again; rename your presentation by typing a new name in the textbox that appears.

Printing the show

You can easily print a copy of your presentation. Click the File menu and choose Print from the menu that appears or press Ctrl+P. Presentations then prepares the presentation for printing in the window that appears, as shown in Figure 17-6. Click the down arrow below the Layout label in the top-right corner, and from the pull-down menu choose the number of slides you want to appear on each printed page.

You also have the option to print your speaker notes if you choose. (The speaker notes check box is shown in Figure 17-6.) However, if you choose this option, you're limited to one slide per page.

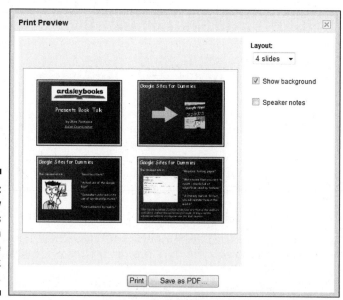

Figure 17-6: Choose how many slides you want on each page and click Print.

Click the Print button and your slideshow is converted to a PDF file for printing purposes. When you're ready to print your PDF copy of your presentation, click the PDF print command.

You can click the Save as PDF button to save a PDF version. These can be printed as handouts or uploaded and saved in your Docs Home. (See the next section.)

Saving a PDF copy of your presentation

You can save a PDF copy of a presentation on your hard drive or USB flash drive in case you ever need a backup. This is particularly handy if you're presenting from a computer that doesn't have an Internet connection. To do this, click the File menu, choose Download Presentation As and then pick PDF from the menu that appears. By choosing this command, you can save a small, compressed copy of your presentation.

If you have Adobe Reader installed (you can download it at `http://www.adobe.com/reader`), the PDF may appear directly in your browser window. Click the Save button on the Reader toolbar to show a dialog box and choose where you want to save your file. Otherwise, a dialog box appears directly in your browser, asking whether you want to open or save your file. Click the Save button, and browse to a location on your hard drive or USB flash drive to save the File. After you save the file, you can open it later with Adobe Reader to view it.

To present your PDF slideshow, open your PDF file in Adobe Reader, and then choose File➪Full Screen Mode, or press Ctrl+L (Windows) or ⌘+L (Mac). Use the arrow keys on your keyboard to move forward and backward.

Uploading existing PowerPoint presentations

You may have a few PowerPoint presentations on your desktop computer that you want to convert into the Google Presentations format and then save online. In fact, you may want to preserve a copy of all your PowerPoint presentations on Google servers so that you don't lose all your hard work if a computer crashes. To upload a PowerPoint presentation, follow these steps:

1. **Click the File menu and choose Upload a Presentation from the menu.**

   When the Upload a File screen appears, you can see the limitations on your PowerPoint uploads. For example, your uploaded presentation can't exceed 10MB.

2. **Click the Browse button to locate your PowerPoint presentation. (You can also convert other open source presentations.)**

3. **(Optional) If you want to rename the PowerPoint presentation, click the What Do You Want to Call It textbox and type a new name.**

4. **Click the Upload File button.**

Integrating other slides into a show

When you create a slideshow, you may want to insert a slide, or series of slides, that you already created for another presentation. You can integrate both PowerPoint and Google Presentations slides. To integrate individual slides from another file, click the File button and choose Import Slides from the menu that appears. The Import Slides dialog box appears, as shown in Figure 17-7. In this dialog box, just follow the steps — the first step asks you to choose the presentation from which you want to import slides.

Thumbnails of the slides from the presentation that you choose appear in the Import Slides dialog box. You can then select the check box to the left of each slide that you want to integrate into your presentation. The slides that you select are copied into your existing presentation. As soon as you select the slides you want, click the Import button; the dialog box closes.

You may need to move the newly integrated slides up or down to place them in the order that you want, as we explain in the section "Organizing Slides," earlier in this chapter. Right-click any thumbnail in the slide pane and choose Move Slide Up or Move Slide Down, as needed.

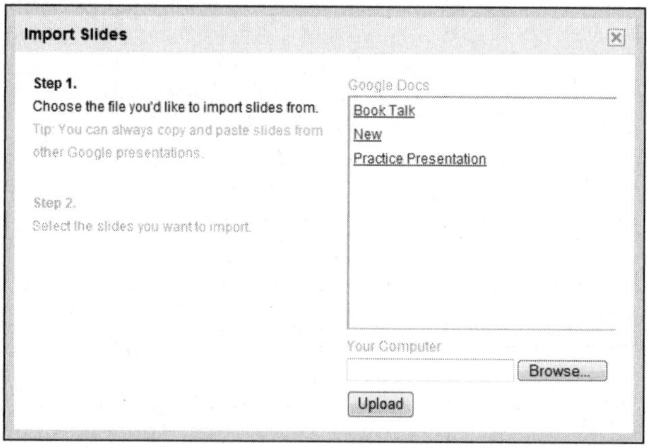

Figure 17-7:
Pick the
document
containing
the slides
that you
need.

Import Slides

Step 1.
Choose the file you'd like to import slides from.
Tip: You can always copy and paste slides from other Google presentations.

Google Docs
Book Talk
New
Practice Presentation

Step 2.
Select the slides you want to import.

Your Computer
Browse...
Upload

Viewing Revisions

What if you make a mistake or add too many slides and you need to retreat to an earlier version of your presentation? Like with Docs and Spreadsheets, Presentations tracks every change that you and your collaborators make to your presentation by selecting the File menu and picking Revision History. The revision screen looks like Figure 17-8.

You can always revert to an earlier version by clicking a Revision # link on the left side of the Revisions tab. A preview of the older version appears in the Presentations window. If you want to use that version, click the Revert to This Version button.

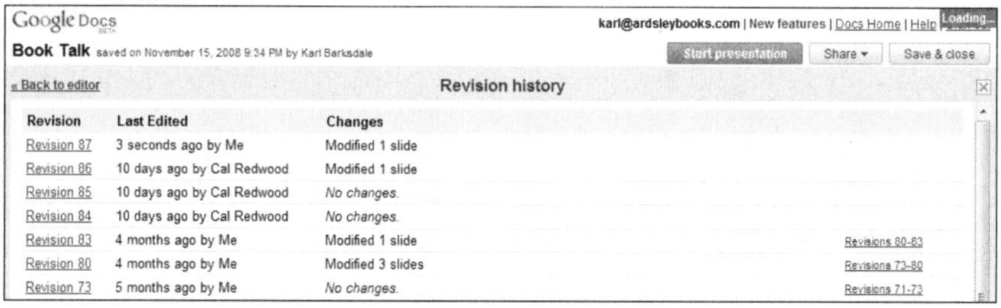

Figure 17-8: Google Presentations keeps track of your presentation changes and revisions.

Revision	Last Edited	Changes	
Revision 87	3 seconds ago by Me	Modified 1 slide	
Revision 86	10 days ago by Cal Redwood	Modified 1 slide	
Revision 85	10 days ago by Cal Redwood	No changes.	
Revision 84	10 days ago by Cal Redwood	No changes.	
Revision 83	4 months ago by Me	Modified 1 slide	Revisions 80-83
Revision 80	4 months ago by Me	Modified 3 slides	Revisions 73-80
Revision 73	5 months ago by Me	No changes.	Revisions 71-73

Giving Your Presentation

Google Presentations gives you two great ways to present your slideshow. First, you can display your presentation from any computer in the traditional way — by projecting it to an audience in a meeting room, classroom, or auditorium. This is a great way to present to a group of people gathered in a room. Second, you can give your presentation on the Web and let other remote participants follow along on their computers and interact with you in a group chat. This is an excellent way to share your ideas with people in different locations or around the world.

Projecting your slideshow

To begin a large group presentation, first make sure that you have an Internet-enabled computer that is connected to a projector. Then log into your Google Apps account, open your slideshow, and click the Start Presentation link in the header at the top of the screen, or press Ctrl+F5 on your keyboard.

Your presentation loads into a new browser window that fills up the screen. However, you probably still see the window border. To hide the window and see your presentation full screen, press the F11 key on your keyboard if you are using Internet Explorer (IE) or Firefox. If you are using Chrome, click the Maximize button. For IE and Firefox users, when you finish viewing your presentation, press F11 again to restore your browser window. Don't worry; if you forget about the F11 key, Google Presentations shows a temporary, transparent box at the top of your screen when you first start your presentation to remind you about it.

You'll also notice the Audience panel that appears on the right side of the presentation. We talk more about the Audience panel in the "Discussing the presentation with your audience" section, later in this chapter. To hide that panel, simply click anywhere along the left edge of the panel (look for the little arrow), as shown in Figure 17-9.

To move from slide to slide, either forward or backward, click one of the arrows in the bottom-left corner of the presentation screen. These arrows appear in a transparent box, so you need to scroll over them to make them fully visible. You can also use your arrow keys, Page Up, Page Down, or the spacebar to advance slides.

If you use Internet Explorer, you can exit full-screen mode by pressing either F11 or Esc. You can also move your mouse to the top-right corner of the screen; the Close button appears. Click the Close button to end the presentation.

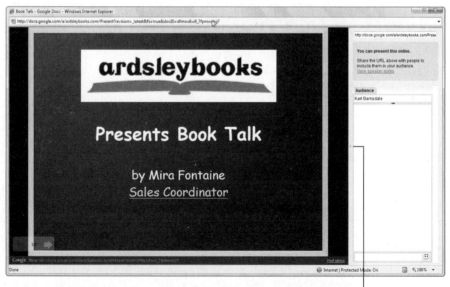

Figure 17-9:
Start your presenta-
tion.

Click here to minimize the discussion panel

Inviting collaborators and viewers

Use the Share tab to invite people as either collaborators or viewers. (See Chapter 15 for more details.) Collaborators can not only co-present with you, but also make changes to the presentation itself. Moreover, viewers don't have to participate in your presentation to flip through the slides on their own time.

Start inviting people by following these steps:

1. **Click the Share button and pick Share with Others.**

2. **Select the As Collaborators radio button to allow the people you invite to edit your presentation; select the As Viewers radio button to allow the people you invite to only view the presentation.**

3. **Click the Invite People textbox and enter the e-mail addresses of the people you want to invite, as shown in Figure 17-10.**

   You can further increase the security of your presentation by not selecting the Advanced Permissions check boxes.

4. **When you finish specifying your security settings, click the Invite Collaborators (or Invite Viewers) button.**

   An e-mail invitation screen appears, letting you send an e-mail message to your collaborators or viewers. This e-mail provides its recipients with a link to access the presentation.

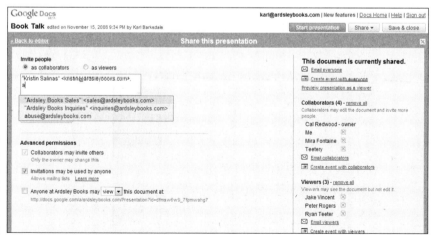

Figure 17-10: Invite people to join your presentation.

If you need to send additional e-mail updates concerning your presentation, click the Share tab and click the Email Collaborators link. The Email Collaborators window appears and lets you write a message to your team. You can also create Calendar events by clicking the Create Event with Collaborators link and filling in the details on the Events Details window that appears. If you need to add or delete collaborators, you can do that from the Share tab, as well, by clicking the X to the right of each contact's name.

Leading an Online Web presentation

One of the great advantages of Google Presentations is that you don't have to present your slideshows face to face with your audience. With Web presentations, you can invite others to follow along with your presentation while you chat about it directly in your presentation, talk about it with Google Talk, or have a conference call on Skype (check out `http://www.skype.com` to find more).

To start a Web presentation, you must first send each member of your audience a link to your presentation. After they have this link, they can view the presentation, print slides, and participate in group chat. Here's the easiest way to create an audience:

1. **Log into Google Docs, open your presentation file, and then click the Share button in the top-right corner of the screen and pick Share with Others.**

   A screen similar to Figure 17-10 appears.

2. **Click inside the textbox below Invite People on the left side of the screen, and enter the e-mail addresses of the people you want to join your presentation.**

3. **Select the radio button to the left of As Viewers and then click the Invite Viewers button. Alternately, to add co-presenters, repeat these steps, select the radio button to the left of As Collaborators, and then click the Invite Collaborators button.**

   The Email Presentation window appears. If you enter e-mail addresses for participants that are outside of your domain, you'll see a dialog box asking you to confirm that you want to invite them. Click OK to load the Email Presentation window.

4. **Compose an e-mail message in the textboxes that appear with a short message and details about your presentation and then click the Send button to return to your Share screen.**

Your message is sent to your participants along with a link to view your presentation. In the message, you may want to include the specific date and time when you will discuss your presentation online. Also, participants should have a Google Account or create one to be able to participate.

5. **(Optional) In the bottom-right corner of the Share screen, click the Create Event with Viewers link to create a Calendar event with your viewers.**

   On the new Event Details window that appears, enter the date and time for when you want to meet and click Save Changes. You may be warned about sending an invitation outside your domain (click OK). If you want to send an e-mail invitation, click Send. When you finish creating your invitation, close the Event Details window. *Note:* The event will include a link to your presentation as well.

6. **Click the Back to Editor link to return to your presentation.**
   When you're ready to start your Web presentation, click the Start Presentation link at the top of the screen, or press Ctrl+F5.

When you start a Web presentation online, you're initially in control. Each member in your audience who has opened your presentation appears in a list in the Audience panel. You can deliver the presentation to your audience slide by slide, just as you would to an audience in an auditorium. When you click the Forward or Back button, your audience sees the slides in the order that you present them, as shown in Figure 17-11.

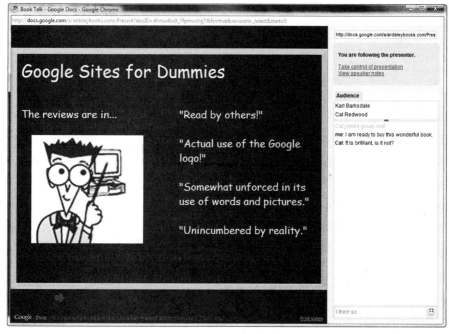

Figure 17-11:
Audience members can go at their pace or follow the presenter.

Audience members can choose to stop following you and flip through slides at their own pace on their screens by clicking the left and right arrows on their screen. When doing this, they see a small slide in the top-right corner of their screen that reflects your current position. To start following you again, they click the Follow the Presenter link,.

To add any latecomers to your presentation who weren't invited previously, copy the presentation address that appears in the textbox in the top-right corner of the Audience panel (see Figure 17-12) or the link along the bottom of the screen. Paste it into Google Talk, Gmail, Chat or an e-mail message and then send it to your contacts. These contacts must be users in your domain to join immediately; otherwise, you must add them as viewers (as described in the preceding steps).

Discussing the presentation with your audience

The Audience panel has similar features to Google Talk (see Chapter 20). You can discuss your presentation with your participants while you collectively view the presentation. This panel can serve another purpose: Your collaborators can chat about the presentation collectively and hammer out details while you all make changes. (See Figure 17-12.)

When new people join your presentation, they appear in your Audience list, as shown in Figure 17-12. You can track the names of who's coming and going with a quick glance at your Audience panel.

Participants can also print hard copies of the slides in your presentation by clicking the Print Slides link in the bottom-right corner of the presentation. (See the section, "Printing the Show," earlier in this chapter for more details.)

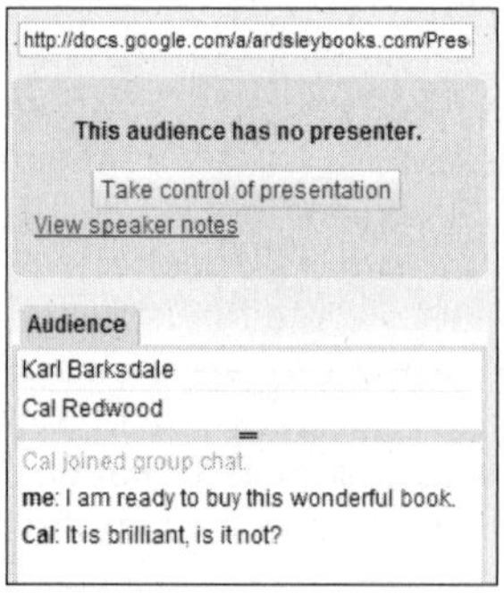

Figure 17-12:
Another presenter can take control of a presentation.

> http://docs.google.com/a/ardsleybooks.com/Pres
>
> **This audience has no presenter.**
>
> Take control of presentation
> View speaker notes
>
> **Audience**
> Karl Barksdale
> Cal Redwood
>
> Cal joined group chat.
> **me:** I am ready to buy this wonderful book.
> **Cal:** It is brilliant, is it not?

Relinquishing control

You can hand the presentation off to a co-presenter by clicking the Stop Presenting link at the top of the Audience panel. Another presenter (whom you invite as a collaborator, as described in the section, "Giving Your Presentation," earlier in this chapter) can then take over the presentation by clicking the Take Control of Presentation button that appears in the Audience panel.

If you're participating in a presentation and think that the current presenter is going too fast or too slow, you can always click back and forward through the presentation at your own pace.

Sharing and Publishing a Presentation

As with Documents and Spreadsheets, Google Presentations allows you to collaborate with other team members or contacts on your presentation without having to e-mail files back and forth and worry about having too many versions of the same slideshow. (See Chapter 15 for more details on sharing and collaboration.)

In this section, we cover how to e-mail your presentation link to other users, set up collaborators, and finally, publish your presentation to a Web page so anyone can view it.

E-mail a presentation

You can easily share a presentation by e-mailing your audience a link to it. If you want to send the presentation to others, click the Email link under the Share button. A simple e-mail form appears, as shown in Figure 17-13. Click the Subject textbox and type a subject, and then click the Message textbox and type a message (we like to keep it short and sweet). Click Send. (You may want to Cc yourself by selecting the CC Me check box below the message.)

The e-mail message that your friend, family member, or colleague receives includes a link to the actual presentation itself. Remember that you're sharing only one copy of the presentation with however many people need it (*singledocumindedness*). After your contact receives the e-mail, he can view the entire presentation — and even make changes if you give him collaborative rights, which we discuss in the previous section. The presentation appears in his Docs Home list.

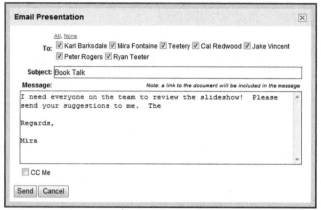

Figure 17-13:
Send your
presentation
to your audi-
ence via
e-mail.

Nervous? Add speaker notes

Speaker notes can help you stay on target with your message while you present. Notes can keep you from forgetting what you want to say, and they can
be added easily. Adding speaker notes is as easy as clicking the Speaker
Notes button when you prepare your presentation and entering the text you
want to appear to remind you of what you want to say. (See Figure 17-14).

After you start your presentation, which we discuss in the next section,
you can simply click the Speaker Notes button again. Doing so opens your
speaker notes window so you can remember exactly what you want to say at
the precise time you need to say it.

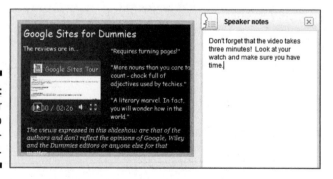

Figure 17-14:
Add speaker
notes to
your pre-
sentation.

Publishing a presentation

You can publish a presentation online with two or three simple clicks. Click the Share tab and then click the Publish and Embed option.

After a few seconds, the URL (Web address) of the published presentation appears on the screen. You can copy the URL and send it to anyone who you want to see your presentation. Additionally, the option to embed a mini player that presents your slideshow on a Web page appears. (See Figure 17-15.) Copy the code in the textbox on the left and paste it into a Web page you've created to have your presentation appear.

If you want to limit publication to just the members of your Google Apps domain, select the Viewers Must Sign In with a *<YourDomainName>* Account to View the Published Document check box.

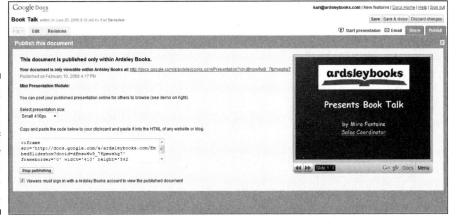

Figure 17-15: Share the Web address of your newly published presenta-tion.

If you decide that you want to stop publishing your presentation online, return to the Publish tab and click the Stop Publishing button, as shown in Figure 17-15.

Chapter 18

Using Google Calendar

*I*t seems that every time we become more efficient, we quickly find something else to fill the extra time. While Google Calendar can't help us with our type A personalities, it can help us organize our time and manage our daily events — whether it's a Little League game, a proposal for an important meeting, or a well-deserved power nap.

Google Calendar is extremely useful because it's online. In fact, you can access Calendar from virtually any device with an Internet or SMS connection. With a few taps or clicks, you can view your agenda on your iPhone, schedule a meeting on your PC, and share a calendar with a colleague from an Internet café in Mumbai.

Using Calendar

You can set up your calendar (or multiple calendars) in a snap. (See Figure 18-1.) To do so, you need the prerequisite username and password. If you're a Google Apps user, you may need to authenticate your account.

 The first time you log into Google Calendar, you're asked to set your time zone. Establishing your time zone helps you coordinate schedules with colleagues in different time zones. (You can change the time zone later by clicking the Settings link at the top of your calendar screen.)

Figure 18-1:
Use Google
Calendar to
keep on top
of your day.

You can access Google Calendar in two ways:

✔ **Open Google Calendar from a Start Page or Sites Page gadget:** Open your start page or Sites page. Look for a Calendar gadget, like the one shown in Figure 18-2. (You can use this gadget to view your upcoming appointments quickly.) Click the Google Calendar link in the title bar of the gadget to open your full calendar.

✔ **Go directly to Google Calendar:** You can log into your Google Calendar directly at `http://calendar.google.com`. Access team or Apps calendars by typing **calendar** and the domain name of your organization in the address bar of your Web browser — `http://calendar.ardsleybooks.com`, for example. Team Edition users should go to `http://calendar.google.com/a/`*yourdomain.com*.

Creating and changing events

The most important Google Calendar procedure to know is how to add and change events. A blank calendar, after all, isn't very useful. You have multiple ways to add events easily to your calendar:

✔ **Quick Add:** Click the Quick Add link or press Q, and then simply click the textbox that appears and type your event details. For example, you can enter something like, "Brunch with Cal 11am Wednesday." It even creates recurring events, such as "Carpool with John 6:30am every Tuesday and Thursday."

✔ **Highlight a time:** Using your mouse, click and drag to highlight a block of time. A white speech bubble appears. Click the What textbox, type your event, and then click the Create Event button.

If you want to add more event details, such as notes, locations, recurring options, or to add guests, click the Edit Event Details link rather than the Create Event button. Doing so takes you to the Event Details screen, as shown in Figure 18-3.

✔ **Create Event:** Click the Create Event link or press C to specify additional event details. On the Event Details screen that appears, you can choose What, When, Where, and add a Description, as shown in Figure 18-3.

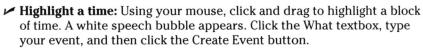

Figure 18-2: Use a gadget to launch and track your calendar.

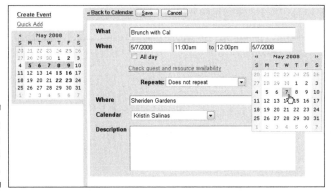

Figure 18-3: Specify the particulars of an event.

Here are some hints for entering event details:

- *What:* Enter a brief description of the event in the What textbox. Is it a meeting? A softball game? A trip to the stylist?

- *When:* Click the When or To textboxes to make a popup calendar appear. This calendar helps you pinpoint the day on which an event begins or ends. When you click the time textboxes, a drop-down list featuring the time of day in half-hour increments appears. Selecting the All Day check box makes the event appear at the top of that particular day on your daily or weekly calendar.

- *Repeats:* From this drop-down list, choose whether you want your event to repeat daily, weekly, monthly, or yearly. Additionally, depending on what option you select, more options appear so that you can choose how long you want the event to repeat.

- *Where:* Enter a description of where the event takes place. If you enter a street address, the next time you look at your event, a Map link appears in the event speech bubble or in the Event Details screen. Clicking that link loads the address in Google Maps, which opens in a new window.

- *Calendar:* By default, events that you enter go to your main calendar (the one titled with your name). When you add multiple calendars, a Calendar drop-down list appears and you can choose to add the event to a different calendar by choosing that calendar from the list.

- *Description:* Add details, such as directions to an event, who you're meeting, what you need to bring, or your goals for a meeting.

When you finish entering the event's details, click the Save button to save the event and place it in your calendar.

- ✔ **Receive an invitation:** If another Google Calendar user invites you to a meeting, that meeting appears automatically on your calendar with a question mark in the corner. Click the event to see the event bubble. You can tell the event host whether you can attend or not by clicking the Yes, No, or Maybe links. The event host receives your response automatically when you click one of these links. Declined events appear faded out in your calendar.

- ✔ **Add an event in Gmail:** If someone sends you an e-mail with some dates and times, Gmail asks whether you want to add the events discussed in the e-mail to your calendar. To add the events to your calendar from Gmail, click the Add to Calendar link that appears to the right of your e-mail message.

Moving your events around

The only constant in life is change. Fortunately, making changes is easy in Google Calendar. When your meeting is rescheduled, you can change the event in your calendar in these ways:

✔ **To change the time of an event:** Simply click the shaded area of the event and drag it to the new time slot.

✔ **To extend or shorten an event:** Click and drag the double white lines along the bottom edge downward to extend the event, or drag upward to shorten the event.

✔ **To make more specific changes to an event:** Click the event and click the Edit Event Details link in the speech bubble that appears.

If you change an event that you didn't create (such as a lunch your supervisor invited you to), the event doesn't change in the host's calendar. Make sure that you call or e-mail your host so he or she can change the event in his or her calendar, too.

Deleting events

To delete an event, simply click an event, and then click the Delete link in the speech bubble that appears. Also, if you double-click an event, the Event Details screen appears, and you can click the Delete button at the top of that screen to delete that appointment.

Setting Up Calendar Notifications

Google Calendar can send you a reminder before an event. Depending on how you set your notifications, Google Calendar shows you a popup reminder, sends a text message to your mobile phone, or sends you a friendly e-mail.

To see popup reminders, you must have a browser window open and Google Calendar loaded. To receive text messages, you must register your mobile phone (which we tell you how to do in the "Registering your mobile phone to receive notifications" section, later in this chapter).

Creating universal event reminders

By default, your primary calendar displays a popup window ten minutes prior to every event you create. Changing this setting is as easy as pie. Just follow these steps:

1. **To change your notifications, click the arrow to the right of a calendar (from the list on the left side of the screen), and then choose Notifications from the drop-down list that appears.**

   The Notifications tab appears, as shown in Figure 18-4.

Figure 18-4:
Set default
remind-
ers and
configure
your mobile
phone.

2. **In the Event Reminders section of the Notifications tab, choose Pop-Up, Email, or SMS (text message) from the By Default, Remind Me Via drop-down list. Choose how soon before each event you want to receive the reminder from the Before Each Event drop-down list.**

If SMS doesn't appear in the By Default, Remind Me Via drop-down list and you want to receive reminders on your mobile phone, follow the steps in the next section to register your mobile phone with Google Calendar, and then return to these steps.

3. **Click the Add Another Reminder link to add up to five notifications.**

4. **In the Choose How You Would Like to Be Notified section, select the check box in the Email or SMS column (depending on which method you prefer).**

For example, select the check box in the Email column to the right of New Invitations to receive an e-mail notification when someone sends you an invitation to an event.

5. **To disable a notification, click the Remove link to the right of the reminder.**

6. **When you're happy with your settings, click the Save button to return to your calendar.**

Registering your mobile phone to receive notifications

Before your mobile phone can receive notifications from your calendar, you must first register your phone with Google Calendar by following these steps:

1. **From the Notifications screen, click the Set Up Your Mobile Phone to Receive Notifications link.**

   Alternatively, from your main calendar, click the Settings link at the top of the page, and then click the Mobile Setup tab. The Mobile Setup tab appears, as shown in Figure 18-5.

Figure 18-5: Register your phone to enable SMS scheduling.

2. **Choose your country from the Country drop-down list.**

3. **Click the Phone Number textbox and enter your mobile phone number.**

   It doesn't matter what format you enter your number in. 555-555-1212 will work the same as (555) 555-1212 or 5555551212.

4. **Choose your carrier from the Carrier drop-down list.**

   If your carrier doesn't appear in the Carrier drop-down list, click the What Carriers Are Supported? link. If you're trying to connect from outside of the United States and the Carrier drop-down list doesn't appear, click the See Help Center for Supported Providers link. A list of the supported carriers worldwide opens in a new window. If your provider appears on the Help Center page and is supported, return to your calendar notification settings, leave the Carrier field blank, and continue to Step 5.

5. **Click the Send Verification Code button.**

   A text message appears on your phone within a few minutes.

6. **Click the Verification Code textbox, type the code that you receive in your phone's text message, and then click the Finish Setup button.**

Although SMS notifications are free from Google, your mobile carrier may charge you for each text message that you send or receive. Be sure to check your phone's plan before you use SMS reminders extensively.

Adding reminders to individual events

You can easily set reminders for individual events. Follow these steps to make sure that you don't miss that important meeting or softball game:

1. **Click an event that you want to add a reminder to and then click the Edit Event Details or More Details link at the bottom of the speech bubble that appears.**

   The Event Details screen appears.

2. **In the Options pane on the right of the Event Details screen, click the Add a Reminder link to add up to five different notifications.**

3. **Use the drop-down lists to choose what type of notification you want and when.**

   For example, to receive an e-mail reminder an hour before the event, choose Email from the left drop-down list and 1 Hour from the right drop-down list.

4. **Click the Remove link to disable a notification.**

   The event reminder disappears right away, and you have to rely on your memory.

5. **Click the Save button to save your changes and return to your calendar.**

Changing Your Calendar Views

Google Calendar lets you change how you view your schedule — just click the blue tabs in the top-right corner of your screen. Here are the basic calendar views:

- **Day:** Click the Day tab or press D to view your appointments for a given day, starting with the next upcoming event.

- **Week:** Click the Week tab or press W to see a full week's worth of events. All day events appear at the top of the calendar.

  You can customize your Week view to start on a day other than Sunday or to hide weekends. Click the Settings link in the top left of the screen, click the arrows to the right of Week Starts On and Show Weekends, and then choose the options you want from the drop-down lists that appear. Scroll to the bottom of the Settings screen and click Save to return to your calendar.

- **Month:** Click the Month tab or press M to see your month at a glance.

✔ **Next 4 Days:** Click the Next 4 Days tab or press X to see this custom view. To change the time period, click the Settings link at the top of the screen and locate the Custom View section (it's halfway down the Settings screen). Click the arrow to the right of the drop-down list in the Custom View section and choose your favorite custom time frame, from Next 2 Days to Next 4 Weeks.

✔ **Agenda:** Click the Agenda tab or press A to see your agenda. The agenda is handy because it lists all the calendar items in a condensed, easy-to-read format. When you click any event, it expands to show you the details.

You don't have to be limited to the options in the preceding list. You can view any number of days, from one day to seven weeks, by highlighting the days on the mini calendar on the left of any calendar screen.

After you find a view that you like, use the arrows at the top left to move forward and backward in increments of that time period. You can also press N to move forward and P to move backward. To return to the current day, click the Today button or press T.

Printing Your Calendar

You can print a copy of any calendar view. You can also save your calendar to a PDF file that you can send to others. Simply select your preferred calendar view (see the preceding section for details), and then click the Print link to the left of the tabs. The Calendar Print Preview window appears, as shown in Figure 18-6.

In the Calendar Print Preview window, you can adjust the font size by clicking the arrow to the right of Font Size and choosing a size from the drop-down list. Choose which direction you want the calendar to print by clicking the arrow to the right of Orientation and choosing a direction from the drop-down list. Print the calendar in black and white by selecting the Black & White check box. To print in color, make sure the Black & White check box is deselected. Click the Print button to complete printing. Click the Save As button to download a PDF version to your desktop.

To print a blank calendar, return to your calendar screen and click the name of each of your calendars in the My Calendars list so they are no longer highlighted, and then click the Print link. When you finish, click the names of your calendars again to make your events reappear.

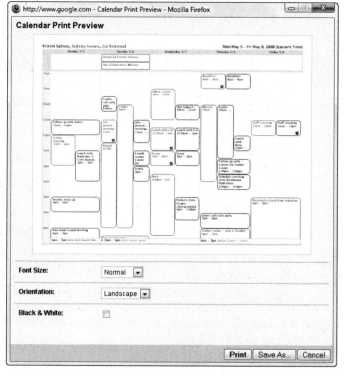

Figure 18-6:
In the
Calendar
Print
Preview
window, you
can set print
options and
save the
calendar as
a PDF.

Using Multiple Calendars

In the following sections, we show you how to create multiple calendars (for example, one for work, one for your bowling league, and one for your weekend adventures). We also cover how you can add public calendars, such as sports schedules, daily closing stock prices, and holidays. Put all your cares on Google Calendar so you can spend less time remembering appointments and more time doing the stuff you love.

Adding calendars

First things first — check out the Add link at the bottom of the My Calendars list. Using the options in this menu, you can add public calendars, import events, and more. Here's what each option in the Add menu does:

✔ **Add a public calendar:** Select this option to explore calendars that others have made, including calendars announcing holidays, your alma mater's football game schedule, or important stock quotes. When you click this option, you see a screen that lets you browse the most popular public calendars. You can also use the search box at the top of the Calendar gallery screen to search any hundreds of others. To add a public calendar, simply click the Add to Calendar button. The Calendar gallery is similar to the Gadget gallery that we discuss in Chapter 6.

To follow stocks, enter the ticker symbol of your favorite company in the Search textbox at the top of the Calendar gallery screen and then click the Search Public Calendars button. Look for the Google Finance calendar for the company you want and click Add to Calendar. Each day's closing price appears at the top of each day on your calendar.

✔ **Add a friend's calendar:** Co-workers who use Google Calendar have shared calendars by default. To show a friend's or colleague's calendar alongside your calendar, first click this option and then enter your contact's e-mail address in the textbox on the screen that appears. Finally, click the Add button to the right of the textbox and your contact's shared calendar appears automatically. If she doesn't have Google Calendar, you can invite her to create one.

✔ **Add by URL:** When you come across a Web site that has a calendar feed that you want to add to your Google Calendar, copy the URL, and then return to your calendar. Click the Add menu in the My Calendars list on the left-hand side of the screen, select Add by URL, and in the screen that appears, paste the URL into the Public Calendar Address textbox. Don't forget to click the Add button when you finish.

✔ **Import Calendar:** Use this tool to add events from another calendar program, such as Outlook or iCal.

To create a new calendar, click the Create link below your calendars. Use this link to create a separate calendar for your bowling league, child's soccer schedule, or other events that you don't want to appear on your main calendar.

Changing colors and settings

Whether you have only a few calendars or a plethora, you can easily manage them from the My Calendars list. To hide calendar events tied to a specific calendar, uncheck the box to the left of each calendar name. Check the box again when you want to show that calendar. You may find hiding calendars particularly handy if your calendar is bursting with events.

In addition to selecting or deselecting the calendars' check boxes, clicking the down arrow to the right of a calendar gives you some more options including specifying colors for that calendar:

- ✔ **Display Only This Calendar:** Selecting this option shows only the events on a single calendar on your main calendar screen. Other calendars and events disappear from your main calendar screen until you check each calendar's check box again.

- ✔ **Hide This Calendar from the List:** This only appears on additional calendars. Selecting this option makes the calendar disappear from the list. Click the Settings link at the bottom of the My Calendars list for options to reveal, hide, and delete your calendars.

- ✔ **Calendar Settings:** Selecting this option opens the Calendar Details screen. You can change the calendar name and description, and see the calendar address. In the Calendar Details tab, you can also access the tool that you can use to embed your calendar on a Web page.

- ✔ **Create Event on This Calendar:** Selecting this option does the same thing as clicking the Create Event link at the top of the main Calendar screen, except it automatically assigns the event to the specific calendar. (When you have multiple calendars and click the Create Event link, you can specify on which calendar you want to create your event by choosing from the Calendar drop-down list on the Create Event screen.)

- ✔ **Share This Calendar:** Selecting this option shows the Calendar Details screen, where you can choose how much information you want to share for each calendar.

- ✔ **Notifications:** New calendars don't have notifications by default, but you can change those settings by selecting Notifications and choosing your options on the Calendar Details screen. (See the section "Setting Up Calendar Notifications," earlier in this chapter, for details.)

- ✔ **Color:** Clicking a color box changes all the events associated with that calendar to the selected color. In addition to being visually appealing, choosing different colors for different calendars can help you tell at a glance what's going on with multiple calendars and if you have any scheduling conflicts.

Feel free to adjust these settings until you find a calendar that makes you smile. For more control over these settings, click the Settings link at the bottom of the My Calendars list.

Be careful not to click the trashcan icon on the Calendars screen (click the Settings link to go to the Calendars screen) unless you're certain that you want to delete a calendar. You can add public calendars again, but if you delete one of your main calendars without sharing it with someone first, you have no way to get it back.

Searching Your Calendar

Search is one of our favorite features in Google Calendar. Sometimes, you may forget an event. You may even forget on which calendar the event is located. No problem. Click the Search box at the top of your Calendar screen or press / (the forward slash key); type a few words about the event, such as **lunch**; then click the Search My Calendars button. A list of all the lunches on your calendars appears, as shown in Figure 18-7. Type in even more information and you can find more specific events. Click the Search My Calendars button to see results from all your calendars.

Figure 18-7: You can find events easily by using Google Search.

Your search results appear in a new tab at the top, so you can switch between your normal calendar views and compare results. In your search results, click the date to the left of an event to see that day's agenda. Click the event time or name to see and edit the event's details.

You can also use the Search box to find public calendars at any time, as discussed in the earlier "Adding calendars" section.

You can usually use the Search box at the top of your Calendar screen to find the event that you can't remember. Suppose, however, that you want to see only meetings with your colleague, Janice, in a certain time period, and you can't remember any of the meeting specifics. Google has the answer. The Show Search Options link appears (in tiny type) to the right of the Search box. Click that link to reveal more specific search boxes, as shown in Figure 18-8. You can add details, such as a date range, that narrow the search results. Click the Search button, and your results appear.

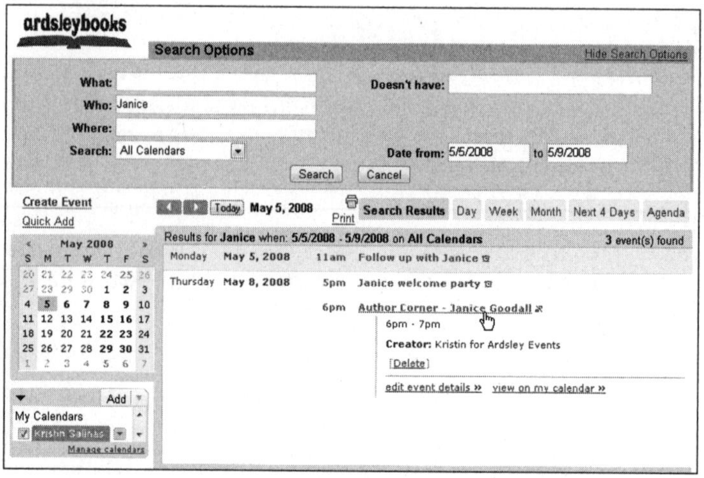

Figure 18-8:
Narrow your
calendar
search
with spe-
cific event
details.

When you finish with the advanced search, click the Cancel button or the Hide Search Options link in the top-right corner to hide the search options and return to the basic calendar screen.

Sharing Invitations with Others

Although it can't add an extra hour to every day, Google Calendar can be a huge timesaver for organizations, schools, businesses, and families. You can send meeting and event invitations, and track people's responses, even if they use other calendar programs.

Now, families can keep track of those family reunions, and parents can coordinate their kids' schedules from home or work. Salespeople can track leads and follow up with their customers. Schools can let teachers book time in the library, share a mobile computer lab, or work with parents to help their students. And don't forget about college students — they can follow a class schedule and book time with their study group by using the campus-wide Google Calendar.

Creating invitations

You can easily send invitations to any kind of event, whether it's a business meeting or poker night. Anyone can receive your invitations, even if they don't use Google Calendar or don't have a Google Account.

Sending event invitations is a breeze; just follow these steps:

1. **To invite guests to a new event, click the Create Event link on the main Calendar screen; to invite guests to an event that already exists on your calendar, click the event to reveal its speech bubble and then click the Edit Event Details link.**

   On the Event Details screen, look for the Guests pane.

2. **In the Guests pane's textbox, enter the e-mail addresses of people that you want to invite to your event. Separate each address with a comma.**

   You can also click the Choose from Contacts link to select guests from your Contacts list.

3. **Select the check boxes in the Guests Can section if you want to allow guests to invite others and see the guest list.**

4. **When you finish adding your guests, click the Save button at the top of the Event Details screen.**

   The Send Update dialog box appears, giving you the option to send an e-mail to invite your guests.

5. **Click the Send button to send the invitation or the Don't Send button to save your event without notifying your guests.**

   Each of your guests promptly receives an e-mail message that asks him whether he plans to attend. Those guests who use Google Calendar see the event appear automatically on their calendars with a question mark in the event's top-right corner. Guests who use Outlook can respond directly from the e-mail, and the event appears automatically on their Outlook calendar, as well.

Responding to invitations

You (or your guests) can respond to invitations in one of two ways. First, you can click a link in the e-mail that you receive. Simply click the link that says Yes, No, or Maybe, and the host's event is updated to indicate your response.

Alternatively, you can respond directly from Google Calendar by clicking an event that shows a question mark in the top-right corner, and then clicking Yes, No, or Maybe in the event bubble that appears. If you click Yes, the question mark disappears. If you click No, the event becomes faded out and the question mark disappears. If you click Maybe, the question mark remains, but your host will know that you're considering attending. You can always change your response later by clicking the event again.

Checking guest status and e-mailing guests

When your event draws near, you may want to see how many people are planning to attend. You can check the status of your guests' responses by double-clicking the event, as shown in Figure 18-9.

Figure 18-9:
View who plans to attend in the event's details.

If you decide to change event details later in the Event Details screen, click Save; a dialog box appears, asking whether you want to notify the guests about the change. To get in touch with your guests at any time, click the Email Guests link in the Guests pane to send a quick message. An e-mail window appears, similar to Figure 18-10. Don't forget to select the Send a Copy to Myself check box if you want to receive a copy of the message.

Sending invitations directly from Gmail

Gmail likes to help you play the part of super scheduler, too. Click the Add Event Info link just below the subject line in the Compose Message window. In the expanded event info area, enter the details for an event, as shown in Figure 18-11. The event is automatically added to your Calendar!

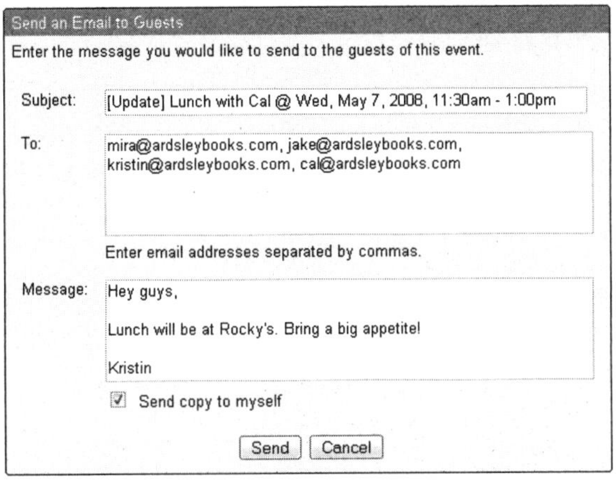

Figure 18-10: E-mail your guests if you want to give them updates or reminders.

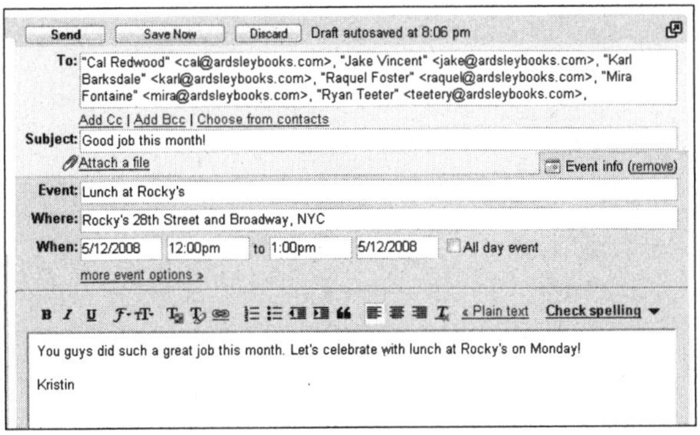

Figure 18-11: Add event details while you're sending an e-mail.

Making a Calendar Available to Others

You can share your calendar with your friends, your soccer team, your family, and your colleagues. When you share with others, you see each other's calendars side by side. By default, your main calendar can be accessed by other Google Apps users in your organization (or Internet domain), but no one outside of it. In the following sections, we cover how to adjust your sharing settings and make your calendar private, if you want.

Sharing options

For each calendar that you manage, you can select how you want to share your events with others. To change these settings, click the down arrow to the right of a calendar in the My Calendars list and choose Share This Calendar from the drop-down list that appears. The Events Details screen appears with the Share This Calendar tab active, similar to Figure 18-12.

We think it's a good idea to create a separate "public" calendar to share with others. This way you can keep your personal events on your main calendar and share your family reunions, work meetings, and so on, without telling people about your doctor appointments.

Figure 18-12: Choose how much information you want to share.

> Ardsley Events Details
>
> Calendar Details **Share this calendar** Notifications
>
> **Share with everyone:**
> Learn more
> ◯ Do not share with everyone
> ◉ Share all information on this calendar with everyone
> ◯ Share only my free / busy information (hide details)
>
> Google Calendar
> Use this button on your site to let others subscribe to this calendar. Get the code
>
> **Share with my domain:**
> Ardsley Books
> ◯ Do not share with everyone in my domain
> ◉ Share all information on this calendar with everyone in my domain
> ◯ Share only my free / busy information with my domain
>
> **Share with specific people:**
> Share with other people or edit who has access.
>
> | PERSON | HAS PERMISSION TO | DELETE |
> |---|---|---|
> | Kristin Salinas <kristin@ardsleybooks.com> | Make changes AND manage sharing | |
> | Cal Redwood <cal@ardsleybooks.com> | Make changes AND manage sharing ▾ | 🗑 |
> | ADD A NEW PERSON: | | |
> | | See all event details ▾ | |
> | | Add Person | |
>
> « Back to Calendar Save Cancel

Depending on what your administrator chooses, you may or may not be able to share details from your main calendar with people outside your organization. Be sure to click the Save button after you make any changes.

The Share This Calendar tab has the following areas:

- ✔ **Share with Everyone:** Choose how much event information you want to make publicly available. If you select any option besides the Do Not Share with Everyone radio button, anyone can search your calendar.

- ✔ **Share with My Domain:** Choose how much information you want your co-workers or colleagues to see.

- ✔ **Share with Specific People:** Allow individuals to view and/or manage events on your calendar. We cover this section in depth in the section that follows.

For the first two sections in the preceding list, you have the following options, which you can change at any time:

- ✓ **Do Not Share with Everyone:** If you select this radio button, no one other than individuals to whom you specifically give permission can access your calendar. This is the most private setting.

- ✓ **Share All Information on This Calendar with Everyone:** Select this radio button if you want your co-workers or anyone, in general, to see your event details. Although we don't recommend using this setting to share your main calendar outside of your domain, you must select this radio button for calendars that you want to post on a Web site.

- ✓ **Share Only My Free/Busy Information (Hide Details):** Select this radio button to allow others to see when you have openings in your schedule but not allow them to see event specifics. They see only blocks labeled Busy in times you have events scheduled, as shown in Figure 18-13.

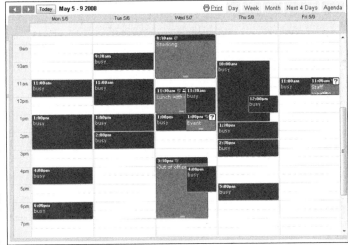

Figure 18-13: Share your time without giving away any details.

Sharing with specific people

Not only can you let others see your calendar events, you can give your friends and co-workers permission to make changes and add events, as well as invite others to join in.

Follow these steps to give a specific person permission to make changes on your calendar:

1. **In the My Calendars list, choose Share This Calendar from the appropriate calendar's drop-down list.**

   The Share This Calendar tab appears (refer to Figure 18-12).

2. **In the Add a New Person textbox, enter the e-mail address of the person with whom you want to share your calendar.**

   If the e-mail address that you're adding is one of your contacts, the name appears automatically below the textbox while you type.

3. **From the drop-down list in the Add a New Person section, choose what permissions you want to give that person. You can choose one of the following options.**

   - *Make Changes AND Manage Sharing*: Your friend or colleague can add, delete, and change events and also allow or deny other people access to make changes to your calendar.

   - *Make Changes to Events*: Your friend or co-worker can add and delete events or make changes to event details on your calendar.

   - *See All Event Details*: Other users can see all of your event details on your calendar, but can't make any changes.

   - *See Free/Busy Information (No Details)*: Other people can see when your events are scheduled, but can't view event details. Events will only read, "Busy." (Refer to Figure 18-13.)

4. **Click the Add Person button.**

   Google Calendar sends an e-mail to that user to let her know that you've shared a calendar; it also adds your calendar to her Google Calendar automatically.

5. **Repeat the steps for any other people with whom you want to share your calendar.**

Scheduling Resources

One of the benefits of having a Google Apps account is that Google Calendar lets you easily find the best time and place for everyone to meet. When you share calendars across your organization, you can view other people's schedules and immediately find the slot that works well for everyone. Coordinating schedules has never been so simple. If you're using Google Apps Premier and Education Edition, you can schedule rooms, equipment, and other resources — so that end-of-year party can go off without a hitch. (Sorry, regular Google Calendar users, you don't get to work with other people's schedules, so go ahead and ignore this section.)

When you need to schedule a meeting and you're not sure what time is optimal for everyone, follow these steps:

1. **Click the Create Event link.**

   You see the Event Details screen, where you can add the specifics of your meeting or party.

2. **Click the Check Guest and Resource Availability link.**

   The Find a Time window appears.

3. **Add a person to the list of attendees by clicking the textbox below the timeline, entering the name or e-mail address of the person that you want to attend, and then clicking the Add button.**

   Every time you click the Add button, each person's schedule appears in the timeline, showing blocks of time that already have events. If your organization is using Google Apps Premier or Education Edition, you also see a Room Finder section below the timeline. The following section explains more about using the Room Finder.

   Now you can find a time that's free for everyone. To move forward or backward a time period, click the blue arrow bars to the right or left of the timeline, or click and drag the gray bar along the top of the timeline left or right.

4. **Highlight a block of time on the timeline that works best for everyone, and then click the OK button in the lower-right corner of the Find a Time window.**

   The thin bar directly below the hours in the schedule shows how heavily people are scheduled. Each busy person at a particular time makes the bar darker. If you can't find a free slot (which appears white in the bar), look for light gray striped areas — only one or two people are busy at that time. Hover your mouse on a busy guest's scheduled block to see the details of that particular event, and then check with that person about the possibility of changing a conflicting appointment.

5. **On the Event Details screen, enter your additional event details, such as a description and reminders, and then click Save.**

   Just as you see when you add guests (see "Creating invitations" earlier in this chapter), a dialog box asks whether you want to send invitations to your attendees.

6. **Click the Send button to send the invitations or the Don't Send button to leave your attendees in the dark (the event will still appear on their calendar).**

With Google Apps Premier and Education Edition, you can schedule rooms and equipment, such as lecture halls, projectors, or company vehicles. When you click the Check Guest and Resource Availability link in the Event Details screen, the Find a Time window opens, and the Room Finder section appears below the timeline. Use the Filter Room list box to quickly find the room or object that you're looking for. If it's available, a green box appears to the left of the room name. If it's not available, a red X appears to the left of it, instead. Just as you do when you add attendees, select a room from the list and click the Add Room button to show the room's schedule.

Using Calendar on Your Mobile Device

If you don't have a cellphone, go to your nearest cellphone store and buy one. They really are cool. Plus, when you have one, you can access Google Calendar events from it or virtually any mobile device. Woohoo!

The following list describes the two ways that you can access your calendar on a mobile device (we cover both in more detail in the sections that follow):

- ✔ **Google Calendar for Mobile:** This method allows you to access a feature-rich version of your calendar on an iPhone, BlackBerry, or other XHTML-capable phone.

- ✔ **Short Messaging Service (SMS):** That's a fancy name for text messaging. Send a text message to Google, and it messages you back with your schedule details. This method is perfect for when you're on the run and need to know where you're heading next.

As always, text messaging and mobile phone data plans generally aren't free. Please check with your mobile provider first to see whether you have access and can afford it. Don't blame us if your next cellphone bill rivals your rent or mortgage payment.

Using Google Calendar for Mobile

To access Google Calendar for Mobile, open your mobile Web browser and enter your direct calendar address (it's probably similar to the address you use to access your normal Google Calendar; for example, `http://calendar.ardleybooks.com`). A login screen may appear, asking you to enter your username and password. After your calendar loads, a simplified version of it appears in Agenda mode, similar to the image on the right of Figure 18-14.

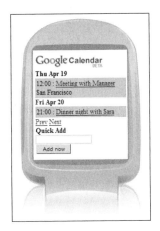

Figure 18-14:
Access your
calendar
from your
smartphone
(left) or
other mobile
device
(right).

To navigate your calendar, click any of the links on the screen. Clicking an event reveals its details. Click the Quick Add textbox, enter the event's information, and then click Add Now to add a new event.

You can enter Quick Add events in phrase form, such as `Tennis lessons every Thursday at 9am.`

Scheduling with SMS

Text messaging is a quick, easy way to find out what's coming up on your schedule — especially when you're away from your computer. You need to register your phone with your calendar first, though. Flip to the earlier section, "Registering your mobile phone to receive notifications," which explains how to set up calendar notifications on your mobile phone.

After you set up your phone with Google Calendar, you can simply send a text message with one of the commands in the following bullet list to GVENT (48368), and you receive a text message giving you the event information you request.

Although you can use the GVENT service free, your mobile carrier may charge for each text message that you send and receive. Check your plan before using GVENT extensively.

Send any one of these commands in a text message to GVENT and wait for a response:

More resources for Google Calendar

If you want to know more about Google Calendar than we cover in this book, we're happy to point you to some great resources:

✔ **Google Calendar Help Center:** Go to www.google.com/support/a/users to find answers to frequently asked questions, find out how to communicate with other calendar programs, or troubleshoot an issue. You can also get to the Help Center by clicking the Help link at the top of your calendar page.

✔ **What's new with Google Calendar:** Google Calendar is always changing, so find out what new bells and whistles those amazing engineers are adding by going to www.google.com/googlecalendar/new.html.

✔ **NEXT:** Receive the upcoming event for the day.

✔ **DAY:** Receive an agenda of today's events.

✔ **NDAY:** Receive an agenda of tomorrow's events.

✔ **"Meeting tomorrow at 2pm":** Send event details to create a new event on your calendar via Quick Add. Remember that Google Calendar breaks down your Quick Add requests into common phrases and tries to guess what you meant. Pretty smart, if you ask us.

✔ **HELP:** Receive a list of these commands.

✔ **STOP:** Remove your phone number from Google Calendar to stop notifications and other calendar messages. You have to reregister your phone to use GVENT again.

Chapter 19

Communicating with Gmail

Does the daily ritual of purging your Inbox besiege you? Messages appear unrelentingly. Responding to e-mail can eat into your day, taking valuable time away from more important tasks, such as enjoying a leisurely lunch. Many of these e-mails are trivial, others are inane, and then you have *spam* — unsolicited ads for products too bizarre to mention. For businesses, schools, and agencies, e-mail has become a necessary evil. It's costly to maintain, mailboxes are limited, and service is often hurt by a lack of local resources.

Gmail is Google's answer to the daily e-mail onslaught and the hassle businesses, schools, and agencies face maintaining their own systems. It's Google's interpretation of how e-mail should work. Gmail can help you battle back and get control of your Inbox, eliminating many of the frustrations associated with the spam-clogged, virus-ridden e-mail systems of the past.

Setting Up E-Mail

Electronic mail finds its way through the Internet by following an address. Every e-mail address, such as `calredwood@ardsleybooks.com`, has three parts:

✔ The username, nickname, buddy name, or handle of the account owner. In our example, the username is `calredwood`.

✔ The characteristic @ sign (pronounced "at").

✔ The name of the domain or Web site that hosts the e-mail service. In our example, the domain name is `ardsleybooks.com`.

Starting Gmail

You can get to your Gmail account a couple of ways. The most convenient method is to use the Email gadget on your organization's start page or on a Sites page that you've designed.

If, for some reason, you don't want to use a gadget, you can access your e-mail directly at `http://mail.google.com` if you have a personal account. If you are a Google Apps user, enter **mail** followed by the domain name of your organization in the address bar and press Enter; for example, an employee of Ardsley Books would use the address `http://mail.ardsleybooks.com`. This address takes you to your Gmail login page, where you can log into your e-mail account.

You need to log in with your username and password every time you begin a new session of Gmail unless you select the Remember Me on This Computer option when it appears.

Getting to Know the Inbox

Any message coming to you arrives in your Inbox. From your Inbox, you can access any feature within Gmail by using the Navigation panel on the left side of the screen and the other links around the page. Here are the key parts, as shown in Figure 19-1:

- ✔ **Links to other Google Apps:** Quickly jump to your start page, calendar, documents, and more by clicking the links in the top-left corner of the screen.

- ✔ **Your e-mail address:** In case you forget, Gmail gives you a friendly reminder at the top.

If you have more than one Gmail account, you can always tell which account you're currently using by looking at your e-mail address at the top of the Gmail window.

- ✔ **Search Mail and Search the Web:** Enter a term in the textbox and click the Search Mail button to search your messages for the term; click the Search the Web button to do a normal Google search.

- ✔ **Compose Mail:** Click this link to open a message window in which to write a new e-mail message.

- ✔ **Inbox, Starred, Chats, Sent Mail, Drafts, All Mail, Spam, and Trash:** These links in the left column take you to the standard folders that hold your messages.

✔ **Contacts:** This section lets you manage your Contacts list, not just for Gmail, but also for your Video Chat, Talk, and Calendar apps. Jump ahead to Chapter 20 to find more about this essential tool.

✔ **Incoming messages:** Your messages appear in the center of the screen, and any new messages appear in bold. Messages that you already read have a shaded background.

✔ **Labels:** Your messages can be tagged with multiple labels. Labels are similar to traditional folders but are much more flexible.

Figure 19-1: Find everything in Gmail's Inbox.

Gmail encourages users to archive old messages, not trash them. With so much storage available, you don't need to delete messages that may have possible importance later. Google can make this suggestion confidently because, no matter how many messages you archive, you can find the one you need quickly with Google's powerful search technologies. If Google can find exactly what you need from the billions of pages on the Internet, imagine what it can do when searching a relatively tiny Inbox. More on Search later!

Composing Mail

When you're ready to create an e-mail message, click the Compose Mail link in the left column of your Inbox, which opens an e-mail form. E-mail forms are organized into fields. A few fields are required; others are optional. We discuss each of these fields in detail in the following sections. As shown in Figure 19-2, the main parts of the mail form are

Figure 19-2:
The
Compose
Mail form.

✔ **Header:** The header section includes the To and Subject textboxes. It also includes the Add Cc, Add Bcc, and Attach a File links, as well as the Send, Save Now, and Discard buttons.

- *To:* Enter the e-mail address of the primary recipients in the To box. (If you can't remember an e-mail address, click the Choose from Contacts link to choose a name from the Contacts list.)

- *Add Cc:* Referred to by its historical name, carbon copy, or by an updated name, courtesy copy. Enter an e-mail address in the Cc box if you're simply informing someone of a message sent primarily to others.

- *Add Bcc:* Known as blind courtesy copy. Enter e-mail addresses in this box for those who you want to inform about a message, but need to hide from others that they received it. Sneaky, isn't it?

- *Add Event Invitation:* Click this link to add appointment details to your message and create a new event on your calendar. If your recipient uses Google Calendar or Outlook, the event will appear on their calendar, as well.

✔ **Body:** The meat of the message goes in the message, or body, field. This section also includes the Formatting toolbar and Check Spelling tools.

To send an e-mail message, follow these basic steps:

1. **Click the To textbox and enter the addresses of those to which you want to send the message.**

    This is a required field. If you don't put at least one e-mail address in this textbox, you get a plea from Gmail reading, "Please specify at least one recipient." Optionally, click the Add Cc link to see the Cc and Bcc textboxes.

2. **(Optional) Type a comma and then enter another e-mail address.**

   You can add as many e-mail addresses as you want. Gmail automatically enters the open (‹) and close (›) angle brackets that appear before and after e-mail addresses. You don't need to enter them.

3. **Click the Subject textbox and enter a subject.**

   In the Subject textbox, enter a few descriptive words to let your reader know what the e-mail message is about.

4. **Click the message field and type what you want to say.**

5. **Click the Send button.**

Gmail automatically adds the e-mail address of anyone you e-mail, or anyone who e-mails you, to your Contacts list. When you begin entering a few letters in the To or Cc textbox, Gmail anticipates the address you're typing and displays recipient names containing those letters. Arrow down to select the correct e-mail address. When it appears highlighted, press Enter or just choose it from the list. (You can find out much more about your Contacts list later in this chapter.)

Composing and formatting messages

You compose all of your great one-liners, tell your jokes, speak your mind, and set things straight in the message (or body) field. Simply click the body textbox and start typing.

You can use the formatting buttons just above the body textbox to apply bold, italic, colors, highlighting, and other formatting to your text. To apply text formatting, simply highlight the text that you want to format and then click the appropriate formatting button.

Attaching files

You can attach any file to an e-mail: a word processing document, a spreadsheet, a picture of your dog Charlie, or that video of your recent fishing trip. To attach a file to your message, follow these steps:

1. **Click the Attach a File link that appears below the Subject textbox.**

2. **Browse to the particular file that you need, select it, and then click the Open button.**

   The name of the attached file appears just below the subject line in your e-mail form.

3. **If you want to add another file, click the Attach Another File link that appears below the name of the file you attached.**

Sending, saving, or discarding

After you finish composing your message and adding attachments, you have three options:

✔ **Send:** Click the Send button and your message whisks across the Internet.

✔ **Save Now:** If you're having second thoughts about sending a particular e-mail message, or if you simply haven't finished it yet, you can save it and work on it later. To save your message, click Save Now.

✔ **Discard:** Okay, you vented, exaggerated, or suddenly realized you don't know what the heck you're talking about. No harm done. Just click the Discard button and forget the whole thing.

Stacking Up a Gmail Conversation

Gmail records the back-and-forth between people as though it were a natural conversation. Gmail stacks replies, one on top of another. The most recent replies appear at the top. In Google parlance, this is a *conversation stack*.

The Inbox displays each message's subject line, followed by a snippet of the message. These bits of information give you clues as to what the conversation is about. You can tell how many reply cards are in the stack by the number that appears in parentheses after the senders' names, as shown in Figure 19-3. You can also see the date a message or reply was sent at the end of the snippet.

Figure 19-3: View conversations in your Inbox.

A conversation appears as a stack of messages, as shown in Figure 19-4. Think of a stack as a pile of cards, each containing the next part of a conversation. To view any part of the conversation in the stack, pick it from the list by clicking on the message's sender, subject line, or date.

Stacked headers give you a lot of information and several options. First, you can tell exactly when the reply was sent by looking in the top-right corner of any message in the stack. Also, you can send related e-mails from each stack in the conversation as follows:

- **Reply:** Reply only to the sender. You can find a Reply link at both the top and the bottom of the message.

- **Reply to All:** Click Reply to All to send a reply to everyone involved in the conversation. (Find Reply to All by clicking the down arrow next to the Reply button or jump to the bottom of the message window.)

- **Forward:** Send a copy of the e-mail message to anyone you want: the news media, your boss, the Federal Trade Commission, Homeland Security . . . (Find Forward by clicking the down arrow next to the Reply button or jump to the bottom of the message window.)

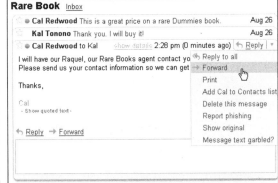

Figure 19-4: Quickly reply to a conversation.

Very few people enjoy sifting through replies that don't apply to them. The Reply to All command has annoyed millions of unhappy cubicle inhabitants in offices all over the world, so click it thoughtfully. If you're sending a reply intended for a single recipient, don't send it to everyone listed in the header.

Collapsing and expanding stacks

After you open a conversation stack, it appears in a collapsed view with the most recent reply at the bottom. To expand the stack so that you can view all the conversations, click the Expand All link (it's to the right of the conversation stack). To collapse the conversations, click the Collapse All link. To read just one reply or part of the conversation, click the snippet or header at the top of the particular message.

To break away from a conversation stack, start by replying to the last message. Click the Edit Subject link, enter a new subject, and send your new message. Any replies to this new message appear in a separate stack.

Marking important messages

Gmail gives you a simple way to highlight important messages. Whether you're in the Inbox or viewing a conversation, simply click the Star icon on the left side of the message header, and a bright, shiny star appears in the icon's place. (See Figure 19-5.) Remove a star by clicking the Star icon again.

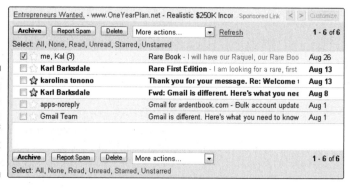

Figure 19-5:
Mark the stars to the left of important messages.

To view just the messages that you've starred, click the Starred link in the left column. (Clicking the Inbox link shows you all of your current messages again.)

In the Inbox, the check boxes to the left of the Star icons allow you to select multiple messages at the same time. After you select the check boxes, you can perform the following actions to all the selected messages.

✔ **Archive:** Archiving conversations places selected messages in storage and removes them from your Inbox. Archiving is a great way to save your messages, but still remove them from your Inbox so you don't have to deal with the clutter.

✔ **Report Spam:** If you receive spam, select that message's check box and let Gmail know about it by clicking the Report Spam button. Reporting spam helps Gmail do a better job of stopping it.

✔ **Delete:** Clicking the Delete button removes conversations from your Gmail account. Deleting a message only places the message in the Trash folder. To get rid of the message permanently, you must go into the Trash folder and delete it again from that screen (or leave it — any mail in the trash more than 30 days gets automatically deleted).

Searching Your Messages

You can use the same powerful Google Search tools that allow you to find exactly what you need on the Internet to find a lost message in your Inbox or in your Archived messages folder. To search your e-mail account for a particular message, follow these steps:

1. **Click the search box that appears at the top of every Gmail account page and enter a search term.**

   You can search for e-mail addresses, subjects, or even text within a message. For example, say you remember only a snippet of an e-mail sent to you, such as *Uncle Jake is having a birthday*. Enter the keywords **jake birthday**. The same rules that apply to a Google search on the Internet apply to your e-mail searches, as well:

   • Statistics point out that a phrase of two to five words is better than a single keyword in narrowing a search.

   • If you put words in quotation marks (" "), Google searches for that exact phrase.

   • You don't need to use capitalization.

2. **Click the Search Mail button.**

   As shown in Figure 19-6, Gmail returns a list of messages that contain the term(s) you enter in the search box in Step 1.

Figure 19-6:
Search your
conversa-
tions by
using the
Search Mail
feature.

Opening Attachments

Every time you receive documents, spreadsheets, images, or presentations as attachments, you have several ways you can open them directly from Gmail:

✔ **View as HTML:** The first option is to view the attachment as a Web page right in your browser. You don't need any special plug-ins or software to view an attachment as HTML because Google uses special tools to extract the text and graphics so that you can preview the document right away. This method is also the fastest way to get to your important proposal or budget report. It works for PDF attachments, too.

✔ **Open as a Google Document or Spreadsheet:** Rather than save the document to your computer, you can simply choose to open the attachment as a Google document or spreadsheet, or view a presentation as a slideshow, directly in your browser.

When you open an attachment in Google Docs, you can view and edit the document right away. Gmail copies the document into your Docs Home, and you can access that document any time you login to Google Docs.

✔ **Download:** For documents that have advanced formatting, or don't open easily as HTML or a Google document, you still have the traditional file download method. Click the Download link to the right of the attachment. The File Download dialog box appears, asking whether you want to open or save the file. If you would like to find the file on your computer later, we recommend that you click the Save button to save the file. The Save As dialog box appears, giving you the option to navigate to the folder on your computer where you want to save the file. Finally, click the Save button to save the file.

Mail messages that contain multiple attachments also give you the option to download all your files at the same time in a Zipped archive. Click the Download All Attachments link to start saving yourself a lot of time by downloading one smaller file.

Don't forget, Google automatically scans your attachments for viruses. To keep you extra safe, Gmail never accepts attachments that contain executable files (files that end in .exe) or archives that contain executables. If you need to send or receive those types of files, you have to resort to another method of transporting the files, such as using an FTP or file transfer site (such as YouSendIt.com).

If you really must send an executable file using Gmail, try this: On your computer, change the .exe extension to .zip or .ppt and attach it to your e-mail. Then let your recipient know that they should change the extension back to .exe when they download it to their computer.

Creating Signatures and Vacation Responses

If it's imperative that people can readily get in touch with you, it's a good idea to let them know alternate ways of contacting you other than via your e-mail address. You can do this by adding a signature that contains your contact information. A *signature* is a block of text automatically appended to the end of your outgoing e-mail messages. Additionally, *vacation responses,* which send an automated response to all your incoming e-mail messages while you're away, help people know when you're unavailable, whether you're on a trip to Hawaii, or spending a quiet weekend at home.

Adding a signature

To add a signature, log into your Gmail Inbox and click the Settings link in the top-right corner. Halfway down the Settings page, look for the Signature box.

You can type whatever you want in the Signature box, but most people include their name, a phone number, perhaps a Web site URL, and a random quote (such as a Zen saying that makes absolutely no sense to anyone who's not a monk). To make your signature active, make sure that the radio button to the left of the signature box is selected, and then click the Save Changes button at the bottom of the Settings page. After you activate your signature, it appears in the message body automatically, as Figure 19-7 illustrates.

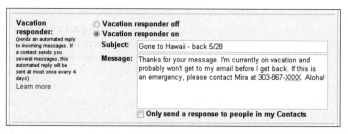

Figure 19-7:
New
messages
add the
signature
auto-
matically.

Mira,

Could you please send me that slideshow for the upcoming meeting?

Thanks,
Cal

--
Cal Redwood
President, Ardsley Books
303-867-XXXX
cal@ardsleybooks.com

Send   Save Now   Discard

Turning the vacation responder on and off

When you're ready for your break from the everyday onslaught of e-mail, flip the switch to turn on your vacation responder. A vacation responder lets people know that you're on vacation, out of the office, or don't want to get back to them right away. When they e-mail you, Gmail automatically sends a message of your choosing informing them that you are unavailable, so they don't have to worry when you don't get back to them in two seconds flat. To turn your vacation responder on, follow these steps:

1. **Log into Gmail.**

2. **Click the Settings link in the top-right corner of the screen.**

   Near the bottom of the page, you can see the Vacation Responder section, as shown in Figure 19-8.

Figure 19-8:
Add a
vacation
responder
on the
Settings
page.

Vacation
responder:
(sends an automated reply
to incoming messages. If
a contact sends you
several messages, this
automated reply will be
sent at most once every 4
days)
Learn more

○ Vacation responder off
⦿ Vacation responder on
Subject: Gone to Hawaii - back 5/28
Message: Thanks for your message. I'm currently on vacation and
probably won't get to my email before I get back. If this is
an emergency, please contact Mira at 303-867-XXXX. Aloha!

☐ Only send a response to people in my Contacts

3. **Select the Vacation Responder On radio button.**

4. **Click the Subject and Message textboxes and enter a subject and message that lets people know you're on vacation (or otherwise unavailable).**

If you use your Gmail for business, give contact information for someone who can cover for you while you're unavailable.

5. **(Optional) If you don't want everyone to know that you've snuck off on a weekend getaway to Rome, select the Only Send a Response to People in My Contacts check box.**

   When you select this check box, only people you know receive the message from your vacation responder.

6. **Click the Save Changes button.**

When you activate your vacation responder, a peach-colored notification bar appears along the top of your Gmail page. To turn off your responder, click the End Now link on the right side of the bar (or select the Vacation Responder Off radio button in Step 3). If you want to make changes or update your e-mail response, click the Vacation Settings link to the right of the End Now link.

Vacation responders send only one e-mail per address every four days, and you can have only one vacation responder active at a time. Hopefully, your friends and associates catch the drift the first time.

Using Labels and Filters

You can whip your Inbox into shape by using labels and filters. *Labels* are like folders, only better — they sort and organize your messages so that you can easily find a particular message later. *Filters* are sets of rules that every new e-mail message is checked against; if the message matches a rule, then Gmail performs an action with the message, such as starring or deleting it.

How can labels and filters help you? Imagine sending all your incoming work-related messages to one folder and your travel plans to another. Filters let you tell Gmail exactly where the messages should go, and labels help you organize messages that you've already received.

Labeling your messages

If you've used other e-mail programs, you're probably used to creating folders and storing your messages in them. The problem is you have to remember in which folder you placed those messages. Labels alleviate memory lapses by allowing you to tag messages and view all your similarly tagged messages in a list, much like a folder. Unlike folders, however, you don't have to move any messages around, and you can easily tag a message with multiple labels.

To create labels, click the Edit Labels link in the Labels list in the bottom-left corner of any Gmail screen. You can also click the Settings link at the top of the screen and then click the Labels tab, as shown in Figure 19-9. On the Labels tab, you can do the following:

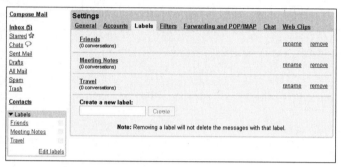

Figure 19-9: Click the Edit Labels link to add, rename, and remove labels.

✔ **Add a new label:** Click the Create a New Label textbox, enter the new label's name, and then click the Create button.

✔ **Rename a label:** Click the Rename link to the right of the label that you want to change. A blue box appears, allowing you to change the label name or enter a new label name. Click OK when you're done, to return to the Labels Settings screen.

✔ **Delete a label:** Click the Remove link to the right of the label name. A dialog box appears, asking whether you really want to remove the label. Click OK, and the label disappears.

When you're ready to tag a message or two, return to the Inbox. Select the check box to the left of the message(s) that you want to tag, and then choose a label from the More Actions list at the top of the screen. The label that you choose now appears to the left of your message's subject, and your message now appears when you click the corresponding label link on the left side of the screen.

You can also customize your labels by adding colors. Click the color square to the right of a label in the Labels list and choose the color that you want. Dark and bold colors can really make more-important messages stand out.

Creating new filters

Filters help keep your Inbox free of clutter by automatically performing an action on a message as soon as it's received, such as deleting any message from a certain e-mail address. You can create as many filters as you want; you can best keep your Inbox clutter free by creating a good number of filters.

Creating effective filters involves two steps. First, choose the type of messages that you want to filter; second, choose an action that you want Gmail to perform on those messages.

To create a new filter, follow these steps:

1. **Log into your Google Apps Gmail (if you haven't already).**

2. **Click the Settings link at the top of the screen.**

3. **Click the Filters tab. (See Figure 19-10.)**

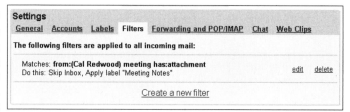

Settings
General   Accounts   Labels   Filters   Forwarding and POP/IMAP   Chat   Web Clips

The following filters are applied to all incoming mail:

Matches: **from:(Cal Redwood) meeting has:attachment**   edit   delete
Do this: Skip Inbox, Apply label "Meeting Notes"

Create a new filter

4. **Click the Create a New Filter link.**

5. **Describe what messages you want the filter to catch by filling in the Choose Search Criteria textboxes. (See Figure 19-11.)**

6. **Click the Next Step button and then select the appropriate check boxes on the Choose Action screen that appears.**

   See the later "Choose an action" section for details.

7. **Click the Create Filter button to create your filter.**

Choose your search criteria

You have six different ways to filter the messages, and you can use any combination to help you narrow your list of filtered messages further.

- ✔ **From:** Enter an e-mail address or the name of a person or company that you want to filter, such as **cal@ardsleybooks.com** or **Cal**.

- ✔ **To:** Find messages that were sent to another person. You can also use this option to find messages that were sent to a mailing list.

- ✔ **Subject:** Enter keywords that appear in the message's subject line.

- ✔ **Has the Words:** Enter keywords that may appear anywhere in the message, including the subject and address fields.

- ✔ **Doesn't Have:** Enter keywords in this textbox to show messages that don't contain a specific word or e-mail address.

The keywords in all the fields work together to limit your search results. For example, enter **wall** in the Has the Words textbox and enter **facebook** in the Doesn't Have textbox to find messages from the *Wall Street Journal,* but not messages notifying you that someone wrote on your Facebook Wall.

✔ **Has Attachment:** Select this check box to filter messages that contain attachments. This setting is also useful in conjunction with keywords in other fields.

Figure 19-11: Choose your filter's search criteria.

If you want to use the same action for messages that have many different fields, type **OR** or a comma between the keywords, such as **delta OR united OR american airlines OR continental** for travel-related messages and **facebook, myspace, linkedin** for messages from social networking sites.

After you enter the keywords, click the Test Search button to see how well the filter works on your existing messages. A list appears just below your filter box, showing you all the messages that match your search criteria.

Choose an action

In the Choose an Action screen, you need to decide what to do with your newly filtered messages. You can choose from six different options, and you can select more than one action to perform, as shown in Figure 19-12.

Figure 19-12: Add an action or two to your filtered messages.

Create a Filter

Choose action - Now, select the action you'd like to take on messages that match the criteria you specified.

When a message arrives that matches the search: **from:(Cal Redwood) meeting has:attachment**, do the following:

☑ Skip the Inbox(Archive it)
☐ Mark as read
☐ Star it
☑ Apply the label: Meeting Notes ▾
☐ Forward it to:
☐ Delete it

Show current filters | Cancel | ‹ Back | **Update Filter** | ☐ Also apply filter to **0 conversations** below.

You can choose one or more of the following actions:

- ✔ **Skip the Inbox (Archive It):** Select this option to have the message automatically sent to the All Mail label.

- ✔ **Mark as Read:** Choose this action and filtered messages no longer appear bold and therefore don't show up as new messages.

- ✔ **Star It:** Highlight important messages with a Star icon.

- ✔ **Apply the Label:** Select this check box, click the arrow to the right of Apply the Label, and choose a label from the drop-down list. Filtered messages will have this label attached automatically, allowing you to access them quickly by clicking the label on the left side of your Gmail screen.

- ✔ **Forward It To:** Select this check box, click in the textbox to the right of Forward It To, and enter the address to which you want the message forwarded.

- ✔ **Delete It:** Select this check box to create your own spam filter — you never even have to see the message.

Adjusting filters later

After you set up a filter, you may find that it doesn't run quite how you want it to. Follow these steps to adjust a filter you've set up:

1. **Click the Settings link at the top of the screen and then click the Filters tab.**

   The Filters tab lists all the filters you've created.

2. **Click the Edit link to the right of the filter that you want to change.**

   The Choose Search Criteria screen appears and shows what you previously entered for the filter.

3. **Change the options in the Choose Search Criteria screen as desired. (Refer to the earlier "Choose your search criteria" section for details.) Click the Next Step button.**

4. **Change the options in the Choose Action screen as desired. (Refer to the preceding section for details.) Click the Update Filter button.**

If you don't like the filter after all, click the Delete link to the right of the filter, and that filter disappears forever.

Alternative Access: Forwarding, POP/IMAP, and Mobile

In the following sections, we cover how to enable forwarding so that you can send your e-mail somewhere other than your Gmail Inbox (if your administrator allows you to), how to sync Outlook with your Gmail mailbox with POP or IMAP, and even how to check your messages on the go from your Web-enabled mobile phone.

Turning forwarding on and off

E-mail forwarding is one of the best ways to consolidate e-mail from multiple addresses. If your Google Apps Gmail account isn't your primary account, you can turn forwarding on in two clicks and pass your Gmail messages on to your primary account.

If you have a personal Gmail account, you can also use this option to forward your personal e-mail to your Google Apps account. Then you only have to look in one place for all your messages.

To set up forwarding for your Google Apps e-mail, log into Gmail and click the Settings link in the top-right corner of the screen. Click the Forwarding and POP/IMAP tab, as shown in Figure 19-13.

Figure 19-13:
Decide what
you want
to do with
forwarded
messages.

Settings
General Accounts Labels Filters Forwarding and POP/IMAP Chat Web Clips
Forwarding: ○ Disable forwarding
◉ Forward a copy of incoming mail to cal@mydomain.net   and
keep Ardsley Books's copy in the Inbox ▾
keep Ardsley Books's copy in the Inbox
Tip: archive Ardsley Books's copy   ng a filter!
delete Ardsley Books's copy

Here's a brief description of what you can do in the Forwarding and POP/IMAP tab:

- ✔ **Disable Forwarding:** Select this radio button if you don't want your messages going anywhere.

- ✔ **Forward a Copy of Incoming Mail:** Select this radio button to send a copy of all incoming messages to another address. Enter the address that you want your messages to go to in the textbox, and click the arrow below Forward a Copy of Incoming Mail, and then choose one of the following options from the drop-down list that appears:

- *Keep Gmail's Copy in the Inbox:* Everything happens invisibly. Your messages are forwarded, and Gmail never knows.

- *Archive Gmail's Copy:* New messages don't appear in the Inbox, but you still can read them from your Gmail account by clicking the All Mail link.

- *Delete Gmail's Copy:* Gmail deletes forwarded messages from your Gmail account.

If you want to forward only certain messages, create a filter (flip to the section, "Creating new filters," earlier in this chapter) and check the Forward It To check box in the Choose Action screen. Enter an address in the Forward It To textbox, and Gmail passes on only those select messages to the address you specify.

Sending mail from different accounts

When you have several e-mail addresses to manage, such as your personal one, one for work, and one for your soccer league, Gmail makes it easy to send and receive all your messages in one place, from up to five different accounts.

To add an account, follow these steps:

1. **Click the Settings link in the top-right corner of the Gmail main page.**

   The Gmail Settings screen appears with tabs along the top.

2. **In the Settings screen, click the Accounts tab, which you can see in Figure 19-14.**

Figure 19-14: Use the Accounts tab in Settings to send e-mail from another address.

3. **In the Send Mail As section, click the Add Another Email Address link.**

   A new window opens, asking you for the name and address that you want to add.

4. **Fill in the information and click the Next Step button.**

   The screen that appears asks you to verify that you are, in fact, the owner of the address you enter in this step.

5. **Click the Send Verification button.**

   The next screen asks you to enter a verification code. When you click the Send Verification button, the Gmail team sends a message to your other e-mail account. Because the message contains a link that will automatically verify your account, you can skip entering the verification code at this time and simply close the verification window. This should take you back to your Gmail screen.

6. **In a new browser window, log into the e-mail account that you enter in Step 4 and look for the new message from the Gmail team.**

7. **Open the message and click the very long, cryptic-looking link to verify your address.**

   If you leave the window open in Step 5, you can copy and paste the verification code from the message into that window and click the Verify button.

Congratulations! Now your other e-mail address is verified. The next time you compose a new message in Gmail, the From field is a drop-down list from which you can select your Google Apps e-mail address or your other e-mail account.

Activating POP or IMAP

POP (Post Office Protocol) and IMAP (Internet Message Access Protocol) both provide you access to your Gmail messages from other e-mail programs, such as Microsoft Outlook, Apple Mail, and Mozilla Thunderbird.

To activate POP or IMAP, follow these steps:

1. **Log into Gmail and click the Settings link at the top of the Gmail page.**

2. **Click the Forwarding and POP/IMAP tab.**

   Your screen should look similar to Figure 19-15.

3. **To turn on IMAP, select the Enable IMAP radio button.**

4. **(Optional) To turn on POP, select the Enable POP for All Mail radio button or the Enable POP for Mail That Arrives from Now On radio button.**

5. **Click the Save Changes button.**

POP Download: Learn more	1. **Status: POP is disabled** ⦿ Enable POP for **all mail** ○ Enable POP for **mail that arrives from now on** 2. **When messages are accessed with POP** [keep Ardsley Books's copy in the Inbox ▾] 3. **Configure your email client** (e.g. Outlook, Eudora, Netscape Mail) Configuration instructions
IMAP Access: (access Ardsley Books from other clients using IMAP) Learn more	1. **Status: IMAP is disabled** ⦿ Enable IMAP ○ Disable IMAP 2. **Configure your email client** (e.g. Outlook, Thunderbird, iPhone) Configuration instructions
	[Save Changes] [Cancel]

Figure 19-15:
Enable POP
or IMAP
from the
Settings
screen.

Configuring Outlook to work with Gmail

Many users are familiar with Microsoft Outlook, so we put together some step-by-step instructions to get your Gmail account up and running in Outlook using IMAP.

Google has instructions online to help you configure many other e-mail software programs for IMAP or POP. To access these instructions, log into your Gmail account, click the Settings link at the top of the screen, click the Forwarding and POP/IMAP tab, and click the appropriate Configuration Instructions link.

To configure Outlook for Gmail access:

1. **Make sure IMAP is enabled (see the preceding section to find how to enable IMAP), and then open Outlook.**

2. **Choose Tools⇨E-mail Accounts.**

   A new window appears with Outlook's e-mail accounts setup screen.

3. **Select the Add a New E-mail Account radio button and then click Next.**

4. **On the Server Type screen that appears, select the IMAP radio button and then click Next.**

5. **In the Internet E-mail Settings screen that appears, fill in all necessary textboxes with the following information (as wehave in Figure 19-16):**

   • *User Information:* Enter your name in the Your Name textbox how you want others to see it when they receive mail from you. In the E-mail Address textbox, enter the full Google Apps e-mail address (**user@*yourdomain.com***).

   • *Server Information:* In the Incoming Mail Server textbox, type **imap. gmail.com**. In the Outgoing Mail Server (SMTP) textbox, enter **smtp.gmail.com**.

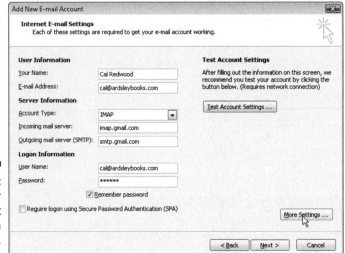

Figure 19-16:
Enter your
account
settings in
Outlook.

- *Logon Information:* Type your full Google Apps e-mail address (**user@*yourdomain.com***) in the User Name textbox and enter your password in the Password textbox.

6. **Click the More Settings button and then click the Outgoing Server tab in the Internet E-mail Settings window that appears.**

7. **Select the My Outgoing Server (SMTP) Requires Authentication check box and then select the Use Same Settings as My Incoming Mail Server check box.**

8. **Click the Advanced tab.**

9. **Below Incoming Server (IMAP), click the arrow to the right of Use the Following Type of Encrypted Connection, choose SSL from the drop-down list that appears, and then enter 993 in the textbox to the right of Incoming Server (IMAP).**

10. **Below Outgoing Server (SMTP), click the arrow to the right of Use the Following Type of Encrypted Connection, choose SSL from the drop-down list that appears, enter 465 in the textbox to the right of Outgoing Server (SMTP), and then click OK.**

11. **Click the Test Account Settings button to make sure that everything works correctly.**

12. **Click the Close button to close the Congratulations dialog box.**

13. **On the Internet E-mail Settings screen, click Next and then click the Finish button.**

Be sure to download the latest updates for Outlook at http://update. microsoft.com.

Accessing Gmail from your mobile device

We're not sure whether you're the type of person who sits on the edge of your seat waiting for your next e-mail to arrive and responds to those messages as fast as they come, or whether you're the casual type who's content with just checking your e-mail occasionally. No matter your level of e-mail anxiety, Gmail makes it easy to check your messages, even when you're away from a computer.

Google's new Android phones are perfectly suited for Gmail and the other Google Apps. If you have an Android-enabled phone, Gmail and Calendar icons appear in your launcher. Simply open the apps and log into your account to access your messages on the go.

If you're a BlackBerry debutant, open your mobile browser and go to `http://m.google.com/a` to download a special Gmail client. This application gives you many of the same features as the normal Gmail interface. Simply log in by using your Google Apps account username and password, and you're good to go.

iPhone fanatics can use the iPhone's built-in Mail client to access Gmail, as well. If you want your messages to sync back to the main program, be sure to set up a custom IMAP account. (See the earlier "Activating POP or IMAP" section to find out how to set up an IMAP account.) You can find detailed instructions for setting up Gmail on your iPhone by logging into Gmail, clicking the Settings link at the top of the screen, clicking the Forwarding and POP/IMAP tab on the Settings page, and finally, clicking the Configuration Instructions link.

If you have a simple Web-enabled phone, open your phone's Web browser application and navigate to `www.gmail.com` or `http://mail.your domain.com`. Enter your Google Apps account username and password on the login page that appears, and then press the Sign In button. Links to your messages and your labels appear in a very simple, easy-to-use format.

Chapter 20

Enhancing Communication with Google Contacts, Chat, and Talk

*T*his chapter is all about creating, adding to, and using your Contacts list with Gmail, Gmail Chat, and Google Talk. Your Contacts list also fuels your Google Calendar (which we talk about in Chapter 18). After all, you need to keep track of the people you communicate with, and Google helps you in that task with its sophisticated *Contacts list.*

The Contacts list is a powerful database where you keep track of your friends, co-workers, and other online acquaintances. In addition to e-mail addresses, the Contacts list lets you add address, phone numbers, photos, important dates, and other notes about your favorite people. If you have a Google Apps account, other users in your domain are added automatically. When you invite people to chat, they appear in the Chat panel to the left of your Gmail screen and in Google Talk.

Growing Your Contacts List

If all you need from the Contacts list is a little help addressing your e-mail, that's valuable enough. But if you want to get the most out of this potent tool, take a few minutes and browse through the following pages.

Gmail automatically adds a contact to Suggested Contacts when you reply to a message from someone. The Contacts list also accumulates addresses and information when you're using the Google Chat and Talk Apps. You can use your Contacts list a little or a lot, depending on your needs. For instance:

✔ In Google Talk and Chat, your contacts are monitored to see who's online and who's available.

✔ In Gmail, the Contacts list allows you to enter just part of a name and have the most likely choices appear so you don't have to type the entire e-mail address in the To textbox .

✔ In Google Calendar, you can use your Contacts list to facilitate the scheduling of attendees, rooms, and resources for meetings and events.

Viewing your contacts

Want to find your Contacts list? Okay, pay attention. If you blink, you may miss this:

1. **Open Gmail.**

2. **Click the Contacts link in the left panel.**

If your Google Apps administrator has set everything up according to Hoyle, you should see a list of the people in your organization — that is, all the colleagues in your domain listing. For example, all the employees at Ardsley Books were automatically added into the Contacts list shown in Figure 20-1. Groups that the organization created are also included in the Contacts list. We discuss groups in more detail in the "Sorting Contacts into Groups" section, later in this chapter.

Figure 20-1:
View your
Contacts list
by clicking
the Contacts
link.

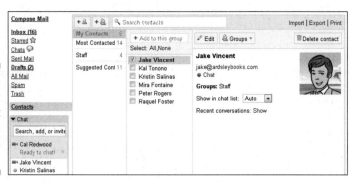

And it doesn't stop there. Gmail keeps track of anyone you e-mail, reply to, or show the slightest interest in and adds them to the Suggested Contacts list. In Figure 20-1, you can see contacts from both inside and outside the `Ardsleybooks.com` domain. For instance, `jake@ardsleybooks.com`, an employee of the bookstore, is automatically added to the Contacts list for future reference.

Gmail automatically groups your contacts by these four categories:

- ✔ **My Contracts:** A list of everybody in your Contacts list. (Think of the proverbial kitchen sink.)

- ✔ **Most Contacted:** An abbreviated list of the most frequently used contacts in your Contacts list. This list may include contacts that are not in your official list.

- ✔ **Groups:** A list of groups that either you or your organization creates. Groups facilitate e-mailing large numbers of people. Instead of repeatedly entering multiple e-mail addresses individually, a group can e-mail dozens, even hundreds of people with one common e-mail address.

- ✔ **Suggested Contacts:** These are people that you exchanged e-mail messages with but that are not in your official list. Click a contact in this list and then click the Move to My Contacts button to add them to your contacts.

Rolling through your Contacts list

Take a second to roll your mouse cursor slowly over the list of e-mail addresses that appears in your Contacts list. Pop, pop, pop, up come little contact cards with descriptions of each individual contact, as shown in Figure 20-2. Unless you or your contacts add more robust information, these listings appear rather plain. However, you can add more pertinent information, including pictures, which can help you remember what some of these people actually look like. (See the "Adding or Updating Contacts" section for details.)

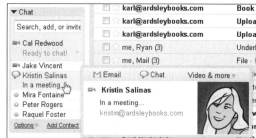

Figure 20-2: Popups display detailed contact information.

Using Quick Contacts in Gmail

The Quick Contacts list, just as the name implies, is designed to save you time and add convenience to your Gmail, Chat, Talk, and Calendar apps. You can view your Quick Contacts list by clicking the triangle in the side panel beneath the Contacts link. Clicking this triangle opens an abbreviated list called the Quick Contacts list, as shown in Figure 20-3. Notice that you can search for contacts or click the Contacts link to view your entire Contacts list.

Figure 20-3:
The Quick Contacts list.

Knowing when your contacts are online

A green dot appears to the left of Cal Redwood's name in Figure 20-3. (Okay, in this black-and-white book, the dot looks gray — but trust us, it's green.) A green dot means that person is online — a useful bit of information if you want to have a real-time conversation with that person by using Gmail Chat or Google Talk.

If you don't want someone to see your green dot, you can block certain contacts so they don't interrupt you while you're working, playing, or attending a meeting. To block visitors, set your status by clicking the down arrow next to Set Status Here. Look just below your name in the left panel. Read the following section for details.

Prioritizing Quick Contacts

The Quick Contacts list displays your most frequently contacted people based on your e-mail and chatting habits. The automatically generated list may not always reflect your wishes, so you can make changes and prioritize your contacts to your liking. By adjusting your list, you can see at a glance which contacts are online and available for a quick chat. Also, contacts that you e-mail most often appear on the list, so you can simply click a name to launch a new Gmail message preaddressed to that person.

You may have other contacts that you need to banish to the background so they don't take up valuable space in the visible portion of your Quick Contacts list. Not that you consider them second-class contacts; you simply don't need to contact them frequently or in any great haste.

To customize your Quick Contacts list, display all of your contacts by clicking the Show All link at the bottom of the Quick Contacts list (refer to Figure 20-3).

After you display all your contacts, decide which contacts you want to show in your Quick Contacts list by selecting one of the following options in the Show in Quick Contacts column (see Figure 20-4):

- ✔ **Always:** Selecting Always shows this contact in your Quick Contacts list, well, always.

- ✔ **Auto:** Selecting Auto means that Gmail decides whether a contact is high frequency and will appear in your Quick Contacts list.

- ✔ **Never:** Selecting Never keeps this contact out of your Quick Contacts list.

- ✔ **Block:** Selecting Block prevents this person from contacting you via Chat. (However, this person can still e-mail you.)

Figure 20-4:
Prioritize who appears in your Quick Contacts list.

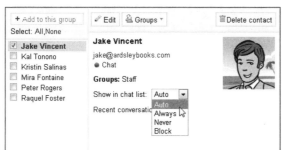

Unearthing lost contacts

Even if you select Never or Block for a contact (see the preceding section for more on the Quick Contacts list options), you can still get to that person's contact information whenever you need it by using the search tool in the Quick Contacts list. After you enter only a few letters in the search box, a list of contact names appears.

After you find the contact that you're looking for, the Quick Contacts search box displays several options for that contact. Click the option that you need:

✔ **Mail:** E-mail that contact.

✔ **Invite to Chat:** Invite the contact to a quick chat, plan lunch, share gossip, and maybe even get some work done.

✔ **Show in Quick Contacts:** Restore this person to your Quick Contacts list if you have deleted them for some reason.

✔ **View Recent Conversations:** Look up what you and your contact said while chatting.

✔ **<*Name*>'s Profile:** Open a contact's profile. You can view his statistics, or add your own data to his contact information. (Your changes only appear in your copy of another's profile.)

Adding or Updating Contacts

In the detailed Edit Contact window, you can change a contact's information, alter details, or even change someone's picture. You can also add e-mail, phone, and address information at any time, so you can reach out to anyone and remind them to pick you up for that preposterous office party. You have three ways to update a contact:

✔ Roll over any contact in your Quick Contacts list. When the contact card appears, click the More down arrow at the top of the contact card, choose Contact Details from the list that appears, and then click the Edit Contact Information link.

✔ Click the Contacts link in the left panel, roll over any contact in your Contacts list, click Contact Details, and then click the Edit Contact Information link.

✔ Search for a contact in the Quick Contacts list search box. When you find it, select <*Name*>'s Profile, click Contact Information, and finally, click the Edit Contact Information link from the card that appears.

To add a new contact, follow these steps:

1. **Open your Contacts list by clicking the Contacts link in the left panel or the Show All link at the bottom of the Quick Contacts list.**

2. **Click the Create Contact button.**

Entering basic contact information

When you create a new contact, the following fields appear in the Contacts window (shown in Figure 20-5):

You can add more than one address, phone number, and so on by clicking the blue add link next to each field's title.

- ✔ **Name:** Enter the contact's first name followed by his last name in this textbox.

- ✔ **Email:** Enter your contact's primary e-mail address in this textbox.

- ✔ **Phone:** Add a phone number here. Choose a number type from the drop-down menu to the right of the box.

- ✔ **Address:** Enter an address. When you save your contact, a Map link appears where you can quickly find the address on Google Maps.

- ✔ **Instant Messaging:** Add a username here for quick access to IM users. Gmail Chat connects automatically to Google Talk, AIM, and Jabber services.

- ✔ **More Info:** Click the plus button if you want to add more fields of information. Four new sections appear: Title, Company, Notes, and Other.

Click the Save button after you finish entering all the necessary data.

Figure 20-5:
Add contact
informa-
tion in the
Contacts
window.

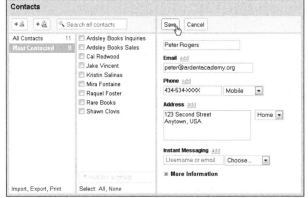

Adding more information about a contact

You may need to add more fields than the basic ones provided in the Add Contact window, particularly if you're entering information for business contacts. Add additional information by clicking the More Information link (refer to Figure 20-5).

You may not always have the data fields that you need for a unique contact, such as fields for a second mobile phone or for a pager. Gmail lets you add fields by clicking the Add link next to any section. From there, you can choose from the standard fields: E-mail, IM, Phone, Mobile, Pager, Fax, Company, Title, or Other. And, if you want to change the name or purpose of a field, click the field box and type whatever name you want.

Adding a picture

You can add your picture to your personal contact information, and the picture is automatically shared with others throughout your network of contacts. So make sure that you add a flattering photo.

You can use any image on your computer as your contact image. The only limitation is that the image must be in one of the following commonly used online file formats:

- ✔ **JPG:** Acronym for Joint Photographic Experts Group, JPG (or JPEG) is a popular online graphics format that uses compression to reduce the size of images.

- ✔ **BMP:** A bitmap file format proprietary to Microsoft Corporation.

- ✔ **GIF:** Acronym for the Graphics Interchange Format. This highly compact, low-resolution format was originally designed by CompuServe for online use.

- ✔ **PNG:** Acronym for Portable Network Graphics. This compressed image format is similar to JPG in many ways, approved by the World Wide Web Consortium as a high-resolution alternative to the GIF format.

After you identify the picture that you want to use, click the name of your target contact. *Note:* You add your picture by choosing your name from the Contacts list.

Follow these steps to add a picture to a contact:

1. **Click the Contacts link in the left panel.**

2. **Click the contact that you want to change and then click the Add a Picture link.**

    The Choose a Picture window appears.

3. **Click a link from the left side of the window, depending on where you want the picture to come from, and follow the instructions here:**

    • *My Computer:* Click the Choose File button, locate your photo in the Browse window that appears, and click Open.

- *Picasa Web Albums:* Type in the username (or yours) in the textbox and click through the online albums that appear. Click the image you want.

- *Web Address (URL):* Type in the URL for the image you want. If the address is correct, a preview of the image appears below.

- *Their Picture:* If the user has their own image chosen already, this option will show their choice and update it whenever they change it.

- *No Picture:* Click Apply Changes to remove any picture and leave it blank.

4. **Depending on your choice in Step 3, click either the Apply Changes or Select Image button.**

5. **(Optional) Crop the image, and click Apply Changes.**

    To keep anyone from getting a big head, Gmail asks you to crop the image down to size. It displays the image in the Crop Your Picture dialog box. To crop your image, follow these steps:

    a. *Drag the selection box into a flattering position.*

    b. *Drag the corners of the selection box to expand or reduce the selection box, as needed.*

    c. *When you're satisfied, click the Apply Changes button.*

    The Edit Contact window reappears, and the picture you just uploaded and cropped now appears in the My Pick picture box. After a little adjustment, you can have nearly anyone, even your cross-eyed accountant friend down the hall, looking like a million bucks. The cropping doesn't change the original file, so if you make a mistake cropping the image, you can always go back and try, try again.

    After you save a picture for a contact, the Suggest This Picture to <*Name*> dialog box appears, enabling you to share the picture you choose with that contact.

6. **(Optional) If you have a flattering picture that you want to send to your boss or another colleague, enter a short note in the textbox to the right of the picture in the Suggest This Picture to <*Name*> dialog box and then click the Yes, Suggest This Picture button.**

    If you click the No, Keep This Picture to Myself button instead, Gmail doesn't send the contact the picture that you use for her in your Contacts list. (We suggest that you resist the temptation to add a picture of a donkey to your boss's contact information, however, in case he happens to see it when looking over your shoulder one day.)

Sorting Contacts into Groups

Groups make it a snap to contact large numbers of people at the same time; for example, create a group of contacts who use your site and contact them in one click. Gmail assigns a single e-mail address (the group's address) that contains multiple e-mail addresses including each member of the group. When you enter a group name in the To field, Gmail enters all the e-mail addresses for the entire group's membership in a flash.

If you belong to a heads-up organization, an administrator may have created some of the key groups within your organization for you. Your company might create groups consisting of all employees, employees in a specific department, all senior managers, and so on. You can create a group of your friends, your immediate family members, or people who share your hobbies.

Creating groups

The best way to figure out how groups work is to create a group of your own. To create a group, follow these steps:

1. **Open your Contacts list and click the group from the list on the left.**

   If you haven't yet added a group, you see the screen shown in Figure 20-6.

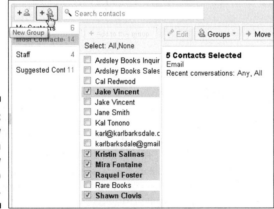

Figure 20-6:
Add a new group with the New Group button.

2. **Click the New Group button.**

3. **In the Create Group window that appears, click the Group Name text-box and enter a name that describes the group. Click OK to save the new group.**

4. **In the Add Contacts textbox, enter however many e-mail addresses you need to define as the group's membership.**

5. **Click the Create Group button to save the group information.**

Viewing and editing an existing group

If you have a contact that you want to add or remove from a group, you can always edit the contacts in the group. You can also rename the group. To view or edit a group, follow these steps:

1. **Click Contacts and then click a group from the list on the left.**

2. **Make any changes that you want, including the following:**

   - *Edit:* Click the Edit link to change the name of your group.

   - *Add to this group:* Type e-mail addresses into the Add Contacts textbox and then click the Add Contacts button to add members to the group.

   - *Delete Group:* Click the Delete Group button.

E-mailing a group

Groups become part of your e-mail address database; consequently, you just have to enter the first few letters in the To textbox, and your group's name appears. Select the name of the group, and the members' e-mail addresses suddenly appear in the To textbox.

Understanding Gmail Chat and Google Talk

If e-mail has a downside, it's that sometimes it just isn't instantaneous enough. That's why instant messaging and SMS (short messaging service; *text messaging* to you mobile phone users) were invented. Google takes care of your instant messaging and SMS needs with Gmail Chat and Google Talk.

In this chapter, we cover how to use Gmail Chat and Google Talk to have a real-time conversation with one or more of your contacts. We also cover how you can use Google Talk to have a voice conversation. Here's some more information on these tools:

✔ **Gmail Chat:** A basic instant-messaging program that's built right into Gmail.

✔ **Google Talk:** A more robust instant-messaging program that you can use as a gadget on your start page or Sites pages or download and use as a stand-alone program. With Google Talk, you can type messages to a contact so you can chat in real time, just as you can in Chat. You can also use a microphone and speakers (or a headset) to have a voice conversation with a contact or to leave a voice message.

When you're ready to start chatting, you first need to figure out who's online and available. You can see who's ready to chat pretty simply; sign into Gmail (if you haven't already) and look for a green dot to the left of a contact's name in your Chat list. If you see the green dot, the contact's ready to chat.

Inviting someone to chat in Gmail Chat

After you identify whether the person you want to instant message is online, starting up a chat in Gmail Chat is simple. Follow these steps:

1. **Sign into Gmail (if you haven't already).**

2. **In the Chat list on the left side of the screen, roll over the contact that you want to chat with and click the Chat button on the contact card that appears. (See Figure 20-7.)**

Figure 20-7:
Click the
Chat button
to invite
someone
to chat.

If you want to chat with someone who isn't in your Chat list, click in the Chat search box, start to type the contact's name, select his name from the list of contacts that appears, and then select Chat from the Options list that appears. This lets your contact know you want to talk. (At this point, you can also add the person to your Chat list by selecting Show in Chat from the Options list.)

3. **In the Chat Invitations window, select the check box to the left of the contact(s) with whom you want to chat, and then click the Send Invites button. Others that you can chat with will also appear so you can make a group invitation.**

After you send an invitation, a message appears in your invitee's Gmail window, asking if he wants to chat with you. (See Figure 20-8.) Don't be offended if he declines. Your contact may just be busy.

Also, if others want to chat with you, you receive an invitation similar to the one shown in Figure 20-8. You need to accept the invitation if you also want to chat.

Figure 20-8:
Click Yes if you want to chat with someone.

Chatting away in Gmail Chat

After you set up everything for your chat and your contact has responded, start chatting! (See Figure 20-9.) Click the textbox at the bottom of the chat window, type a message, and press Enter to send the message.

Figure 20-9:
Chat away!

Clicking the Pop-out option separates your entry window from your conversation, which allows you to see more of your conversation. Also, to help you know what your partner in chat is doing, a message indicating that the person is typing will appear.

You can hold multiple chats at the same time. You can open several contacts in separate chat windows and talk to each of them independently. You can also have a chat with multiple participants in the same window (say you invite more than one person to a chat, or you are invited to a chat with multiple participants). If someone is chatting way off topic, click the arrow to the right of Options and select Block *<Name>* to block someone from your chat, as shown in Figure 20-10. Ah, the power you'll feel blocking people right and left!

Figure 20-10:
Use your
options
to block
undesirable
elements.

Starting a voice/video chat

If you have a microphone or webcam, you can make voice or video calls to users directly from Gmail. Users with video enabled show a camera icon next to their names in the Chat list.

Before you can use voice/video chat features in Gmail, you have to install a special plug-in. To do so in Internet Explorer, click the yellow ActiveX bar at the top of the screen. For Chrome, Safari, and Firefox, go to `www.gmail.com/videochat` and click the Install Voice and Video Chat button. The plug-in installer starts automatically. Restart your browser to start video chatting.

To start a voice call, click a contact. In the new chat box that appears in the bottom-right corner of the screen, select the Video & More option and then choose Start Voice Chat from the list that appears. A ringing sound plays until your contact answers, just like a regular telephone. Click the Microphone button on the left to mute the call. To end the call, click the Hang Up button.

To start a video call, select the Video & More option in your contact's chat box and choose Start Video Chat from the menu that appears. The ringing sound plays while you wait for your contact to answer, and a preview of your video appears in a screen above the chat box, similar to Figure 20-11.

Keeping track of chats

If you need to keep a record of a chat you had in Gmail Chat or Google Talk for any reason, Gmail makes it easy by sending you an e-mail message containing the entire chat's text. And, because you can store and archive all your e-mail, you can always get to the chat record any time you want.

You can search for old chats as easily as you can search all your mail messages. Simply enter any part of the chat that you can remember in the search window (a few key words will do), and options start appearing. You can also search for chats by contact name or by date.

Make your video chat go full screen by hovering over the video and clicking the full screen button that appears in the top left corner of the video. Click the button again or press the Esc key to return to the smaller view. For more control of your video size, click the pop-out button (it's the arrow to the right to the chat close button).

Figure 20-11:
Meet face
to face with
Gmail Video
Chat.

Changing your Chat status

If you're signed into Gmail, you normally show up as online and available to chat to other people. To change your status (say you're busy and don't want your status to appear as online), follow these steps:

1. **To customize your personal chat settings, in the Chat section in the left panel, click the down arrow to the right of Set Status Here and choose one of the following options from the list that appears:**

   - *Available:* Lets people know you're available and willing to chat.

   - *Custom Message (for availability):* Write a customized message that people see when they check your availability.

   - *Busy:* Let people know that you're busy and can't chat right now.

   - *Custom Message (for busyness):* Write a customized message that everyone sees when you're busy.

   - *Sign Out of Chat:* Close Chat temporarily.

2. **(Optional) To create a custom message, select the Custom Message option, click the empty textbox that appears, and type a short message to your chat buddies. Clear this message later by accessing the Set Status Here option as described in Step 1 and choosing Custom Message.**

   Your custom message appears in your list of options. You can create several custom messages and apply them whenever you want.

Accessing Google Talk

If you need a more powerful instant messaging application than Gmail Chat, Google Talk is your answer. Google Talk is a gadget that you can add to your start page or Sites pages, as shown in Figure 20-12. (See Chapter 6 if you need help adding this gadget.)

Figure 20-12: Add Google Talk as a gadget to your start page.

If you're running Windows, you can add functionality to your Google Talk gadget, such as voice calls and file transfers, by downloading the Google Talk client. Go to www.google.com/talk and click the Download Google Talk button. Run the setup program and then log in using your full e-mail address and password.

Inviting a contact to chat in Google Talk

After you have Google Talk working, either from a gadget or from the client itself, you may need to sign in. Your existing Gmail contacts automatically appear. To begin chatting, you pick users the same way you do in Gmail Chat.

To invite a contact to chat, follow these unbelievably easy steps:

1. **Click a name from the list.**

2. **Start typing or click Call to have a "phone call." Honestly, isn't a simple call more personal than a bunch of typed text? (For more on calls, see the "Making a call" section, later in this chapter.)**

Use the search box (you know, the box with the magnifying glass in it) to find people to talk with by entering part of their names or e-mail addresses. After you locate chat buddies, you can add them to your Contacts list and invite them to chat.

Chatting with a contact in Google Talk

Google Talk (see Figure 20-13) works a lot like the chat application in Gmail, described earlier in this chapter. In fact, it's almost 100 percent the same when it comes to chatting, so we will skip to a few new things you can do with Talk and Chat.

Figure 20-13:
Talk with a contact by using the Google Talk gadget.

TIP

To add some fun, you can insert an emoticon into your message by typing any of the common symbols, such as **;)**, which Google Talk replaces with a winking smiley in your message when you press Enter. You can also click the smiley to the right of the textbox and select a face from the menu that appears.

You can keep chats private by not creating an e-mail record of the messages in your Gmail. (See the sidebar "Keeping track of chats" for more information about storing and searching chats.) Have a chat on the sly by clicking the down arrow in the upper right of the chat window and choosing Go Off the Record from the list that appears.

Chatting with a group

After you establish your list of contacts, you can chat with any or all of them as a group. After you start a basic chat with a contact, click the Group Chat button in Google Talk (see Figure 20-14). (To add additional people to your conversation in Gmail Chat, choose Options⇨Group Chat.) In the textbox that appears at the top of the chat window, enter the e-mail addresses of other users and press the Enter key. Right away, they can begin chatting along with you (assuming they're online, of course).

To talk to someone privately outside of the group chat, click that user's name in the Chat list and a separate tab (Talk) or chat window (Gmail Chat) appears.

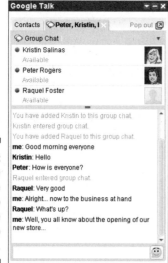

Figure 20-14: Invite multiple contacts to participate in a group chat.

Making a call

If you and a contact are both online, you can use Google Talk to make voice calls.

Both you and your contact must have the Google Talk client installed on your computers for this function to work. For best results, use a high-quality headset microphone and double-check to make sure that the sound levels are set properly before you begin.

To start a call, pick the name of the person you want to call. When their card appears, click the Call button or phone icon to the right of your contact's name. You can then start *a talkin'* . . . it's that easy.

When you're having a voice conversation in Google Talk, the talk window features the following options and indicators, as shown in Figure 20-15:

- ✔ **End Call:** Click this button to terminate the voice call.
- ✔ **Email:** This button loads Gmail in your browser so you can send a quick message to your contact.
- ✔ **Send Files:** Click this button to locate a document or photo on your computer that you want to send to your contact. You can also drag a file from your computer desktop into your chat window to send it immediately.
- ✔ **Mute:** Click this button to turn your microphone off temporarily.
- ✔ **Sound indicators:** Shows with a volume indicator whether your Talk software is receiving input from a microphone.

  If you want to adjust your audio settings, click the Settings link in the upper-right corner of the Google Talk client window, and then choose Audio from the options on the left. You may also have to adjust your volume settings in your operating system's control panel.
- ✔ **Internet connection strength:** Like bars on your mobile phone, these bars indicate your Internet connection's speed. The more bars, the better.

If a contact doesn't answer when you try to call, you have the opportunity to leave a voice mail.

Figure 20-15:
Share
pictures
and files in
Google Talk.

Sending a voice mail

Voice mail options are the same as the options for regular voice calls. You can send voice mail to any of your contacts, even if they don't use Google Talk or Gmail. When you want to send someone a voice mail, click the down arrow to the right of the Email button and choose Send Voicemail from the list that appears.

Voice mail messages appear alongside regular messages in Gmail, and you can either play them directly from Gmail or download them as MP3 files, as shown in Figure 20-16.

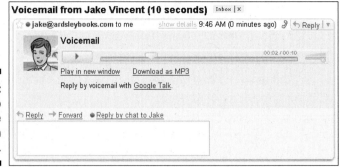

Figure 20-16:
Listen to
your voice
mails in
Gmail.

Part VI
The Part of Tens

"It's web-based, on-demand, and customizable. Still, I think I'm going to miss our old sales incentive methods."

In this part . . .

We know there are a lot of ways to create your Google Site. We won't get in the way of your creativity, but in case you hit a brain block, we begin this part with ten ideas for creating schemes and using Google gadgets to empower your team or fan club.

We end this part by sharing ten more Google apps and services that we think are especially worth looking at. They certainly make our lives easier. Although there are over thirty freebies out there, we've highlighted our favorites, including directory assistance and Sketch-Up.

Chapter 21

Ten More Ideas for Your Scheme

· ·

*W*e've shown you the tools, you've tried the options, and now you're ready to pull out all the stops and put Google Sites to work. In this chapter, we brainstorm a few ideas for Google Sites for your family, school, business, and nonprofit organization. Here are ten of our favorite scheme ideas. We don't have enough room to write full chapters on any of these ideas, but each is a site that has actually been created and used to great success. From the classroom to the boardroom, this list should spark a few great ideas for your site project.

Family Scheme

There is no more enjoyable use of Google Sites than to share online moments with family members. Use Sites to keep in touch with each other no matter how dispersed your family members may become.

Why not have an Announcements page where family can keep up with each other's activities. And don't forget the photo album of that trip to Disney World, your drive along the Blue Ridge Parkway, or the hike up to the base of Mount Rushmore. Post the annual holiday card online instead of mailing it. Each aunt and uncle can have his or her own, individual sub-page. Leave these pages up and updated all year long; why should the holiday ever end?

For the family with busy, tight schedules, creating separate calendars for each family member makes a lot of sense. The calendars can all be displayed together on one page so everyone knows who needs a ride to a swim practice, when that big piano recital will be held, and whose birthday is sneaking up on the horizon.

Little League Scheme

With Google Sites, no group is deemed too small or insignificant. You can make the local Springville Giants Little League team as important as their major league equivalent at AT&T Park in San Francisco by giving them their own Web site.

If you're creating such a site, don't forget to include

- The season schedule
- Information needed by parents, such as the required registration, liability, and medical forms for easy download
- Pictures of the team in action as well as the annual team picture
- Team statistics
- Special awards and recognition for each child
- Safety tips and baseball rules
- Links to sites that teach the fundamentals of the sport

You may even want to include ads for some of your team's sponsors on the team's site. After all, a bit of free advertising can't hurt your chances to win their sponsorship next season. (They may even kick in for some new uniforms.) Also, think about a link to stores that carry equipment that players need along with cost saving and shopping tips. This can be a big help to parents trying to outfit the next A-Rod for the upcoming season.

Book Club Scheme

A book club scheme can work for many different types of groups and organizations that meet frequently. Sites pages can be created to share the club's book list. Don't leave out a calendar of club meetings and special events, such as book signings, and drop in some gadgets that represent RSS feeds from a wide range of literary news and reviews.

Create a page that allows members to wiki about books they are reading. Let all the members contribute to an online review. Pick a moderator to edit the pages just in case one of your members can't spell. (Heaven forbid.)

Links to online literary sites could be very helpful to members. Allow comments so members can talk about the literary sites to which you are linking. For example, you could provide links to book reviews, like those found in *The New York Times* Reading Room (http://readingroom.

`blogs.nytimes.com`). And don't forget to create links to other book clubs, such as Oprah's Book Club (`http://www.oprah.com/entity/oprahs bookclub`), so your members can find out what others are recommending. Most of all, get copies of *Google Sites & Chrome For Dummies* for all your book club members. They will find it as riveting as the latest Grisham, Rowling, or King.

Corporate Retreat Scheme

Corporate retreats can quickly turn into mammoth organizational challenges. Every business, large or small, plans retreats. For example, a large corporation may need to bring its worldwide sales team together for training. Google Sites is perfect for this type of complex operation. For example, create a "Sales Force Conference 2010" page to coordinate all the aspects of the event.

- ✔ Planners can coordinate their own internal planning efforts on a separate conference planning team site.

- ✔ Information including all the important details can be shared directly with those who are attending.

- ✔ Pages can even be translated into most major languages, if needed, by using Google's Web page translation tools.

On the site for your participants, don't forget to include a Countdown gadget leading up to the conference's opening session. And remember the travel itinerary, complete with airport shuttle or cab information. Also, use Google Maps. Conference participants love maps. You can even get digital maps from the convention site staff that you can upload for your attendees. If the site has wireless access, and what convention site doesn't, put the login instructions on your site.

Include preliminary agendas and room assignments. Participants will also need countdown reminders to important deadlines, such as the drop-dead dates for making hotel reservations or flight plans. Don't forget to set up an e-mail group with Google Groups to send reminders to everyone. A clever trick is to tie the group to an RSVP sign-up link. This will help you build the mailing list that you'll need as the conference date approaches.

During the conference, provide instant messaging support from the site for session Q&A or any help desk issues. Post any last minute updates needed by a few confused participants. After the conference, use the same site pages to share highlights, convention notes, pictures, and YouTube videos of the event. If specific training was provided, presentations, transcripts, summaries, and other corporate guidance can be made available on the site after the event is history.

Newsletter Scheme

Printing newsletters is so passé. Put them online. Create your own pre-designed template for your newsletter that you can use for future newsletters. This reduces your development time the next time you compile the latest news.

An online newsletter also gives you more flexibility with your content over the traditional paper versions. You can add gadgets that interest your audience to provide interactivity. For example, you can insert a Finance gadget that tracks your corporate stock performance. You can even have Google translate the newsletter into multiple languages if necessary.

Combine your newsletter site with a Google Groups registration so that everyone who signs up receives the newsletter via e-mail with a link directly to the online version. Adding your organization's logo to the newsletter site places it on every newsletter from then on without much fuss or bother on your part.

Don't forget to archive past editions for reference purposes. In fact, create separate pages for each and index them with a newsletter sitemap. Naming each one by date makes this an easy task. If anyone needs to find something from an obscure past issue, he can use the built-in search tool and find the issue quickly.

Group or Team Project Scheme

Google simply understands collaboration. All the Google tools were made with sharing and teamwork in mind. Sites, Apps, Talk, Gmail, Calendar, and all the other Google Apps and gadgets are designed to be shared. Each can also be opened up to simultaneous group collaboration. This set of tools brings teams together to complete projects and assignments in powerful new ways.

Setting up team meeting schedules, scheduling rooms and resources, and following up with details is a snap when you combine Google Sites with Gmail, Google Calendar, and other Google Apps.

List pages can keep track of every step of a project. Spreadsheet gadgets can be created to keep track of a team's budget or to create charts and graphs to record progress. Plus, you can use thousands of additional gadgets to keep track of everything from deadlines to team To-Do lists. The Google Talk and instant messaging features will keep the conversations rolling.

An Announcements page can keep everyone up-to-date. Sites pages can also be used to communicate to supervisors what the team is working on and how much progress has been made. It's like creating your own internal advertising agency to keep people apprised and interested in the project's progress.

Homeroom Scheme

If you're a teacher at any grade level, Google Sites can add high-tech efficiency to your communications with parents and students. For younger students in particular, be sure to create a page that communicates directly to parents about how their kids are doing and lets them know when assignments are due. The Announcements template would be perfect for this task. You can easily include a calendar of classroom events, such as your testing or activities schedule. These can all be linked to a school calendar as well.

Showcasing student work for the K–8 crowd is easy with Google Sites. Student's written work, such as essays and reports, can be shared from a Filing Cabinet. To show student artwork, scan the pieces you want to share and upload the images to a page created from a Web page template. You can even link to and display student presentations live online, particularly if they are using Google Apps to prepare their presentations.

For older students, create a page where students can download assignments and study guides, and provide a place where they can sign up for and receive course announcements. Don't forget to suggest that students build sites for their own teamwork efforts. Check out the College Scheme ideas explained in more detail in Chapter 12.

Many faculty members are using Google Sites to support teacher in-service and schoolwide teacher support networks. Providing a place where teachers can swap information and curricula, as well as privately discuss student progress, can facilitate school improvement. Make sure that you take full advantage of the security settings to preserve the confidentiality needed in a school environment.

Political Scheme

Whether you are organizing a political campaign for the presidency of the United States or managing a campaign to pass a bond to build a new library in your hometown, Google Sites is the answer. Create separate sites; one for the public campaign that voters see and another to keep campaign volunteers organized and in the loop.

The 2008 Presidential campaign set a new standard for managing campaigns online. A lot can be learned by examining how the campaign involved people in social networking forums, publicized events, and organized the candidates' answers to issues for information seekers. Here are some other ideas:

- Create and publish a calendar of campaign events.
- Use Google Checkout to collect campaign contributions.
- Create a Filing Cabinet to download issue and position papers.
- Create a gadget to track poll results.
- Create a gadget to count down to Election Day.
- Create a site to orchestrate the victory rally.
- Use a wiki to create a profile of your candidate or of your issue.
- Provide ways to contact the campaign.
- Create an online campaign store for yard signs, T-shirts, buttons, and bumper stickers.
- Post your campaign's commercials or link to them on YouTube.
- Create a moderated space where voters can comment and share their thoughts on the issues.
- Link to other organizations that support your issue or candidate.

Investment Club Scheme

In these interesting financial times, it may be good to go online with your investment club info and results. Here are a few ideas:

- Use the Google Finance gadget to keep track of every portfolio in the club.
- Use Google Finance to do "what if" trading scenarios to see how alternative investment paths would have performed. Make it a contest. Have each club member create their own fantasy investment portfolio scenario and track the results. Give the winner a share of Berkshire Hathaway Inc. (NYSE:BRK.A) and a free lunch with Buffet.
- Create an RSS gadget that links you to current investment articles and news feeds.
- Link to CNBC or other investment sites live or link to investment YouTube videos.

✔ Have a wiki or comments section for club members where they can share their ideas and recommendations. Use the site to help members vote to decide what the next investment will be.

✔ Track the biggest movers in each sector.

✔ Give advice on how to protect the value of your club and your member's personal investments.

✔ Stream Jim Cramer's Mad Money every day.

✔ Don't get into credit-default swaps.

✔ Don't buy Lehman Brothers at any price.

Your Scheme Here

Oh, what the heck . . . you can do about anything you want with Sites. You can create a site on pumpkin carving or holiday tree-decorating ideas. Create a hobby site or display your photographs or your award-winning watercolors. Create a site for your church or community organization. Create a site for the county fair. Make a wedding site for that special event, or better yet, create a baby site for the new arrival. Announce a graduation with Google Sites. There's really no limit to the creativity. Do whatever you can think of. Just remember to stay away from illegal online activities. This would be a violation of the spirit behind Google's mantra, "Don't be evil."

Bottom line; enjoy Google Sites!

Chapter 22

Ten More Google Apps for Your Team

● ●

*W*e know that Google Apps is going to make your team more efficient, streamlined, and hip. And just because you're using the basic Google Apps (Sites, Docs, Calendar, Gmail, and Talk) doesn't mean you have to stop there. After all, you can find numerous other free Google Apps and services that can help make your life easier.

So, before we send you off to build your site, we want to take a moment to tell you about some of our favorite Google services. We can't list them all in this chapter, and Google is adding new ones all the time. For a complete list, go to www.google.com/options — and if you're extra adventurous, see what's bubbling in Google Labs at www.google.com/labs.

Creating a Google Account

To use most Google services, you need a Google Account. A Google Account is different from your Google Apps account, but you can use your Google Apps e-mail address to sign up for a Google Account and add some of the additional features that we talk about in this chapter. See Chapter 3 to set up a Google Account.

1-800-GOOG-411

This App has nothing to do with the Internet — at least, not directly. Google offers free phone directory assistance for local businesses. Call 1-800-GOOG-411, and Google not only lists the most relevant businesses that you're looking for, but also sends you an SMS text message with the listing you want and connects you to the company you choose free. You'll be amazed at how good the service is. Here are the key prompts and voice commands, in order:

- **What city and state?** Say the city and state you want information for, such as "Duluth, Minnesota."

- **What business name or category?** Say the name of the business that you're looking for, such as "Dentist" or "John Smith."

- **Say, "Number X":** Listen to the list of results. When you hear the business that you want more information on, say the corresponding number. You don't have to wait until the list ends. Google connects you automatically, or you can say one of these commands:

    - *"Details":* Listen to the full address and phone number of the business. It repeats the information twice, so you can make sure that your pen is working correctly.

    - *"Text message":* If you're using a mobile phone, say this command to receive a text message with the address and phone number of the business.

- **Say, "Go back":** Return to the previous prompt.

- **Say, "Start over":** Begin your search again with the city and state.

AdWords

    http://adwords.google.com

What better way can you get your message out there than to advertise on Google? With AdWords, you can quickly and easily set up an account and decide how much you want to pay for advertising. It's a cost-per-click service, so you decide how many times your ad can appear and be clicked. You're in control of how much you pay.

Visit www.google.com/businesseducators to download a free handbook and discover more about advertising with Google.

AdSense

`http://adsense.google.com`

AdSense is Google's way of renting space on your Web site for advertisements. You have control over the advertisement categories that appear as well as the color scheme. Every time your visitors click a link, you make money. It's as simple as that!

Follow the tutorial on `http://adsense.google.com` to set up your account and begin making easy money.

Google Notebook

`http://google.com/notebook`

We love this tool. Notebook lets you take notes in your Web browser and keep them online and accessible from anywhere. Copy snippets of Web pages (including tables and images), make To Do lists, and more. For added convenience, you can also download the Notebook browser plug-in and note things when you're surfing the Web without having to open another window.

Google Finance

`http://finance.google.com`

Track your stock portfolio or follow your favorite companies from one convenient place. Google Finance brings information from multiple finance and news sites, and places them in one location. Sift through financial statements, check the historical stock prices, and watch the latest videos from the experts. As a bonus, you can add a Google Finance gadget to your Start Page and see how your stocks are doing while you peruse your Gmail Inbox.

Google Product Search

`www.google.com/products`

Looking for a printer or vintage coffee maker? Google Product Search looks through a large selection of Internet stores so you don't have to. Sort your results by price, and you can find the best deal around. Adding Google Checkout (`http://checkout.google.com`) to your Google Account saves time that you'd otherwise spend filling out forms — and it keeps your credit card information safe. Product Search lets you sort your results by price or relevance, and other users have rated the stores, so you know what you're getting into.

Google Reader

`www.google.com/reader`

Instead of taking a lot of time to visit your favorite news sites and blogs, make them come to you. Google Reader helps you corral all your sources into one place, and it automatically updates your top stories. After you log in the first time, be sure to take the tour. Click the Add Subscription button on the left side of the screen and a textbox appears, allowing you to search for your favorite Web site feeds. Click the Subscribe button on the search results page and you'll receive messages and articles right away.

Think of Google Reader as an Inbox for the Web. Rather than messages from people, you get articles from Web sites.

Google Maps

`http://maps.google.com`

Google Maps is intuitive and fun. Find addresses, locate businesses, or get directions from place to place. Our favorite map views include

- ✔ **Street View:** Get down to street level and take a panoramic tour of major cities. Use the plus and minus buttons to zoom, and then drag the little yellow man onto an outlined street to see what passersby see on their way to work.

- ✔ **Traffic:** Google taps into several traffic monitoring sources to give you current traffic conditions. Green is good, red is bad. Google even takes into account bad traffic when giving you directions to your destination.

- ✔ **More:** New Google Maps features are added all the time. Check the Photos box in the list that appears to view pictures from nearby sites. Check the Wikipedia box to show buttons that preview articles about cities, landmarks, or other points of interest.

- ✔ **Map:** Quickly find your way around with the default map view. Search the map for local businesses, get directions from one place to another, print your maps, or e-mail them to your friends.

- ✔ **Satellite:** See a bird's-eye view of your local shopping center or historic statue. When you click the Satellite button, you can also check the Show Labels box to see street names on the map.

- ✔ **Terrain:** See the world in topographical form, including all the nooks and crannies of the Grand Canyon or your ski resort.

There are some hidden features for getting directions to a place on the map. Right-click on the map your starting point and choose Directions from Here from the menu that appears. Then right-click your destination and choose Directions to Here. To customize your route, drag the blue directions line to any other road or point along the way that you'd like to visit. While you drag the line, a tooltip appears that shows you how long your new route will be.

Don't forget to check out the My Maps tab to add your favorite spots, draw borders, and shade in areas.

Google Pack

http://pack.google.com

Google Pack brings together all the free software that you need (and none that you don't) in one easy-to-use installer. These programs include Web tools, Internet security programs, and other productivity software. Pack even keeps your software up-to-date automatically. Here are our favorite Google Pack programs:

- ✔ **Google Earth:** Take Google Maps to the next level with a 3D atlas of the world. Zoom into famous landmarks, search for your house, see community photos of places, and globe-trot without leaving your home.

- ✔ **Google Desktop:** Add Google Search to your computer desktop. Google Desktop helps you quickly find documents, images, and music on your computer as easily as you find pages on the Internet.

- ✔ **Picasa:** Organize and edit your photos with simple yet powerful tools. Picasa also has an online counterpart called Picasa Web Albums (http://picasaweb.google.com), which lets you post your photos into your own online gallery with one click.

- ✔ **StarOffice:** For documents that need a little more oomph than Google Docs provides, try this free alternative to Microsoft Office. It includes all the tools that you need to create documents, spreadsheets, presentations, drawings, and databases.

The Google Installer notifies you of program updates. Check back from time to time for more programs by returning to `http://pack.google.com` in your browser.

Google Translate

`http://translate.google.com`

Get yourself out of a pinch by using Google Translate. With support for over 20 languages and the ability to translate entire Web sites in a single bound, Translate saves the day time and again. Go to `http://translate.google.com` and click one of the tabs along the top. Here's how they work:

- ✔ **Text and Web:** Enter a word, phrase, or paragraph in the Original Text textbox at the top of the page or enter a Web address in the Translate a Web Page textbox at the bottom of the page. Click the arrow to the right of the appropriate language textbox and choose the language combination that you want to translate from/to from the drop-down list that appears. Then click the Translate button. After a moment, a translation appears on the right side of the screen. Web pages will load in their entirety in the same window.

  Google Translate, like other automated translation services, can do a decent job of translating basic text. However, many times, you get a quite literal and not very accurate translation, which can be funny or just plain confusing. If you need to translate an important document, make sure that you have a native speaker read through the translation before you send the document. (You don't want to inadvertently insult someone with an inaccurate translation.)

- ✔ **Translated Search:** Google Translate can help you find a search term in Web pages that are written in a language other than English.

- ✔ **Dictionary:** Use this language translation dictionary when you're stumped by a foreign word you encounter. Enter a word in the Enter Word textbox and choose a language translation in the drop-down menu to the right; the foreign language equivalent appears.

- ✔ **Tools:** Add a Google Translate gadget to your Web page so that your visitors can translate your page in a flash. Simply choose your page's language and then copy the HTML code that appears in the box below Step 2 into your page. If you translate pages often, make life simple — add one of the translate buttons listed at the bottom of the screen to your browser's toolbar by clicking the link and dragging it to your browser's bookmarks or favorites bar. Then when you visit a site, simply click the button to translate the page instantly.

Index

• B •

• *H* •

● **T** ●

INESS, CAREERS & PERSONAL FINANCE

nting For Dummies, 4th Edition*
470-24600-9

keeping Workbook For Dummies†
470-16983-4

nodities For Dummies
470-04928-0

g Business in China For Dummies
470-04929-7

E-Mail Marketing For Dummies
978-0-470-19087-6

Job Interviews For Dummies, 3rd Edition*†
978-0-470-17748-8

Personal Finance Workbook For Dummies*†
978-0-470-09933-9

Real Estate License Exams For Dummies
978-0-7645-7623-2

Six Sigma For Dummies
978-0-7645-6798-8

Small Business Kit For Dummies,
2nd Edition*†
978-0-7645-5984-6

Telephone Sales For Dummies
978-0-470-16836-3

INESS PRODUCTIVITY & MICROSOFT OFFICE

s 2007 For Dummies
470-03649-5

2007 For Dummies
470-03737-9

e 2007 For Dummies
470-00923-9

ok 2007 For Dummies
470-03830-7

PowerPoint 2007 For Dummies
978-0-470-04059-1

Project 2007 For Dummies
978-0-470-03651-8

QuickBooks 2008 For Dummies
978-0-470-18470-7

Quicken 2008 For Dummies
978-0-470-17473-9

Salesforce.com For Dummies,
2nd Edition
978-0-470-04893-1

Word 2007 For Dummies
978-0-470-03658-7

CATION, HISTORY, REFERENCE & TEST PREPARATION

an American History For Dummies
7645-5469-8

ora For Dummies
7645-5325-7

ora Workbook For Dummies
7645-8467-1

istory For Dummies
470-09910-0

ASVAB For Dummies, 2nd Edition
978-0-470-10671-6

British Military History For Dummies
978-0-470-03213-8

Calculus For Dummies
978-0-7645-2498-1

Canadian History For Dummies, 2nd Edition
978-0-470-83656-9

Geometry Workbook For Dummies
978-0-471-79940-5

The SAT I For Dummies, 6th Edition
978-0-7645-7193-0

Series 7 Exam For Dummies
978-0-470-09932-2

World History For Dummies
978-0-7645-5242-7

OD, GARDEN, HOBBIES & HOME

e For Dummies, 2nd Edition
471-92426-5

Collecting For Dummies, 2nd Edition
470-22275-1

ing Basics For Dummies, 3rd Edition
7645-7206-7

Drawing For Dummies
978-0-7645-5476-6

Etiquette For Dummies, 2nd Edition
978-0-470-10672-3

Gardening Basics For Dummies*†
978-0-470-03749-2

Knitting Patterns For Dummies
978-0-470-04556-5

Living Gluten-Free For Dummies†
978-0-471-77383-2

Painting Do-It-Yourself For Dummies
978-0-470-17533-0

ALTH, SELF HELP, PARENTING & PETS

r Management For Dummies
470-03715-7

ety & Depression Workbook
Dummies
7645-9793-0

ng For Dummies, 2nd Edition
7645-4149-0

Training For Dummies, 2nd Edition
7645-8418-3

Horseback Riding For Dummies
978-0-470-09719-9

Infertility For Dummies†
978-0-470-11518-3

Meditation For Dummies with CD-ROM,
2nd Edition
978-0-471-77774-8

Post-Traumatic Stress Disorder For Dummies
978-0-470-04922-8

Puppies For Dummies, 2nd Edition
978-0-470-03717-1

Thyroid For Dummies, 2nd Edition†
978-0-471-78755-6

Type 1 Diabetes For Dummies*†
978-0-470-17811-9

arate Canadian edition also available
arate U.K. edition also available

ble wherever books are sold. For more information or to order direct: U.S. customers visit www.dummies.com or call 1-877-762-2974.
ustomers visit www.wileyeurope.com or call (0)1243 843291. Canadian customers visit www.wiley.ca or call 1-800-567-4797.

WILEY

INTERNET & DIGITAL MEDIA

AdWords For Dummies
978-0-470-15252-2

Blogging For Dummies, 2nd Edition
978-0-470-23017-6

Digital Photography All-in-One Desk Reference For Dummies, 3rd Edition
978-0-470-03743-0

Digital Photography For Dummies, 5th Edition
978-0-7645-9802-9

Digital SLR Cameras & Photography For Dummies, 2nd Edition
978-0-470-14927-0

eBay Business All-in-One Desk Reference For Dummies
978-0-7645-8438-1

eBay For Dummies, 5th Edition*
978-0-470-04529-9

eBay Listings That Sell For Dummies
978-0-471-78912-3

Facebook For Dummies
978-0-470-26273-3

The Internet For Dummies, 11th Edition
978-0-470-12174-0

Investing Online For Dummies, 5th Edition
978-0-7645-8456-5

iPod & iTunes For Dummies, 5th E
978-0-470-17474-6

MySpace For Dummies
978-0-470-09529-4

Podcasting For Dummies
978-0-471-74898-4

Search Engine Optimization For Dummies, 2nd Edition
978-0-471-97998-2

Second Life For Dummies
978-0-470-18025-9

Starting an eBay Business For Dur 3rd Edition†
978-0-470-14924-9

GRAPHICS, DESIGN & WEB DEVELOPMENT

Adobe Creative Suite 3 Design Premium All-in-One Desk Reference For Dummies
978-0-470-11724-8

Adobe Web Suite CS3 All-in-One Desk Reference For Dummies
978-0-470-12099-6

AutoCAD 2008 For Dummies
978-0-470-11650-0

Building a Web Site For Dummies, 3rd Edition
978-0-470-14928-7

Creating Web Pages All-in-One Desk Reference For Dummies, 3rd Edition
978-0-470-09629-1

Creating Web Pages For Dummies, 8th Edition
978-0-470-08030-6

Dreamweaver CS3 For Dummies
978-0-470-11490-2

Flash CS3 For Dummies
978-0-470-12100-9

Google SketchUp For Dummies
978-0-470-13744-4

InDesign CS3 For Dummies
978-0-470-11865-8

Photoshop CS3 All-in-One Desk Reference For Dummies
978-0-470-11195-6

Photoshop CS3 For Dummies
978-0-470-11193-2

Photoshop Elements 5 For Dum
978-0-470-09810-3

SolidWorks For Dummies
978-0-7645-9555-4

Visio 2007 For Dummies
978-0-470-08983-5

Web Design For Dummies, 2nd E
978-0-471-78117-2

Web Sites Do-It-Yourself For Dur
978-0-470-16903-2

Web Stores Do-It-Yourself For Dur
978-0-470-17443-2

LANGUAGES, RELIGION & SPIRITUALITY

Arabic For Dummies
978-0-471-77270-5

Chinese For Dummies, Audio Set
978-0-470-12766-7

French For Dummies
978-0-7645-5193-2

German For Dummies
978-0-7645-5195-6

Hebrew For Dummies
978-0-7645-5489-6

Ingles Para Dummies
978-0-7645-5427-8

Italian For Dummies, Audio Set
978-0-470-09586-7

Italian Verbs For Dummies
978-0-471-77389-4

Japanese For Dummies
978-0-7645-5429-2

Latin For Dummies
978-0-7645-5431-5

Portuguese For Dummies
978-0-471-78738-9

Russian For Dummies
978-0-471-78001-4

Spanish Phrases For Dummies
978-0-7645-7204-3

Spanish For Dummies
978-0-7645-5194-9

Spanish For Dummies, Audio Se
978-0-470-09585-0

The Bible For Dummies
978-0-7645-5296-0

Catholicism For Dummies
978-0-7645-5391-2

The Historical Jesus For Dummie
978-0-470-16785-4

Islam For Dummies
978-0-7645-5503-9

Spirituality For Dummies, 2nd Edition
978-0-470-19142-2

NETWORKING AND PROGRAMMING

ASP.NET 3.5 For Dummies
978-0-470-19592-5

C# 2008 For Dummies
978-0-470-19109-5

Hacking For Dummies, 2nd Edition
978-0-470-05235-8

Home Networking For Dummies, 4th Edition
978-0-470-11806-1

Java For Dummies, 4th Edition
978-0-470-08716-9

Microsoft® SQL Server™ 2008 All-in-One Desk Reference For Dummies
978-0-470-17954-3

Networking All-in-One Desk Reference For Dummies, 2nd Edition
978-0-7645-9939-2

Networking For Dummies, 8th Edition
978-0-470-05620-2

SharePoint 2007 For Dummies
978-0-470-09941-4

Wireless Home Networking For Dummies, 2nd Edition
978-0-471-74940-0

Appomattox Regional Library System
Hopewell, Virginia 23860
06/10